An introduction to INFORMATION DESIGN

גלריה עליונה
Upper Gallery
صالة العرض العليا

An introduction to INFORMATION DESIGN

Kathryn Coates & Andy Ellison

Laurence King Publishing

Published in 2014 by
Laurence King Publishing Ltd
361–373 City Road
London EC1V 1LR
Tel +44 20 7841 6900
Fax +44 20 7841 6910
Email: enquiries@laurenceking.com
www.laurenceking.com

This book was produced by Laurence King Publishing Ltd, London

A catalogue record for this book is available from the British Library

ISBN: 978-1-78067-325-7

Design by Lizzie Ballantyne

Printed in China

Frontispiece: Signage at the Design Museum Holon, Tel Aviv, designed by Adi Stern Design (see pp. 181–183).

Contents

Introduction

Why read this book?

Information is everywhere. We are surrounded by it and it is delivered to us in many different ways. From the moment we get up in the morning, we engage with information that has been designed for specific purposes: the nutritional information on the packets of the cereals we eat; the daily news via a newspaper or a screen; a timetable to see when the next bus is due. We are constantly engaging with the communication of information.

If you are reading this book then the chances are that you are interested in design and are curious to know more about information design. This subject is large and complex and takes in many forms and platforms. The aim of this book is to demystify the process of producing clear information design and to provide some fundamental guidelines to the considerations and processes you may need when communicating to specific users or audiences. This knowledge will better equip you to produce effective solutions to the design challenges you may encounter within your own study and practice.

To demonstrate the breadth and diversity of the subject, we feature the work of an international selection of designers. The purpose is to give a behind-the-scenes look at the journey to a final outcome. These case studies are not just about who information design is for and who created it; their purpose is to show the creative processes behind a successful information design project. These case studies allow us to see the fundamentals of information design being put into action on real projects by practising designers.

Our aim in writing this book was to provide an inspirational guide to the discipline of visualizing information, a discipline that falls within the larger subject of graphic design. Our intention is to explain the subject practically: this is not just an introduction to the theories of information design, but a how-to book that includes hints and tips on the actual design process.

The structure of the book

The basic premise of this publication is: What is information design? How do you do it? How have others done it? The book is structured so you can read the chapters sequentially or dip into the specific areas covered as and when required. Hints and tips are offered throughout to give practical support and guidance to would-be designers.

You will be presented with the fundamentals of information design and guided through the core skills, taking into account the values of the audience, hierarchy, structure, legibility and media. You will be provided with inspirational visual examples and shown why information design is so important in modern life. We cover all aspects of information design, including print media, screen-based solutions and 3D physical environments. The case studies offer vivid insights into the working practices of contemporary practitioners, inviting comparisons and contrasting views on the subject. Our goal is to make readers aware that there is always a variety of methods available to them to answer design problems.

Chapter 1: What is information design?

This chapter aims to provide an insight into the subject of information design, to explain its purpose and the various forms it takes. We outline a brief history of information design to put the discipline in context, then discuss why it is necessary and how we use it in our daily lives. Finally, we look at the various ways in which it is presented and how the approach has to be modified depending on the format.

Definitions of information design

In an age where we are bombarded with information, the boundaries between what is and what is not considered information design have become blurred. We consume thousands of pieces of information every day, often without even noticing, so what exactly is information design?

Many people define it differently. Some feel that it is simply the visualization of data; others see it as the communication of any message in any form. This could take the form of an advertisement or of a safety sign: both communicate a message or meaning to the viewer, and both deal with information, whether it is about selling a product or about preventing risks to health.

'Information design is the defining, planning, and shaping of the contents of a message and the environments in which it is presented, with the intention to satisfy the information needs of the intended recipients.'

International Institute for Information Design (IIID)

'In its broadest sense, all graphic design is "information design". The distinction for me is that graphic design is the organization of elements that are typically capable of communicating independently, like words, photography and illustration. Information design, as I see it, incorporates the more elemental particles of data, and as a result requires more interpretation or authorship on the designer's part for it to speak fluently.'

Nicholas Felton, Feltron (USA)

'It is the organization and display of information, messaging or storytelling in an ordered hierarchy. A journey of information. To present content in a clear and unique and engaging way by engaging and targeting the human senses through the use of graphic devices such as type, colour, imagery, time, light, textures and materials etc. to either warn, teach, explain, entertain or direct.'

Vince Frost, Frost Design (Australia)

'Is there too much design now? Look on the web – is there a different sort of design emerging? A creative world where designers seem to own what they are doing, a showing off if you like. A comfortable designers' world where there is more of the same, time and again. To be a designer you surely need opinions – you must ask why. Why can't you hear the train times? Why can't elderly people understand Bluetooth? Why can't I find the lavatories at Terminal Five? We know and read the words about information design ... Enabling, understanding, making information more useable, clarifying the complex and more ... But think of yourself sitting in a room. No computer, no blogging, no music, with a Pentel sign pen in red and black and just a plan, some words and a problem. And you stay there until you have the answer. That's information design.'

John Bateson, Bateson Studio (UK)

'A certain type of information design sometimes seems to be about displaying a graphic designer's prowess for creating aesthetically pleasing and colourful graphic representations of statistics or facts. Whilst this may look good, it often leads to a piece of work that inspires one to look, rather than read. For me, good information design should engage the reader both visually and cerebrally, offering something beyond a surface impression.'

Dr Alison Barnes (Australia)

Previous page: The Rosetta stone, an irregularly shaped block of black basalt, found in 1799 near the town of Rosetta (Rashid) near Alexandria by Napoleon's armies. The stone is inscribed with a priestly decree issued at Memphis in 196 BCE on behalf of King Ptolemy V. The inscription appears in three scripts – ancient Egyptian hieroglyphs, Demotic script and ancient Greek – and provided the key to the decipherment of hieroglyphs in the modern age.

Opposite: Cave painting showing horses, bulls and stags, in the Lascaux caves in southwestern France. The paintings are around 17,000 years old.

A brief history of information design

It would be impossible to give a detailed history of information design in just a few pages. It is, however, important to establish that information design is not a new invention: it has been with us for a very long time, albeit in different forms, and has been vital to civilization and in communicating between cultures and generations. This section introduces the milestones in the development of information design from both our ancient and our recent past.

Cave paintings

Well before early versions of writing originated in Mesopotamia around 3000 BCE, images had been used as a way of communicating for thousands of years. Markings and drawings have been found all over the world, often carved into stones or drawn on rock faces. The best known of these are the cave paintings of Lascaux and Chauvet in France. Experts consider the latter to be among the oldest, at around 30,000 years old. The paintings show images of animals such as deer and bison, as well as lions, bears and hyenas and even birds from Paleolithic times.

Little is known as to why early humans created these images, but they could be interpreted as a means of recording and educating communities, as well as a form of self-expression. These images could have had some significance in prehistoric pagan cultures, perhaps used by the local shaman to contact spirits and influence the weather, find new hunting grounds and heal the sick. These cave paintings represent the first attempts to convey information visually. They reveal how individuals communicated to each other about their habits, experiences and lifestyles.

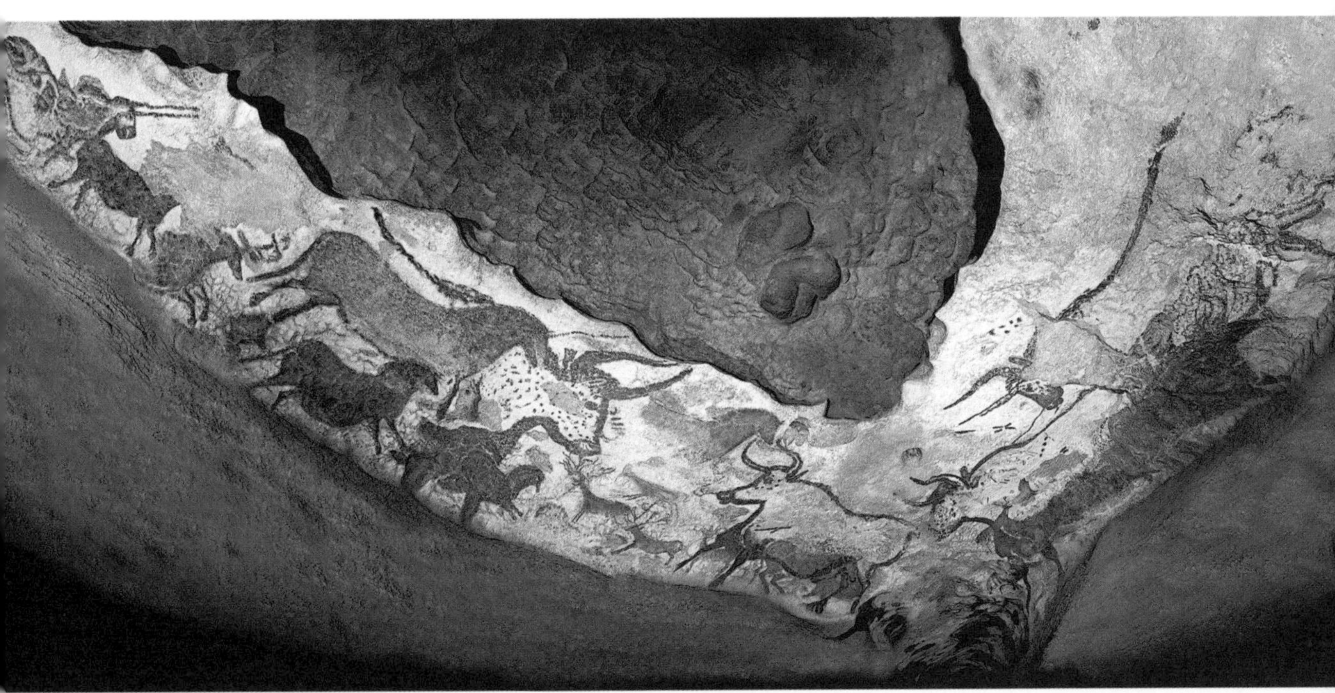

Sumerian clay tablet, probably from southern Iraq, c. 3100–3000 BCE. The tablet is inscribed with cuneiform, an early form of writing inscribed with a sharp instrument. It records the allocation of beer.

Early forms of writing

The earliest evidence of writing did not emerge until around 3000 BCE, in the Sumerian culture of Mesopotamia. This writing system was based on pictographs. It was read from top to bottom and was constructed on a grid with equal vertical and horizontal spacing. It is thought that this early version of writing was a system of accounting, as the first written records are tablets that show commodities listed with accompanying names and numerals organized in columns. As the writing was inscribed, it would often be smeared as the scribe moved his hand across the writing surface. Consequently, scribes turned the pictographs on their sides and wrote the rows horizontally to make the writing easier. The pictographs became less literal-looking and began to represent ideas rather than physical objects, so a pictograph of the sun might mean 'light' or 'day'. This in turn led to a form of rebus-style writing (substituting an image for a letter or word), which then developed into cuneiform – a phonographic writing system in which images represented sounds or syllables.

In Egypt a similar system was utilized to communicate, though, unlike Sumerian script, this did not develop into a more abstract form of writing for almost 3,500 years. The Egyptians did, however, produce illustrated manuscripts using papyrus, a material similar to paper, that was made from the pith of the reed-like papyrus plant. The Egyptians combined both images and words to communicate information on papyrus scrolls, such as their religious beliefs on the afterlife. These are well documented in the tombs of the pharaohs and also the religious scrolls found in Egypt.

Over centuries of development, cuneiform and other ancient forms of pictographic writing turned into the alphabets and styles of writing we use to communicate today. As a result of this, communication between individuals can be more precise. Images can be restricting and open to misinterpretation, whereas words are unmistakable and can communicate complex ideas. Writing allows us to communicate to a mass audience and to document our history down the generations. It also allows us to exchange important information between cultures and races.

Cartography

Cartography, the science, skill or work of making maps, demonstrates the first recognizable form of information design as we know it today. The ancient Egyptians created maps that communicated information about the stars. A star map dating from around 1500 BCE was discovered in the tomb of the great Senmut (a high-ranking official in royal service to Thutmose II) near Luxor. This map apparently shows a gathering of planets in particular positions in the night sky, thereby referring to a specific point in time.

The first maps indicating land or territory are harder to identify. One artifact that could be described as an early land map was found in 1930 at a dig in the ruined city of Ga-Sur at Nuzi (the modern city of Yorghan Tepe), 200 miles north of the site of Babylon in modern-day Iraq. The map is drawn with cuneiform characters and symbols inscribed on a small clay tablet thought to date from 2500–2300 BCE. It represents a district bounded by hills or mountains and bisected by water. It is interesting to note that the hills or mountains are shown as overlapping semicircles – a device used by mapmakers and illustrators for centuries afterwards.

By the 2nd century CE, mapmaking had become more sophisticated. Ptolemy, a Roman citizen of Egypt, was an astronomer and mathematician who wrote *Geographia*, or *The Geography*. This substantial work provided information about map projections on what was known about the world's geography between 127 and 150 CE. Ptolemy was the first recorded person to assign coordinates to geographic features and imposed a grid system on a map, using the same grid system for the entire globe.

It is from the pioneering efforts of early mapmakers such as Ptolemy that we are able to orient ourselves in our surroundings and find our way from one place to another with such accuracy.

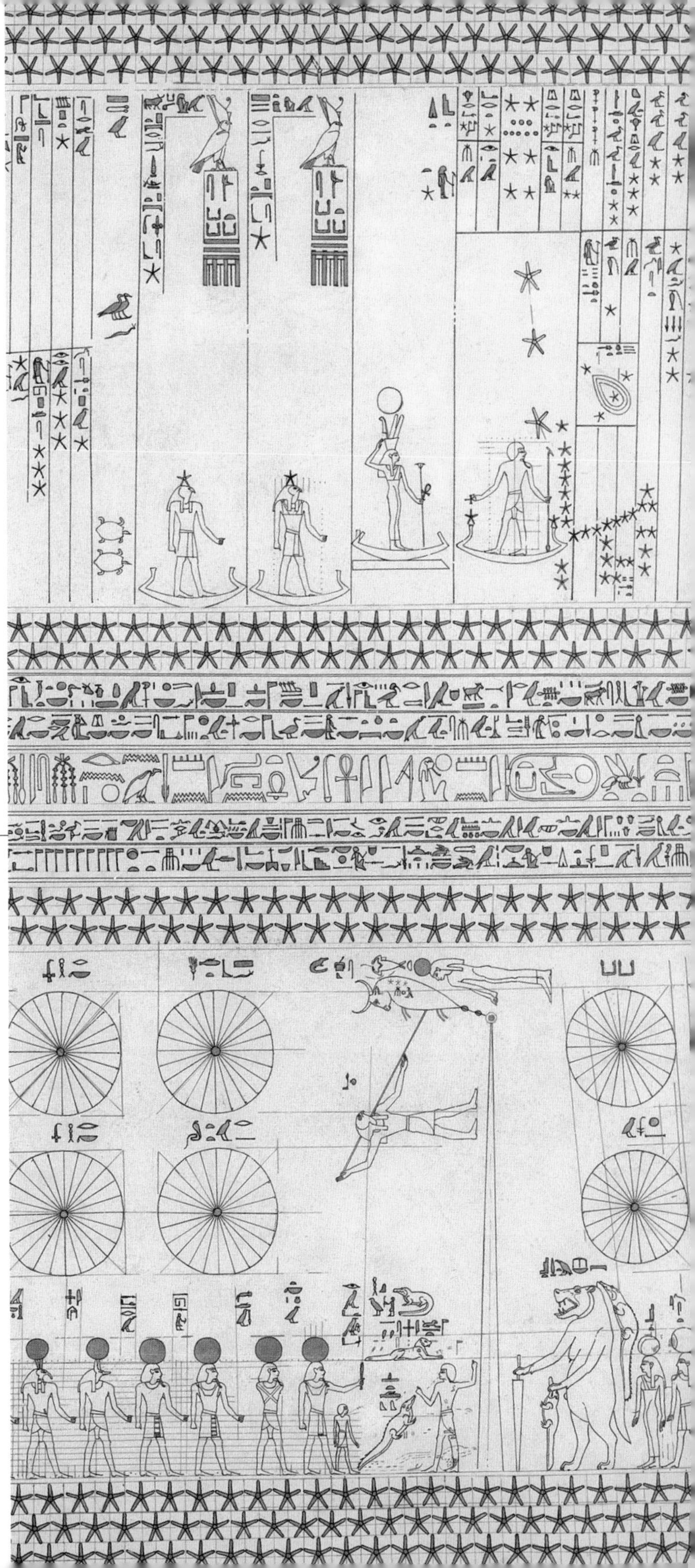

Right (detail): Facsimile painting by Charles K. Wilkinson of the Astronomical Ceiling in the tomb of Senmut, near Luxor, Egypt, c. 1473–1458 BCE.

Below: Cast of a Babylonian clay tablet inscribed with a map, c. 2500–2300 BCE, from Ga-Sur, Mesopotamia (modern Iraq).

Charts and graphs

Today, bar charts and graphs seem such an obvious way of presenting statistical data that it is easy to think anyone could have created them. Scottish economist and engineer William Playfair (1759–1823) is often credited with the invention of bar, line and pie charts. Large amounts of statistical data were available in the 18th century, but this was always presented in printed tabular form. Playfair had the idea of presenting data in illustrative form. The bar chart first appeared in his *Commercial and Political Atlas*, published in 1786. In his *Atlas* he presented information on imports and exports from different countries over the years, which he showed as line graphs. This meant that the reader could see the relationship between the various economic factors in quantitative graphical data. It was the first step towards the visualization of data.

This clever way of presenting data enables the eye to perceive instantly what the brain would take much longer to deduce from a table of numbers. This is what makes graphs work so well for scientists, businesspeople and others. The charts allow the numbers to speak to everyone in the same way. They transcend the boundaries of culture, language and race: a Russian person can understand the same graph just as well as a French person. Graphs make information easy to decode and accessible for a much wider audience.

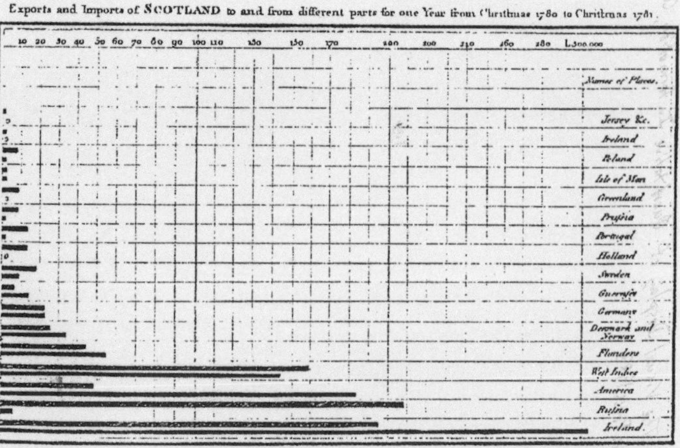

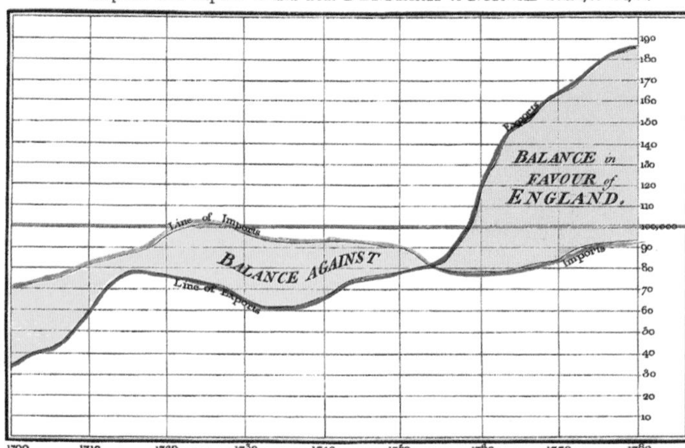

Top: 'Exports and Imports of Scotland to and from different parts for one Year from Christmas 1780 to Christmas 1781', bar chart from William Playfair's *The Commercial and Political Atlas* (1786).

Above: 'Exports and Imports to and from Denmark and Norway from 1700 to 1780', graph from William Playfair's *The Commercial and Political Atlas* (1786).

ISOTYPEs by Otto Neurath representing different groups of people, c. 1945. Otto & Marie Neurath Isotype Collection, University of Reading.

ISOTYPEs

ISOTYPEs (short for International System of Typographic Picture Education) are an attempt to communicate information pictographically, through a standard visual language. They were created by Vienna-born political economist Otto Neurath (1882–1945) between the 1920s and 1940s. Following the First World War (1914–1918), Neurath felt it was vital to communicate important social and economic issues clearly. He believed that information should be comprehensible to all people, no matter their cultural or educational background. He is quoted as saying 'words make divisions, pictures make connections'.

A system of elementary pictographs was developed, completely void of decoration, in order to present complicated data visually. The pictographs were designed to represent subtle qualities within the data, and challenges such as how to represent an emigrant or an unemployed man through a pictograph had to be overcome. Along with scientist and mathematician Marie Reidermeister (later his wife), Neurath converted data from verbal and numerical form into visual layouts.

Inspired by the artistic movement of Constructivism and the avant-garde New Typography movement of the 1920s and 1930s, German artist Gerd Arntz (1900–1988) designed most of these pictographs; by 1940 there were more than 1,000. Simplicity was the key: a strict set of rules governed the pictographs to ensure they were consistent in their make-up and application. These specified the use of text, colour and positioning.

Neurath's work had an enormous impact on information design. The conventions and simplified visual imagery he produced helped to develop a universal visual language that can still be seen in the use of pictographs in signage and information systems worldwide.

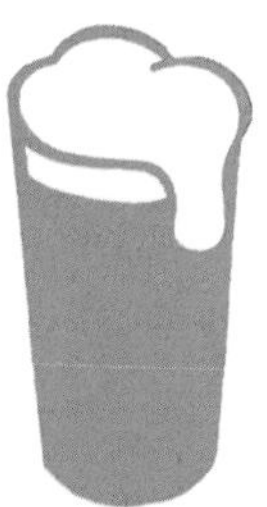

A selection of Gerd Arntz's ISOTYPEs, 1928–1965.

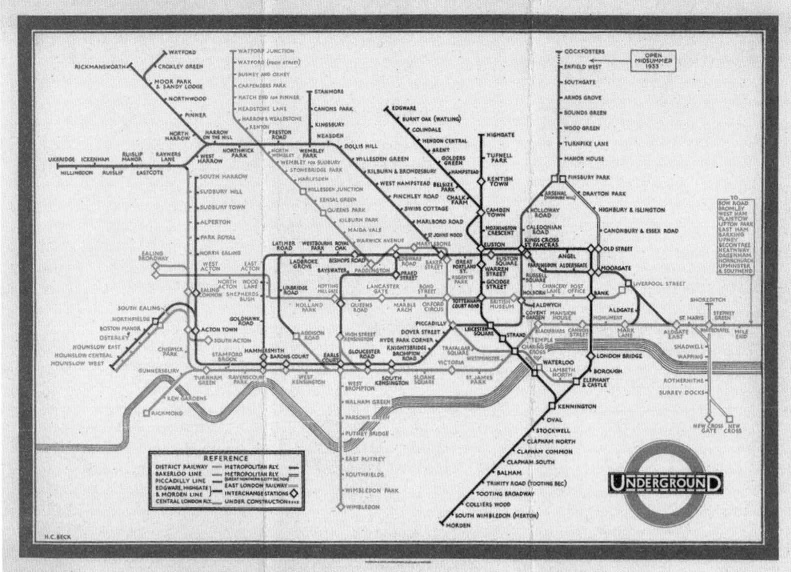

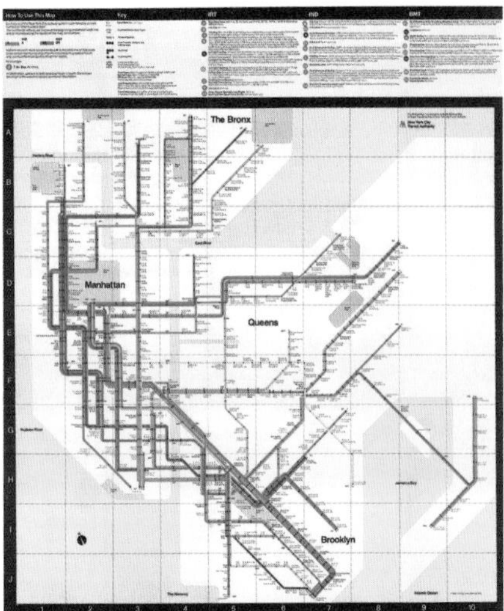

Above: Henry C. Beck's map of the London Underground, 1933.

Right, above: The New York Subway map, designed by Massimo Vignelli, 1972.

Right: Map of the Paris Metro, based on Beck's London Underground map.

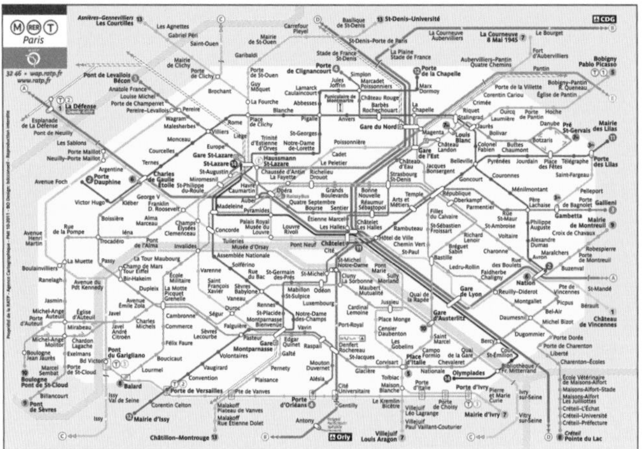

Reproduced by courtesy of RATP

The geographically inaccurate map

Most people are familiar with the iconic London Underground map, designed by English engineer Henry C. Beck (1902–1974) in 1933. This map was a major innovation of its time, because it does not take the form of a traditional, geographically correct, map. It presents a diagrammatic representation of the Underground in which accurate distances and realism are dispensed with (there is no need for such information when one is underground) in favour of clarity and usability. The result is a clear map drawn on a grid of horizontals, verticals and 45-degree diagonals, with bright colour-coding to identify the different lines. The central section of the map is enlarged in proportion to the rest as it contains several complicated interchanges and more stations. Beck was a draughtsman who had worked on electrical circuits: the combination of circuit diagram and map was his idea. London Underground's publicity department was initially sceptical about Beck's design, but it printed a trial run and asked the public for feedback. The new map was found to be easy to read and functional, so it was implemented throughout the Underground system. It is now a design standard and has inspired subway and railway maps across the world.

Right: The first personal computer prototype, the Xerox Alto, 1973.

Below: The Lisa, made by Apple Computers, 1983, was the first personal computer available to the consumer that featured a detachable keyboard, mouse and Graphical User Interface.

Bottom: The Microsoft Windows 3.0 Graphical User Interface, 1990.

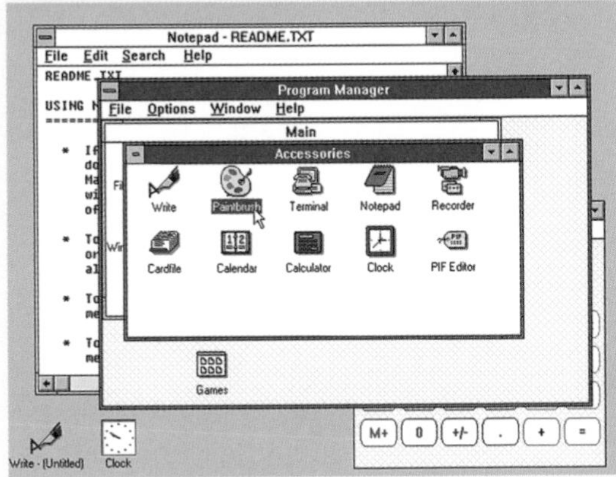

The Graphical User Interface

A Graphical User Interface (GUI) is the representation of information and actions available to a user through graphical icons and visual indicators. The actions are performed through direct manipulation of the graphical elements, rather than typed commands via text.
We tend to take GUIs for granted; they include the word processor on our PC and the mobile phone interface we use to dial numbers and send text messages. Without these intuitive interfaces, we would have to use complicated computer code to control these devices.
The evolution of computers began back in the 1950s, but the home computer, or personal computer, as we know it today, was developed in the 1970s.

Xerox developed the Xerox Alto, the first personal computer prototype, in 1973. It used a keyboard as an input device, a mouse as a pointing device and a video screen as a viewing device. In 1981, the introduction of Xerox Star brought in the first GUI. Graphical icons were used to initiate operations and control the computer rather than typing in long lines of programming code. The machine was not developed beyond the prototype stage, as it was thought to be too expensive to be marketable.

A young Steve Jobs (CEO of Apple Inc. until his death in 2011) had been to a presentation of the Xerox Star system and decided to build a GUI of his own.
The result was the Apple Macintosh, which launched in 1984. The interface used a desktop metaphor, with files, folders and even a wastebasket or trash can. It featured overlapping windows to separate operations. The system also included a keyboard and mouse as input devices. Since the GUI was embedded into the operating system, all the application software employed the same methods to perform tasks, making it easy to learn new pieces of software. In 1990, Microsoft introduced the Windows operating system, which used the same metaphors as the Macintosh.
It became the standard operating system for the personal computer market.

The multi-touch screen revolution

A touch screen is an electronic display that is sensitive to the touch of a stylus or finger within the display area. E.A. Johnson of the Royal Radar Establishment in the UK is credited with the invention of the first touch screen in 1965. The touch screen enables the user to interact with the display directly without the need for a mouse or touchpad. Today, touch screens are widely used with digital appliances such as mobile phones, satellite navigation devices and video games.

Multi-touch technology allows the device to recognize two or more points of contact with the screen. When an object or finger touches the surface, sensors detect the disruption of an electrical field. This information is relayed to the software, which responds to the gesture accordingly. This technology has allowed designers to develop more intuitive and gesture-driven interfaces for handheld electronic devices such as the mobile phone. Interactive designer Mike Matas from the USA has commented, 'If you want to do something (on a computer) you should just be able to reach out your hand and do it, no buttons and no computer interface required.'

Many companies utilize multi-touch screen technology for their smartphones and tablets. Devices such as the Apple iPhone and iPad were designed to be used with a finger, so you control everything with a tap, drag, swipe, pinch, flick or twist of the fingers. Even seemingly complicated tasks can be completed with these simple gestures. These interfaces are now becoming commonplace, with many PCs using the system too.

This technology has allowed electronic devices and interfaces to become more accessible and instinctive. They rely less on complicated menus and keyboards and as a result use fewer moving parts.

Using a multi-touch screen on an Apple iPad.

Why is information design necessary?

Information plays a large part in our daily lives. We are surrounded by information all the time, from the remote control for our TV to the interface on our mobile phone and the webpage we view. We take it for granted, but someone had to design the way in which it is visually presented.

Try to imagine a world where information design didn't exist. Taking a simple bus or rail journey would be quite difficult without it. How would you know which bus or train to catch, where to catch it and what time it departed or arrived at its destination? How would the driver know where he was going without the use of directional road signs? How would you know when to turn and in which direction? Even simple decisions when driving such as when to stop at a junction would be difficult without the traffic-light system. Crossing a busy road could prove difficult without simple aids such as the pedestrian crossing.

Below: The UK road and motorway signage system was designed 1957–1967 by Jock Kinneir and Margaret Calvert. It has since been adopted around the world, for example at Umm Suqeim, Dubai, UAE (**bottom**).

Pedestrian crossing light from the former German Democratic Republic.

Simple inventions like warning symbols and colour-coding allow users to navigate and use machines safely. They provide guidelines that everyone can follow, even if you are unfamiliar with the environment or the equipment being used. Clear instructions are given on what (or what not) to do.

Consider travelling to a foreign country where your native language is not spoken. At the airport, how do you know where to find the departure gate or retrieve your luggage? How do you find the taxi rank or bureau de change? All these dilemmas are solved via information design. It provides clear instructions, facts or data to an audience in a visual language that can transcend international boundaries and bring people together. It helps us to learn complex information, such as the Periodic Table. It can make the complicated very simple and can save time and effort in the transmission.

Above: Signage in two languages at Hong Kong airport.

Right: The Periodic Table.

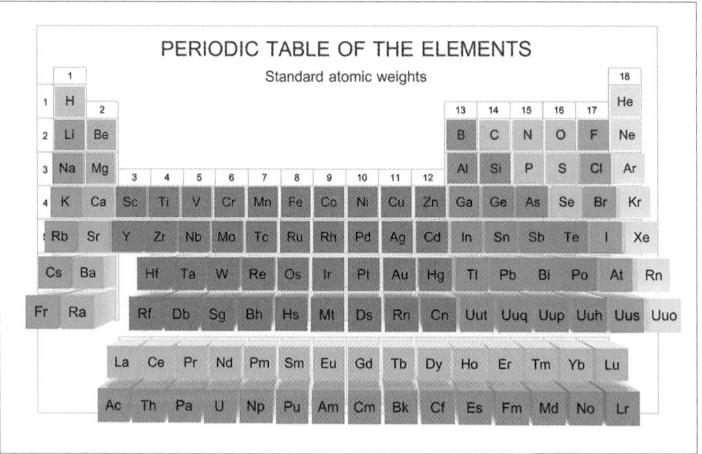

What are the different types of information design?

Information design takes many forms. We break them down into three main categories: print, interactive (including screen-based design), and environmental. These three categories also overlap, as various types of information frequently appear in one or more category. This is not a definitive list and some people may use other categorizations. Each category takes a different approach to the presentation of data, to which we will draw attention.

Print-based information design

If you were asked to give an example of print-based design, what would it be? Something from a textbook at school; a biological diagram of an eye, perhaps? Information is presented to us all the time, and in a variety of ways; we often just don't consider or realize it. Information design is not just the sexy pieces of data visualization we see in graphic design books, it is also the everyday instances that we take for granted. Consider the utility bill that tells you how much electricity you have used, or the instructional diagrams that come with flat-pack furniture. Information is everywhere, and we are not always aware of how much thought has gone into its visualization.

Information in print relies on a single image or sequence of images to convey complex sets of data. It not only uses diagrams or charts, but can also use photography, illustration and text to communicate, for example, a newspaper or magazine article. It is static and the reader is passive in the transmission of the material. The user does not interact with it in any way other than to decode the visual data presented to gain the facts or figures more quickly than by reading long passages of explanatory text.

The complexity of the data has to be considered; an audience may struggle if too much information is presented in one piece. Navigating the information is necessary; unlike interactive information design, where the user can isolate particular sets of data, print presents all the information together. This may mean that a key (sometimes called a legend), such as colour-coding or symbolic pictograms, is required to be able to decipher the material. An example of this is the

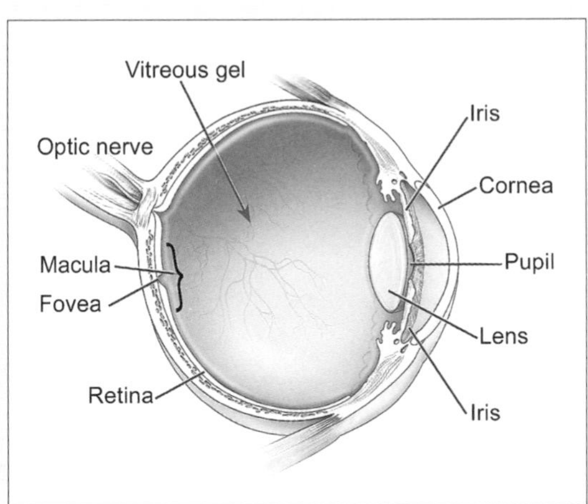

Above: Anatomical diagram of an eye.

Right: Assembly instructions for the IKEA ANSSI barstool.

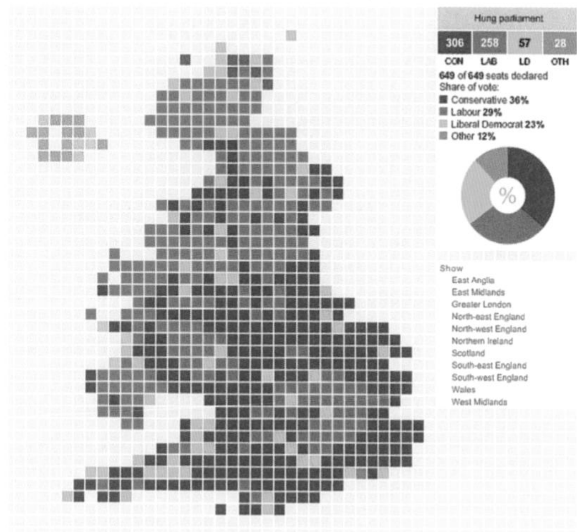

Above: Mark Bryson's map for *The Guardian* newspaper showing results for the 2010 UK general election.

Below: The Sacramento Municipal Utility District bill, designed by Opower, details the addressee's energy usage in relation to that of their neighbours via graphical content.

2010 UK election map designed by Mark Bryson, which shows via colour-coding the number of votes cast for different political parties across the UK.

If done correctly, information design can modify people's behaviour. In an age when we are all concerned about the amount of energy we consume, simple graphics such as that of an energy-efficiency chart allow a user to judge a rating immediately.

In 2009 Robert Cialdini, a social psychologist at Arizona State University, conducted a study in conjunction with the Sacramento Municipal Utility District. 35,000 randomly selected homes were chosen to receive a new style of utility statement. These rated consumers on their energy use by comparing them to their neighbours. Consumers received two smiley faces for very efficient energy use, one smiley face for good, and frowns for using too much energy.

After a six-month period, Cialdini found that the customers who received the personalized statement reduced their energy use by 2 per cent more than those who received the standard statements.

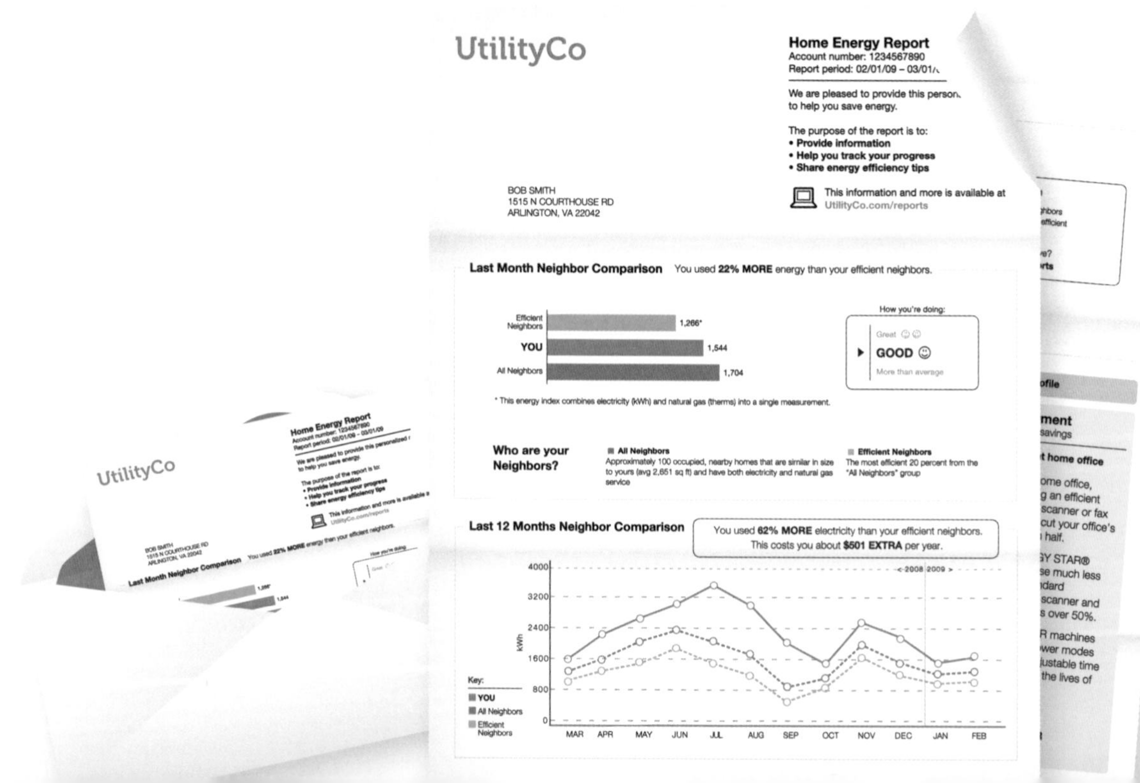

UtilityCo

Home Energy Report
Account number: 1234567890
Report period: 02/01/09 – 03/01/

We are pleased to provide this person
to help you save energy.

The purpose of the report is to:
- **Provide information**
- **Help you track your progress**
- **Share energy efficiency tips**

This information and more is available at UtilityCo.com/reports

BOB SMITH
1515 N COURTHOUSE RD
ARLINGTON, VA 22042

Last Month Neighbor Comparison You used **22% MORE** energy than your efficient neighbors.

Efficient Neighbors 1,266*
YOU 1,544
All Neighbors 1,704

How you're doing:
Great
GOOD
More than average

* This energy index combines electricity (kWh) and natural gas (therms) into a single measurement.

Who are your Neighbors?

All Neighbors Approximately 100 occupied, nearby homes that are similar in size to yours (avg 2,651 sq ft) and have both electricity and natural gas service

Efficient Neighbors The most efficient 20 percent from the "All Neighbors" group

Last 12 Months Neighbor Comparison You used **62% MORE** electricity than your efficient neighbors. This costs you about **$501 EXTRA** per year.

kWh 4000 3200 2400 1600 800 0
2008 2009
MAR APR MAY JUN JUL AUG SEP OCT NOV DEC JAN FEB

Key:
YOU
All Neighbors
Efficient Neighbors

Interactive information design

The computer and the internet have revolutionized how we receive and interact with data. Interactive information design requires a very different approach than print. Since the user is active in making choices, those choices need to be considered and presented. It is not a case of presenting a static image on screen. The user needs to be involved or immersed in the information. This often involves filtering data to show particular facts, figures or statistics. The user selects the criteria by which the data or information is measured or compared. The navigation of this information is very important: the options available have to be clear and should lead to some meaningful resolution.

Think about the interface of your cable or terrestrial TV supplier. The choice of programming has to be presented clearly. What is showing at the moment? What will be next? Can I set a reminder to watch a transmission? How do I record a particular programme at a certain time? Decisions have to be made by the user. There should be no ambiguity or uncertainty as to the on-screen navigation and instructions.

Since information is divorced from the page, the designer can employ sound and moving images as part of the experience. The user is no longer passive. Paul Farrington of Studio Tonne in the UK has created website interfaces for numerous clients, including the navigational interface for record label 4AD's e-commerce site. The navigational tool had to enable the user to search quickly through the label's 25-year back catalogue as well as searching via artist. The decisions made on the tool took the user to specific pages within the site.

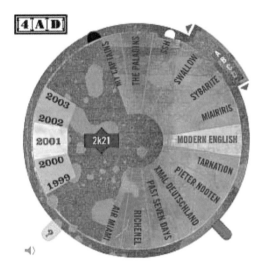

Interface for the 4AD website, designed by Paul Farrington of Studio Tonne. The user selects a year and an artist on the wheel to navigate to the appropriate page of the site.

This Virgin Media television interface displays the programme schedule alongside icons showing what is set to be recorded and which programmes can be accessed via catch-up services.

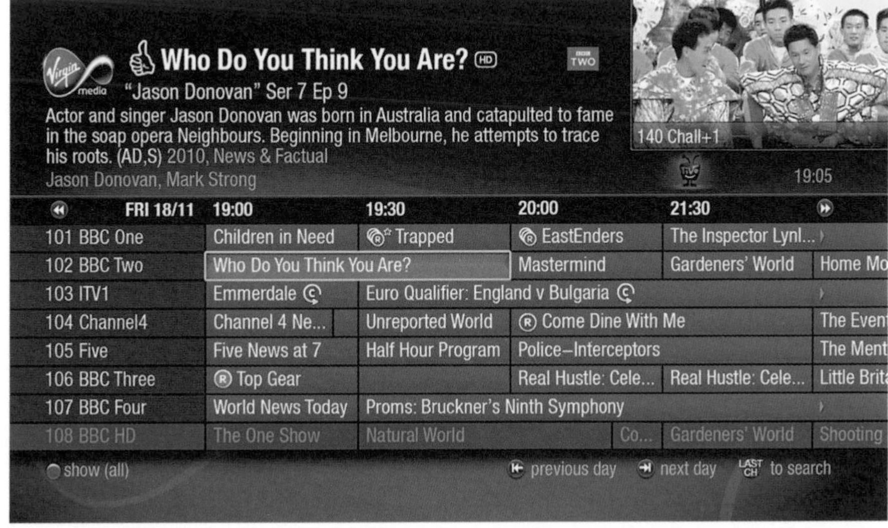

To illustrate how interactive information design differs from print, try comparing the experience of reading a magazine in print form with a multi-media tablet such as an iPad. The iPad application incorporates sound and moving imagery as part of the user experience. It shows behind-the-scenes video features in real time as opposed to static imagery.

The capabilities of an interactive solution allow users to explore content in a variety of ways. Depending on the content, it can be preferable to guide the user through set pathways or allow them to meander through at their leisure. The ability to navigate and make decisions about what and how we view has placed more responsibility on the designer to make the transmission of information easier and clearer. The choices made can separate out data and make distinctions or comparisons more apparent.

We now have information designers who call themselves user experience designers; they understand the difference between telling people about features of a product or service and letting them experience the benefits for themselves. The user experience is explored in more detail in Chapter 2.

Examples of interactive information design include reading a magazine on an iPad (**left**) and using an in-car navigation system (**above**).

Environmental information design

Signage is probably the first thing most people think of when talking about environmental information design, although wayfinding, exhibition design and large-scale installations could also be included in this category.

American urban planner Kevin Lynch first used the term 'wayfinding' in his 1960 book *Image of the City*. He used it to describe navigating through a physical environment using visual cues to orient oneself. This can incorporate signage along with lighting and three-dimensional objects. The function of wayfinding is to inform an audience of where they need to go, how to find it and what to do once they have arrived. The designer must be aware of the physical limitations of an environment and of the needs of the user. They may have to analyze the space and make informed choices based on how real people use the area. A good example of wayfinding and signage in practice is provided in the case study at the Design Museum Holon, Tel Aviv, in Chapter 7.

The challenge with exhibition design is how you communicate important facts or data to a large audience in a specific site. The material presented will have to be at a larger scale, but it is not simply a case of making everything bigger. The designer may have to think about the distance from which a project is viewed, where it is positioned, even the ambient lighting conditions within that physical environment to ensure that it is legible. It is possible to use multiple platforms to communicate, choosing print for some elements and interactive for others. This may depend on the amount of detail required and how the presentation of the information aids comprehension. For example, a piece about kinetic energy will use movement to tell the audience about it. The main thing to consider with environmental information design is visibility and context.

HAPTICA
HAPTICA

Chapter 2: Information design for specific audiences

This chapter explores the issues of usability and the audience. The more you can learn about your audience, the better-informed choices you can make about the design and how it meets the audience's needs. This could mean the difference between a design that has longevity and something that needs costly revisions. In this chapter we explore how to identify the needs and requirements of an audience and the importance of taking these into consideration when designing.

Identifying the audience and their needs

One of the mistakes designers can make when presenting information visually is to only please the client in the process, while neglecting the needs and requirements of the intended audience. Don't assume you know what the audience wants or responds to. You need to try to achieve a balance in your designs so you meet the needs of the audience as well as satisfying the client. This may mean modifying the proposal in relation to what the audience requires, instead of what the client wants to say. When preparing your proposal or brief you need to ask lots of questions. How does the audience make sense of the information? Is it purely visual or does it require sound or even touch? Do any environmental factors need to be considered, such as where the piece will be positioned and how lighting may affect legibility? The more you learn about your audience, the more informed choices you will be able to make about the design and how it meets their needs.

The key with this process is to analyze your audience in detail and get to know what they want and why. If you can design to the audience's requirements you will produce a solution that is both meaningful and functional.

'Usability is the ability of an object or system to be used with satisfaction by the people in the environment and context the object or system is intended for.'

Ronnie Lipton, writer on information design

Previous page: The Haptica Braille watch, designed by David Chavez, enables the user to get a quick and accurate time-reading while maintaining discretion.

Defining the audience

Designers need to be able to identify the audience or group of people to whom they are communicating. This can make the difference between a successful design and an unsuccessful one. Audiences can be defined by a number of factors such as gender, race, age, occupation or income. The analysis of these categories is known as demographics. By examining several of these categories it is possible to define a demographic profile. This profile provides information about a typical member of this group. The information designer can use this material to understand the needs and requirements of a specific audience and adjust their designs accordingly.

An audience for a product or service can be very general, for example, an international audience of 18- to 65-year-olds of varying levels of education and different cultural backgrounds, or very specialist, such as 8- to 12-year-old middle-class British boys who like computer technology. Even though information is on view in public places and visible to all of us, it is not aimed at everyone. There is no single audience. The important thing is to identify the main users and understand the kinds of needs and/or restrictions that should be considered when designing for them.

Shown overleaf are four mobile phones, as an illustration of the way a specific category of audience uses a product and how in turn that audience can influence the development of the product. Each phone is essentially the same product, with the same basic functions. The type of category or audience, however, has had a huge effect on the look, feel and usability of the product.

A simple smartphone has a multitude of functions such as phone, text, email, camera, maps, GPS, music and alarm. The ability to use all of these functions depends on the kind of user and their level of proficiency with the technology. Not everyone will use every function, even if they are available.

The Doro phone, produced in Sweden, has been designed with elderly users in mind. It has a limited number of functions, and the size and visibility of the buttons on the keypad were determined as a result of testing on older people whose sight and dexterity might be impaired.

The Firefly phone from the USA has been designed with children as young as 5 years of age in mind. It dispenses with normal keypad functions and instead of using numerals it uses pictograms to represent mother, father, answer and end. The parent can program the phone, and calls in and out can be controlled by a password to limit usage.

Korean designer Seon-Keun Park has proposed a concept for a Braille phone for visually impaired users. The phone's keypad is presented in Braille characters, but it also has a revolutionary new screen with the ability to fabricate raised Braille characters within the screen area so that the visually impaired can 'read' text messages. The concept won a red dot design award in 2009.

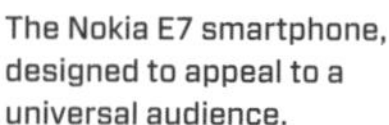

The Nokia E7 smartphone, designed to appeal to a universal audience.

The Doro PhoneEasy® 612, designed for seniors.

Concept for a Braille mobile phone, designed by Seon-Keun Park for Samsung.

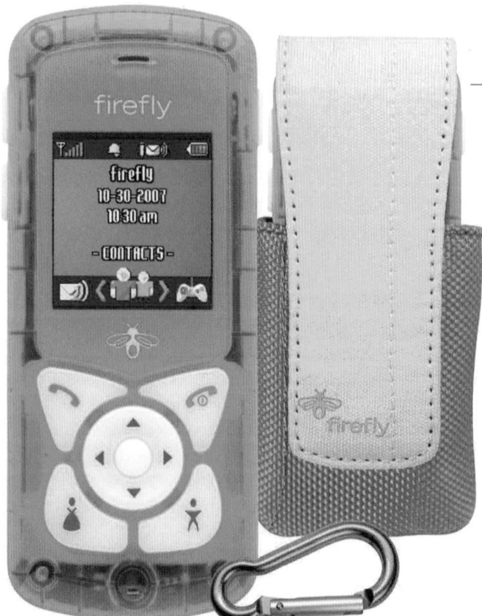

The Firefly mobile phone, designed for children.

Cultural considerations

Cultural backgrounds and population stereotypes can influence the way in which an audience interacts with a product or service. When designing for particular markets such as mainland Europe or the USA, certain simple factors may influence your design decisions. An example of this is a basic electrical switch. In the UK, a switch tends to be flicked down to turn something on and up to turn it off, whereas in the USA the opposite is the case.

Imagine designing a safety system in which a shut-off button had to be included. In an emergency situation people do what they have always instinctively done when switching something off. If your switch is designed for the wrong market and turns on instead of switching off, this could have disastrous results. It is for these reasons that it is important to know whether your audience is global or local. Particular solutions may lend themselves better to one audience than another.

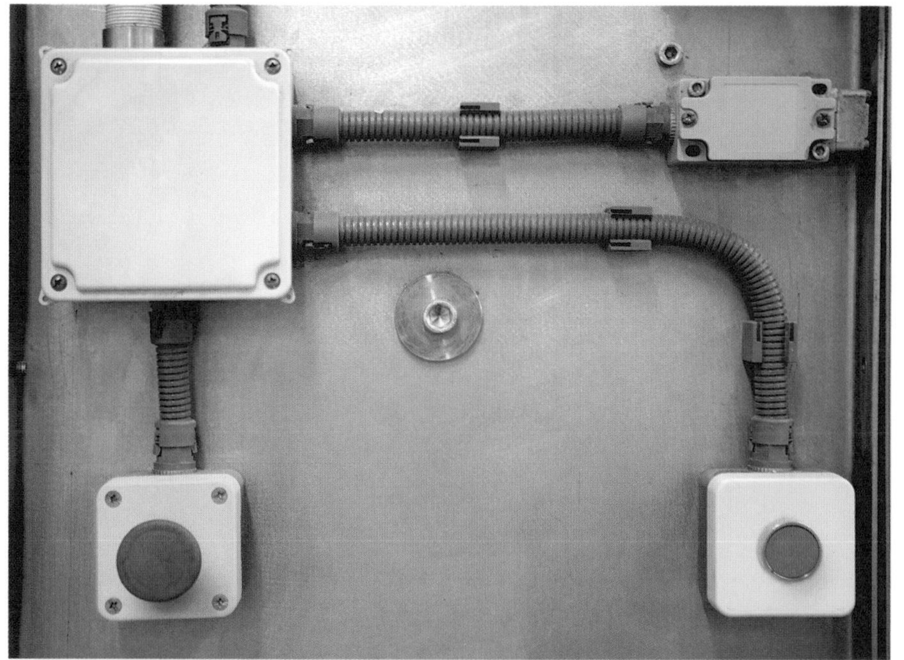

Designers cannot assume that their designs will be viewed only in the country of origin. It is for this reason that using universal symbols, such as those identifying male and female (**above**), or colours for 'stop' and 'go' (**left**), are beneficial to society as a whole. Not everyone speaks the same language and it is this visual representation that makes it easy for visitors to recognize, digest and navigate information.

Ethnography and personas

Ethnography is the anthropological study of human behaviour when dealing with products or services. Many companies employ ethnographic research when designing for specific audiences. By observing a user interacting with a product in their own environment, a designer can gain a clearer understanding of the needs of the audience. Don Tunstall, PhD, states 'Ethnography is a philosophical approach to human knowledge that says it's best to understand people based on their own categories of thought, behaviour and actions.' It is not essential to carry out ethnographic studies with every project, but it does provide a unique insight on how an audience views a product or service.

Since ethnography can be expensive and time-consuming, many designers use the method of fabricating personas to gain a greater understanding of their audience. In simple terms this means constructing a fictitious character who represents a whole group or section of society. The character is given a name, and a description of their attitudes, behaviours, environmental conditions, goals, personal details and skill sets is built up. It is important to base these descriptions on research rather than on the designers' opinion. Once constructed, the personas can be used to test out the functionality or appropriateness of the solution to a design problem. It may be necessary to use several personas to obtain an accurate assessment of the solution. A practical exercise on creating a persona is set out later in this chapter (see pp. 37–39).

Semiotics

Factors such as colour-coding can be treated differently from country to country. For example, the lettering on exit signs in Europe is green, whereas in the USA it is red. The theory of semiotics looks at how meaning is constructed within cultures and explores how ideas are connected with words, images and objects. Colour can be used as a sign to convey a meaning or mood to an audience.

Semiotics is defined as the theory of signs. The word 'semiotics' comes from the Greek word *semeiotikos*, which means 'interpreter of signs'. Signing is vital to human existence because it underlies all forms of communication. Signs are amazingly diverse. They include gestures, facial expressions, speech, slogans, graffiti, commercials, medical symptoms, marketing, music, body language, drawings, paintings, poetry, design, film, Morse code, clothes, food, rituals and primitive symbols. Signs are important because they can mean something other than themselves. For example, spots on your chest can mean you are ill, while a blip on the radar screen can mean impending danger for an aircraft. Reading messages like this seems simple enough, but a great deal hangs on context. Spots on your chest need to be judged in a medical context; similarly, signs are not isolated – their meaning depends on the contexts in which they are read and understood.

Semiotics is about the tools, processes and contexts we have for creating, interpreting and understanding meaning in a variety of ways.

Gender

If you had to produce a design aimed solely at men or women, what differences do you think you would have to take into consideration? It is not simply that designs for women are pink and those for men blue! Although we may not want to admit it, there are distinct differences in the ways the genders interpret and react to information. Much of this depends on how children are conditioned: boys may be brought up to pay more attention to scientific subjects, such as mathematics, physics and computer science, which could lead to males being more confident with technology and high-tech products. In studies conducted by British cognitive psychologists Diane McGuinness and John Symonds in 1977, it was found that male babies responded more to mechanical objects than to faces; female babies had the opposite reaction. This experiment demonstrated that younger males and females differed in their preferences for objects and people.

In many Western cultures, girls are often encouraged more into the arts and social sciences, which could explain why females are thought to possess greater confidence with social relationships and aesthetics than their male peers. This could also explain why more men than women seem to be interested in technology. In simple terms, one key cultural difference between the genders is that men might be encouraged to put function first and then emotion, whereas women might put emotion first and then function. When designing with men in mind you may have to think about the levels of technology and also how it appeals to them on a personal level. Consider the amount of detail that is incorporated; the shapes and colour palettes employed to convey the data and how complicated the data is. It is important to note that designers should base their designs on solid research and not resort to making assumptions based on gender stereotypes.

Age and familiarity with technology

Age can be a huge consideration when deciding what kind of technology should be used to present data. Although we live in a computer-literate society, there are varying levels of competency within the community. Different generations have grown up with different forms of technology. As we age we often find it more difficult to learn new processes. The younger generation are computer-literate from an early age and so feel comfortable with technology, but many seniors do not have the same level of familiarity or proficiency. When designing for seniors it may be necessary to use simple technology that requires a minimum of concentration to use. Think about the mobile phones presented earlier in this chapter (pp. 29–30): for the older market a larger keypad with simple functions was employed, which made the equipment easy to use and the audience less fearful of the technology. Conversely, a younger generation often embrace new forms of technology and equipment and are happy to learn different techniques to retrieve information; they have less fear of the equipment.

One Laptop Per Child project

A good example of designing an interface appropriate for a specific audience is design agency Pentagram's work with the One Laptop Per Child project. This initiative aims to provide durable, low-power $100 laptops to children all over the world. The goal is for children in developing countries to learn about new technology. The laptop's interface has to be universal and so uses an icon-based 'zoom' system to communicate. This interface, called Sugar, was developed by Lisa Strausfeld, Christian Marc Schmidt and Takaaki Okada. It is easy for children to use and has four main categories to navigate: Home, Friends, Neighbourhood and Activity. All the functions are contained within these categories. The laptop is not as complicated as a standard PC, but allows many of the same functions and networking capabilities. Friends and Neighbourhood show which other users the laptop is connected to and arranges them around their current activities. Home shows the user's activities, such as drawings, texts and photographs. The challenge of the project was to develop an interface that multiple users could relate to and understand. It also needed some degree of freedom, such as assigning colours to Friends. The resulting software uses simplified icons to signify features and so does not rely heavily on the use of written text to navigate. The project has been running since 2007, and so far 2 million children have received laptops.

The XO-3 tablet mimics the XO laptop and has a multi-touch display, which can pick up pen and brush strokes as well as gestures. The screen is readable in sunlight.

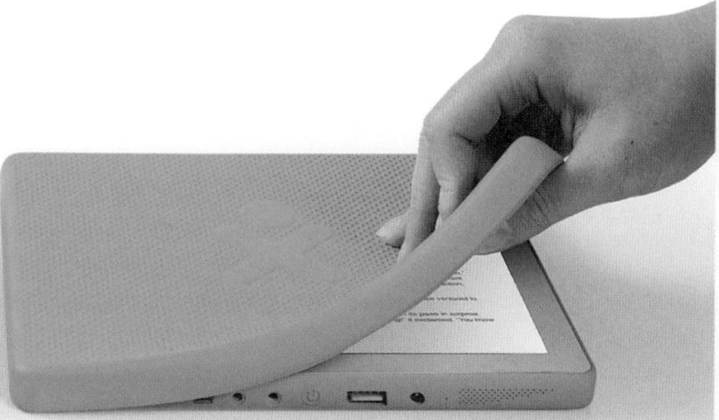

Above: The prototype XO-3 tablet, designed by Yves Behar's fuseproject. The all-plastic tablet is semi-flexible and extremely durable.

Right: The XO laptop is similar in size to a textbook. It has a flexible design with rounded edges, a sealed, rubber-membrane keyboard and an integrated handle. Here it is used by children in Paraguay (**right**) and Nepal (**far right**).

How to identify your audience

Mood boards are a creative tool. They are generally a collection of materials that give a visual direction for any given project. In the way we are presenting them they can also give a visual indication of the attributes and interest of an audience. Design agency Landor Associates uses a specific grid to identify personality attributes for its branding projects. We have adapted this practice to show how to visually identify and clarify your audience.

This is not a mood board in the traditional sense, like one used by an interior designer. This one does not use randomly sourced images to give a visual 'feel'. Instead, it uses strict criteria to identify images for each section of the grid.

The modules can work to give an indication of lifestyle and personal attributes rather than just colour, shapes and objects.

Within the nine squares, identify specific criteria to look for within images. For example, if one square were a car, what car would it be for this kind of audience? If one were a holiday, what kind of holiday would it be and to which destination? By building a collection of imagery you begin to identify links and clarify the perception of the user.

PERSON

HOLIDAY	CAR	ANIMAL
BOOK	FOOD	HOUSE
VEGETABLE	CELEBRITY	GAME

How to create personas

From producing the mood board it is possible to move on to the slightly more complex creation of personas. Since the mood board has identified lifestyle choices you begin to acquire an overall picture of the kind of person you are designing for. This enables you to suggest a fictitious personality for them. Begin with a photograph.

Questions to ask:

Is this person male or female?

How old are they?

Where do they live?

What is their job?

What are their aspirations?

What will they need this product or service for?

How will they use it?

A successful persona is a story of that person. It has some personal details that give an insight into the user. Think about what the person does after work, or what they never get a chance to do but would love to. The questions will change based on the information project you are designing for. You will probably need more than one persona to obtain a fully rounded picture. For example, personas for a wayfinding project may take into account the local community, ranging from mothers going shopping, to national and international city visitors. These may include people of varying age and ability and possibly non-English-speakers. Approaching it from the perspective of a diverse audience will help to identify possible problems early on, so always design with them in mind. This in turn may save money and time as well as producing a more user-friendly solution.

Example of persona: Noah (age 8)

Noah lives just outside a city centre with his mum, dad and younger sister Darcey. He attends an independent Steiner school. He enjoys drawing, reading and playing computer games. He is obsessed with *Star Wars*, collects Lego and also loves programmes about history (anything with battles/ beheadings and weapons in!). In his spare time he goes swimming and is a member of a martial arts club. He is very sociable and enjoys spending time with his friends and extended family. When he grows up he wants to design computer games or planes for NASA.

Example of persona: Iris (age 79)

Iris is a widow. She lives just outside the city centre in a middle-class area with lots of greenery. She lives alone and suffers from arthritis. Since her children have grown up and moved out she spends a lot of time alone. She loves to read and regularly visits the library. Her eyesight is not what it used to be and she needs strong spectacles to be able to read. She is currently waiting for a cataract operation, which should improve her sight. She likes to spend time with her family and regularly travels on public transport to visit relatives. She isn't very good with technology, although she tries. Quite often her family have to leave simple instructions on how to use the DVD player and complicated gadgets. Her health is a worry to her family and they keep in touch as regularly as they can.

Some of Lance Wyman's designs for the 1968 Olympic Games held in Mexico City. The ticket (**top right**) is an excellent example of designing for an international audience. The entrance, row and seat numbers are all communicated through pictograms rather than text.

Internationalism

We live in a global economy and information is disseminated all over the world. One challenge that designers face is that of the international audience. How do you communicate to billions of people worldwide in several languages and still be cost-efficient? This is a very difficult issue to resolve. One method is to use minimal text and instead employ imagery, charts, diagrams and other visual forms as the main method of delivery.

A good example of this is designing for global events such as the Olympic Games, which must cater for a vast multi-national audience. American graphic designer Lance Wyman took on this challenge to produce the graphic identity and information system for the 1968 Mexico City Olympics. The problem was that the information had to be conveyed to all people, no matter what their background or their native language. The solution was to design information and a wayfinding system based on simple pictographic imagery. The icons were constructed using a modular format so that they could be applied across a multitude of platforms. These included site identification, directional signs, posters, maps, uniform patches and even giant colour-coded balloons hanging over the sports arenas. The resulting design was seen as so successful that the *New York Times* wrote, 'You can be illiterate in all languages and still navigate the surroundings successfully.'

The success of Wyman's solution lay in his ability to understand the needs of the audience. He considered the restrictions put in place by such a diverse group. He also thought about the user experience of how to navigate a busy city. This led to the implementation of a functional and user-friendly system that has become a blueprint for several others.

Monochrome pictograms for the London 2012 Olympic Games designed by SomeOne design practice. The images are based on actual photographs of iconic poses taken from each sport.

When designing for an international audience, simplicity and clarity are the qualities to keep in mind. If there are fewer elements to distract, the message will be more efficiently delivered. Again using the Olympics as an example, how do you demonstrate various sporting events clearly without using words? For his graphic identity for the 1972 Munich Olympics, German designer Otl Aicher devised a system based on a strict modular grid of vertical, horizontal and 45-degree lines. Each Olympic sport had a pictograph designed for it based on a simple line drawing of an abstract athlete. The symbols were derived from typical postures or poses from each sport, emphasizing the motion and the equipment involved to aid their identification. The pictographs were used extensively throughout the Games and were applied to signage, information booklets, maps, event documents and tickets. Those attending the Games quickly became familiar with the visual language.

Pictograms designed by Otl Aicher for the 1972 Munich Olympic Games.

Inclusivity

The British Standards Institute defines inclusive design as 'The design of mainstream products and/or services that are accessible to/and usable by, as many people as reasonably possible ... without the need for special adaptation or specialized design.'

Put simply, inclusive design is user-centred; it understands that people are not either disabled or fully abled. There is a wide spectrum of capabilities within the population; inclusivity involves making sure that as many of those as possible are catered for within one design.

Inclusivity may take many factors into consideration. In 2009–2010, the British government commissioned a Family Resources Survey to provide statistics about the typical British household. The survey included questions on disability. Statistics from the survey show that within the categories of cognitive, sensory and motor abilities, 16.8 per cent of the population have less than full ability in one or more. This might include visual impairment, auditory impairment, dyslexia, memory loss, mobility and other cognitive functions such as communication. Out of a population of 61.8 million people, this means that about 10 million people have an impairment of some sort.

It may not be possible to take all of these into consideration when producing a design. However, there are guidelines available on the use of typography, colour combinations and scale of visual elements that may result in a design that works well for a greater percentage of the audience.

Visual impairment

Another important consideration when visualizing information is that of visual impairment. In the UK, more than 1 million people are registered as blind or partially sighted. Almost 700,000 people have a visual impairment, which makes it difficult for them to read standard-size print (categorized as text used in everyday publishing such as newspapers, books and magazines).

There are several different types of visual impairment that a designer should consider. This does not just involve those who are losing their sight, but those who may have less severe conditions such as colour blindness or loss of peripheral vision. Our eyesight deteriorates as we age, and older eyes may have difficulty differentiating colour, especially in low lighting conditions. An estimated 10 per cent of males suffer from some sort of colour blindness, and around 1 per cent of women. It is a hereditary condition caused by a reduced number of a particular type of visual receptor at the back of the eye.

In 1917, Dr Shinobu Ishihara, a professor at the University of Tokyo, designed a test for colour vision defects. Now known as the Shinobu Ishihara colour-blind test, it uses coloured dots placed in a pattern to present a numeral. Certain combinations are extremely difficult for people with particular types of colour blindness to read. Most forms of colour blindness involve difficulty differentiating between either red and blue or blue and yellow, although in some cases colour cannot be distinguished at all.

What design decisions need to be taken when visualizing information for the visually impaired? It would be very difficult to design for every ocular deficiency. The basic rule is to use contrast to maximum effect. Make sure that there is a large enough tonal difference between colours to be able to distinguish them from one another.

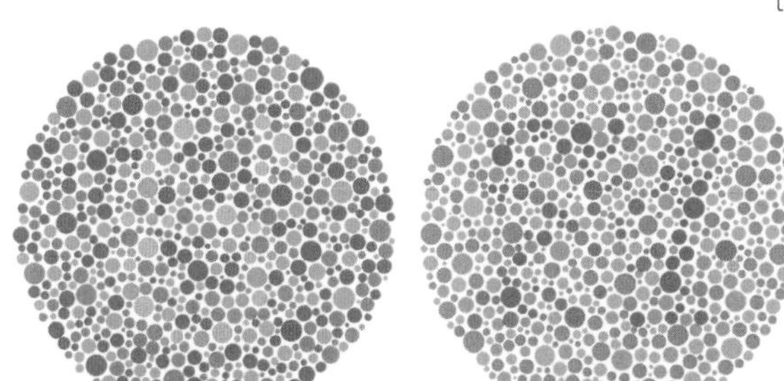

The Shinobu Ishihara tests for colour blindness.

abcdefghijklmn abcdefghijklmn

abcdefghijklmn abcdefghijklmn

abcdefghijklmn abcdefghijklmn

abcdefghijklmn abcdefghijklmn

The four colour bars on the left demonstrate a strong contrast between the background colour and the text. The bars on the right show a weak contrast, making illegibility more likely.

The greater the contrast between elements, the easier it is to tell them apart. Look at the block of four colours with reversed-out text shown above. These would be relatively easy for someone with a visual impairment to read, as the amount of contrast between the elements is strong. Conversely, the other four show poor contrast between the foreground and background. The white text against yellow is very difficult to read. If you compare these combinations they are not as successful as the previous ones.

Field of view

Another important point is to group relevant chunks of information together. Certain eye conditions can lead to a loss of peripheral vision, meaning any elements not in the central portion of our field of vision are obscured. There is also the loss of the central field of vision, which means only areas at the outer edge can be distinguished. Although most people adapt to this kind of visual impairment, it would help when arranging information to try to keep it clustered together so that the area needing to be viewed is reduced.

Technical issues relating to visual impairment

The designer needs to be aware that certain decisions can have a dramatic effect on how legible a design is to a visually challenged audience. These could include choices of colour, scale and weight within a design solution; for example, particular colour combinations can be very difficult for anyone who is colour blind to distinguish. There is software available that designers can employ to mimic some of these visual disturbances (see p. 47). These help to assess how successful a piece of design is to someone with less than 20:20 vision. Braille may have to be incorporated into the design in instances such as medical packaging or wayfinding.

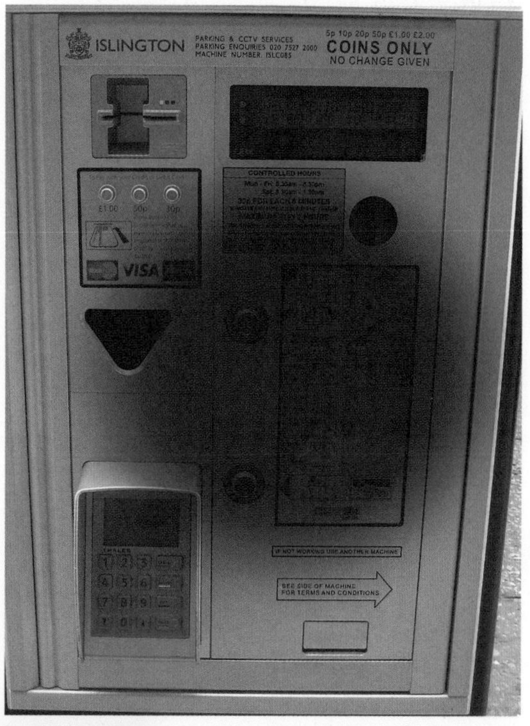

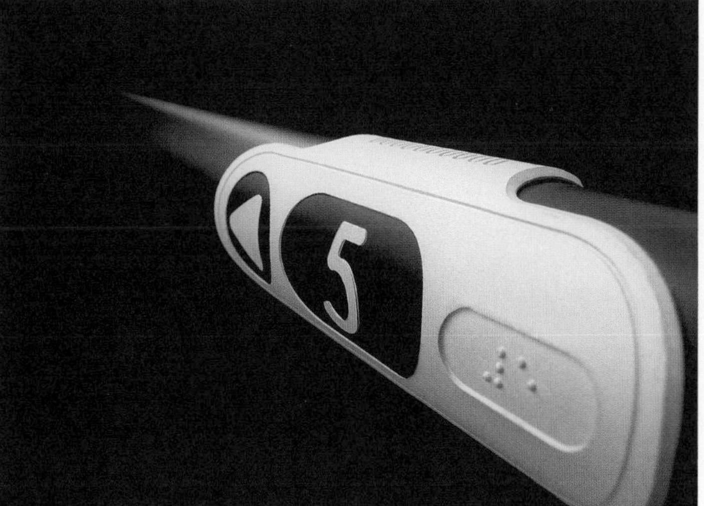

Above: Reconstructions of the field of view that is seen by someone with a loss of peripheral vision (**left**) and by someone with a loss of the central field of vision (**right**).

Left: Pasamano is an award-winning wayfinding product. It has been designed to assist blind and visually impaired visitors, as well as the sighted, by Esteban Marino. The signage element was created for use on handrails on stairs and walkways. Produced in anodized aluminium, there is a strong contrast between the matt aluminium and the black background, which helps the viewer to distinguish between the various elements. The information is displayed in Braille, along with clear and legible numerals and graphic icons such as arrows and pictographs. It provides clear, intuitive signposting for visually impaired visitors to navigate and indicate emergency escape routes in unfamiliar environments with ease.

Contrast

Contrast is a very important element when designing with visual impairment in mind. It is a simple exercise, but squinting your eyes while viewing a design will let you see how close the tonal qualities are of differing colours. If they all look the same shade of grey, the tone is too similar. If you were colour blind, this may result in you not being able to distinguish one colour from another. This could be problematic if you are using typography on a background colour, or need to tell one coloured line from another on a subway map, for example.

When designing something to be viewed or read from a distance, don't just guess what would be an appropriate size. We get a false sense of scale when designing on a computer screen; zooming in and out means you don't get a true representation of the final artwork. Print out sections of type at actual size in draft form and pin them up to mimic real scale and distance. This will help you decide on suitable sizes and weights to use within designs.

There are certain recommendations you should consider when choosing typefaces. The majority of typefaces may work for clear and large print, so long as they are a reasonable size and weight. The deciding factors should be how easily recognizable the characters are and how easily they are distinguished from one another. Try to avoid fonts that have extreme contrasts within their stroke weight, such as Bodoni or Didone: the hairline serifs and bold strokes make it difficult to read at small sizes.

The media used to visualize the design also need to be taken into consideration when designing with type. Screen resolution may mean that certain typefaces have to be discounted, as they cannot be rendered accurately at small sizes on 72dpi screens. In this instance it may be preferable to use fonts specially designed for the screen, such as Verdana and Georgia.

When designing, avoid using light type on a light background. If you are using white type, ensure the background colour is dark enough to give maximum contrast.

abc defghij klmn

abc defghij klmn

abc defghij klmn

abc defghij klmn

abc defghij klmn

abc defghij klmn

abc defghij klmn

abc defghij klmn

HINTS & TIPS

Designing for visual impairment

Think about which colours you use to convey information. Perhaps use complementary methods such as shape and typography to help differentiate them.

Consider using colour contrast to help make things stand out, but ensure there is also sufficient brightness contrast.

Ensure a design is still legible when it is converted to greyscale.

Be careful to position elements within a design so that anyone with a loss of peripheral vision can still see all the components.

abc defghij klmn	abc defghij klmn	abc defghij klmn
abc defghij klmn	abc defghij klmn	abc defghij klmn
abc defghij klmn	abc defghij klmn	abc defghij klmn
abc defghij klmn	abc defghij klmn	abc defghij klmn
abc defghij klmn	abc defghij klmn	abc defghij klmn
abc defghij klmn	abc defghij klmn	abc defghij klmn
abc defghij klmn	abc defghij klmn	abc defghij klmn
abc defghij klmn	abc defghij klmn	abc defghij klmn

abcdefghijklmn

abcdefghijklmn

abcdefghijklmn

abcdefghijklmn

abcdefghijklmn

Above: A piece of software called Color Oracle is available to help those designing for the visually impaired by replicating what people with common colour vision impairments will see. These colour bars show (**left to right**) the original colour scheme and then the results for the conditions deuteranopia (common colour blindness with difficulty distinguishing between red and green), protanopia (difficulty distinguishing between red and black) and tritanopia (a rare form of colour blindness where the sufferer has difficulty distinguishing between blue and yellow).

Left: These colour bars demonstrate the problems that can arise in legibility when converting from colour to greyscale.

Designing for a target audience – children

Project: Letterlab, a typographic exhibition for 6- to 13-year-olds, Graphic Design Museum, Breda, The Netherlands, October 2009–January 2011
2D, 3D, multi-media and type design: Catelijne van Middelkoop and Ryan Pescatore Frisk of Strange Attractors, Rotterdam and New York

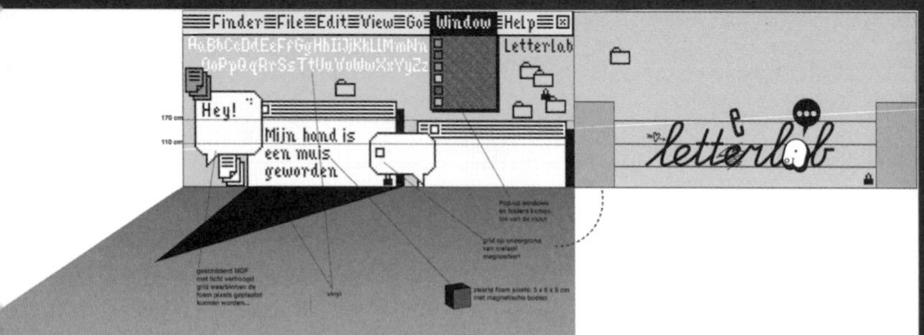

Overview

The Graphic Design Museum in Breda initially approached the designers in December 2008 about creating an exhibition focused on typography for children aged 6 to 13. They were given ten months' lead-time before the scheduled opening.

Strange Attractors were familiar with a previous exhibition at this museum, which had targeted the same audience, albeit with more general content. That exhibition incorporated some interactive elements, but the designers realized that the new exhibition needed to be positioned much more as an interactive experience for the target audience, with spatial and environmental engagement to provoke curiosity and encourage direct interaction.

Initially, it was important to instil the museum staff with an understanding regarding the difference in approach between a passive presentation of flat, static information hung on walls or encased in glass and one that actively embodied content and utilized a holistic expression of experience through the coordination of space, time, sight, touch and sound. The designers began their research and conceptual positioning from the broadest perspective; they believed it was important not to rush to obvious and comfortable solutions, because building a strong fundamental understanding of the problem would achieve the most effective solutions.

Approach

To begin the initial inquiry, the designers asked a simple question: How do you make children experience the history and creative possibilities of typography?

They did not intend on making the children do anything; they wanted the exhibition experience to be so inviting and engaging that children felt compelled to interact with it. If the exhibition could harness the childlike wonder and enjoyment of play, then interaction would occur naturally. They also needed to ensure that the children benefited from an educational experience and gave careful thought to the position and order in which each of the display stations would be encountered. They did not want the target audience to be reminded of classroom-based instruction, or worse, of homework! They structured an active curriculum for children as an engaging experiential journey using digital and analogue media, colours, sounds, and tactile interaction that utilized contemporary memes such as text messaging, touch screens and graffiti.

Above: A computer-generated schematic showing details and measurements for wall graphics along with a cardboard mock-up of the Typo Lounge area.

Opposite: A series of images demonstrating Strange Attractors' process of developing Letterlab from technical drawings and screen mock-ups to maquettes and final visuals.

Letterlab maquette and color indications

Letterlab construction drawings/spatial design and actual construction

Letterlab Type Station (Station 3).

Development

This is a summary of the first presentation the designers made to the clients.

Design problem to solve/goal:
How to make children experience the history and creative possibilities of typography.

Note 1:
Use a selection of 5 different typefaces for the entire exhibition!
1 pixel face + 1 brush script + 1 text letter + 1 slab serif + 1 fat face (marshmallowy)

Note 2:
Combine high- and low-tech where/when possible!
Wood + electronics + screen-printing + laser-cutting

Sketches (thoughts on the interior):
An exhibition space like an emptied-out toy box, spread out over and sunk into the floor, engaging yet surprisingly organized and full of hidden facts.

Thoughts:
Five stations made out of screen-printed plywood, covered with type, child proportions yet accentuating the height of the space
Pixel facts (example: the first Nokia consumer phone had a display of 84 x 48 pixels)
Translucent PVC cubes (c. 10 x 10cm)
LED lights
Micro-controllers

Historical references:
Design for a newspaper stand by Herbert Bayer (1924)
Kiosk by Michel de Klerk (c. 1919–1923)
Dylaby (Stedelijk Museum) by Daniel Spoerri (1961)

Timeline:
From sounds and shapes to letterforms and compositions, gaining meaning, becoming an experience!
(A brief history of typography)

Station 1:
WAF! WAT? W! (Shapes and sounds make letters)
Focus: type and rhythm
Components: Wii remotes/ PlayStation USB controllers, webcams, projector, computer, speakers

Station 2:
a. Geometric wall type (reference: Wim Crouwel, geometric shapes with rare earth magnets)
b. Drawing letters with light (drawing letters with LED sticks)
Focus: type and form
Components: geometric building blocks, rare earth magnets, USB camera, LED light sticks, computer and screen

Station 3:
'Press here!' (based on 'Real Design': Wijdeveld, Crouwel, etc.)
a. From analogue to digital (no overlapping elements)
b. No more boundaries (touch screen enables overlap)
Focus: type and composition
Components: RFID tags and reader, laser-cut and screen-printed wood blocks, interchangeable grids, computer, projector, touch screen (use abstractions of original printing studio)
'Gutenberg press'
'Letterkast'
Base components on originals by Wijdeveld (1931)

Letterlab Pixel Wall (Station 2).

Station 4:
A play with the meaning of type
Focus: type and meaning
Components: computer, projector, green screen, cams
Station: triplex, vinyl (pixels on floor), chroma key green paint

Station 5:
Typo lounge
Focus: type and overview
At this station, a movie will loop through the history of typography, combining aspects from all exhibition stations and providing a comprehensive overview. There is also room for a speaker (teacher, guide) to step on to a stage.
Components: giant foam letter and pixel seats, projector/flat-screen TV, DVD player
Station: vinyl (pixels, half-tone patterns and splashes on floor and wall), triplex, foam

Window front thought:
A set of monitors displaying the action inside triggering children outside to come in and play!
(Windows entirely covered with vinyl except for peepholes at kids' height... Psssst!)

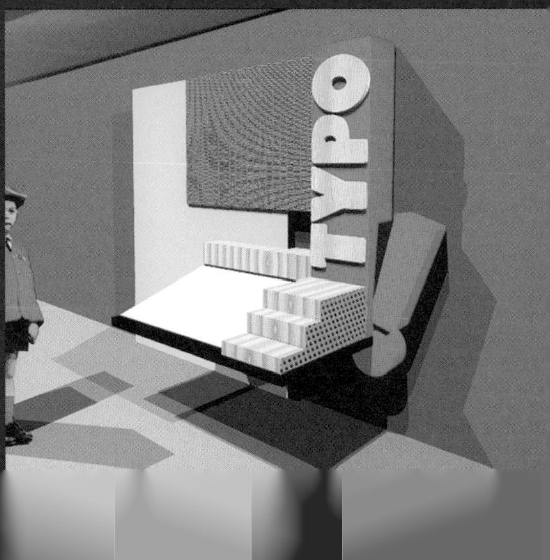

Outcome

Letterlab was all about letters in the broadest sense of the word. In this exhibition, children aged 6 to 13 and their parents discovered that the letters you mostly encounter in books mean a great deal more.

Letterlab made children realize that the letters we use for reading have a history of development, that they are designed, and that the way in which that takes place determines how the letter functions.

The exhibition let the target group view letters from different perspectives:

- Letter and sound: the pronunciation of a letter could very well be closely associated with the shape of the letter. How does that work?

Inside the 'theatre' children could play a custom-designed and programmed game. The game, projected inside a large structure built from letters, could be controlled by playing two oversized musical instruments. Each key launched a different sound as well as a corresponding letter or shape onto the game field.

- Letter and shape: a letter consists of several components, or several forms. That is how you get different fonts. Appropriately, five new fonts were created for Letterlab.

The designers also designed a giant desktop for the exhibition space, including menu, files, folders and pop-up windows. Inside the windows, visitors could manually leave their own pixel message. An example of a pixel font could be found on the desktop as well.

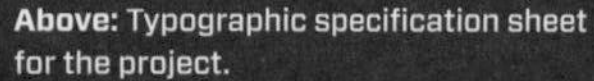

Above: Typographic specification sheet for the project.

Right: Letterlab Typo Lounge (Station 5).

Letterlab Typo Lounge in action.

- Letter and composition: a letter becomes part of a composition; for example, on a poster or in a book or newspaper. The composition is determined by the positioning of the letter in the space.

In Composition, a large letter-shaped printing press offered children the opportunity to discover how newspapers are put together. Large blocks with pre-set texts such as headlines, along with individual letters, formed the toolkit for creating your own Letterlab Courant. A webcam recorded the manual labour and displayed the results on one of two screens mounted on the giant H. The second display was connected to a touch screen on the other side of the press. Using similar design elements but now experiencing the (dis)advantages of the computer, a comparison could be made between two different time periods in modern typography: the analogue and the digital era.

- Letter and meaning: a letter, several letters (a word), and even more letters (a sentence) give meaning. A text can be written through the meaning of the letters.

Behind the theatre a dark alley was created in which children could use light graffiti to leave their name or tag on the wall. Stencils were also supplied, providing pre-set positive words such as: 'good', 'hope', 'beautiful' and 'nice'.

Letterlab was a laboratory where children could find out for themselves how various perspectives of the letter work. Discovery assignments were linked to each sub-theme. The assignments were layered and diverse, so that children of various ages could feel challenged by them.

One of the corners of the exhibition space was given over to a lounge area where visitors could watch a custom-crafted film that provided an abstract overview of the history of typography. The film also showed how all the stations in the exhibition are related to one another.

At the European Design Awards in 2010 the Letterlab project was awarded the Gold in Brand Implementation and the Jury Prize.

Chapter 3: Structuring information

Structure is essential when presenting information to an audience. We need to think about how our audience receive and are guided through information, what they see and when. This chapter demonstrates practical ways in which to structure designs and also gives visual examples of poor structure and hierarchy to use as a comparison. Whether you are designing information for print, interactive or the environment, well-organized information placed within a well-designed structure with application of a clear hierarchy will aid communication of information and content.

Grids

Imagine a page in a book or newspaper, or a webpage full of information. All of the information, text and data are the same size; there is no colour, no space, no varying weight of type, and images are the same size and are placed randomly around the page with no explanation. Where do you start? Where would you look first? How do you know what is the most important information? What do the images and data relate to? Would you take the time to read through everything and try to work it out, or would you just switch off and dismiss the page?

Organizing information visually requires a grid. A grid can be as simple or as complicated as the designer needs. A simple grid will consist of a series of horizontal and vertical lines that form a framework for information to be placed in, such as that illustrated at top right. The design of the grid should be led by the information it is carrying. Put simply, you need to have organized your content and have a clear idea of the different levels, or 'hierarchy', within it in order to design an effective grid. The image at bottom right shows content where there has been no thought to importance. Headings, body text, captions, diagrams, charts, images and quotes may be some of the elements you have to consider within your design. In order to make them stand out, you may want your quotes to be set to a different column width than your body text; therefore, your grid should be designed and constructed to allow you to do this.

A well-constructed grid allows information to be organized effectively and should help the reader navigate through the content presented in a sequential manner. The grid is a powerful and effective tool to utilize when designing and can be applied across a wide range of formats including books, magazines, websites and posters. Alongside a clear hierarchy, the grid controls how information is delivered and received by an audience.

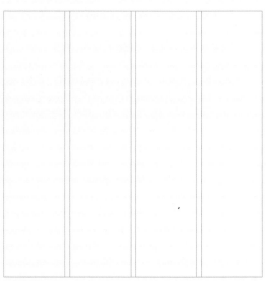

A basic grid.

An exhibition by ceramicist Denise Roberts
Shore Things
A joyous celebration of the vibrant colour and light encountered at the coast. Denise playfully combines colour texture and mark-making to suggest bunting boats and buoys. Denise is particularly passionate about beautiful objects exquisitely made to make you think. She collects photos of flaking peeling surfaces, ceramics and vintage picnic hampers. She runs her own ceramics studio described as a 'beach hut at the end of the garden' and supplies her work to galleries and outlets nationally, including Falmouth, Brighton and Cirencester. She is a Member of Marlborough Open Studios group.
Aug 4 – Aug 25 2012,
The Clay & Glass Studio, Grey Gables, Ogbourne St George, Marlborough, Wiltshire,
SN8 1SL, United Kingdom
http://www.deniseroberts.co.uk

Text in a grid with no hierarchy applied.

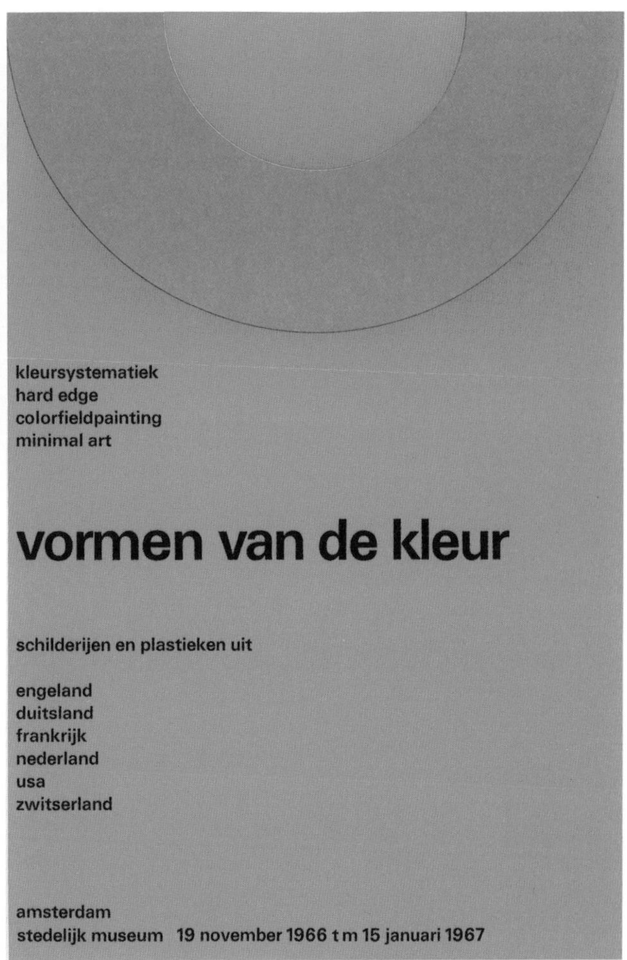

Above: Posters designed by Wim Crouwel: 'Vormgevers', 1968 (**left**) and 'Vormen Van de Kleur', 1966 (**right**). These two posters show examples of the grid system used in practice. You will notice that Wim Crouwel left the grid system exposed on his 'Vormgevers' poster. This 28-column grid allows for maximum flexibility in the placement and alignment of elements; all the letterforms line up exactly. The negative space also plays an important part in the composition of the pieces, allowing the viewer's eyes to be directed to certain elements.

A grid may also be dynamic; in addition to, or instead of, horizontal and vertical lines it may consist of diagonal or curved lines. A grid is as creative as the person designing it! Conventions can be challenged or broken. Many designers have explored the idea of breaking the grid in order to create work that reflects content with more freedom and emotion, allowing their creativity and instinct to guide their work rather than the structure of a grid. A few examples by Rudy Vanderlans for *Émigré* magazine are shown on p. 61. However, it is important to have a clear understanding of the purpose of a grid and to know the rules before you attempt to break them!

'A grid system is an aid, not a guarantee. It permits a number of possible uses and each designer can look for a solution appropriate to his personal style. But one must learn how to use the grid; it is an art that requires practice.'

Josef Müller-Brockmann, graphic designer and author of *Grid Systems in Graphic Design*

Hierarchy of information

Hierarchy concerns the order in which information is presented; having organized your content you will have decided what needs to be seen and read by your audience and in what sequence. To create a clear hierarchy, you should work out what it is they need to see/read/interact or respond to first, second and third.

Remember the page we mentioned on p. 56 when discussing the grid? It would have been difficult to read because we hadn't used any different sizes, colour or a grid to help you navigate through the information. This page had not been organized. There was no hierarchy. We need to identify what the different levels of information are and the order in which they should be seen and read, as in the illustration to the right. Once this order has been established, we can begin to apply a visual hierarchy. This will result in the successful navigation and communication of information.

A visual hierarchy can be created in many ways. Refer to the illustrations at the bottom of this page and consider using variations of scale, weight (light, medium or bold weights of a typeface), colour, tone, graphical elements (shapes/lines), space and placement of elements to signal where you want your audience to go. In some instances, for example when using interactive media, sound and movement may also be utilized.

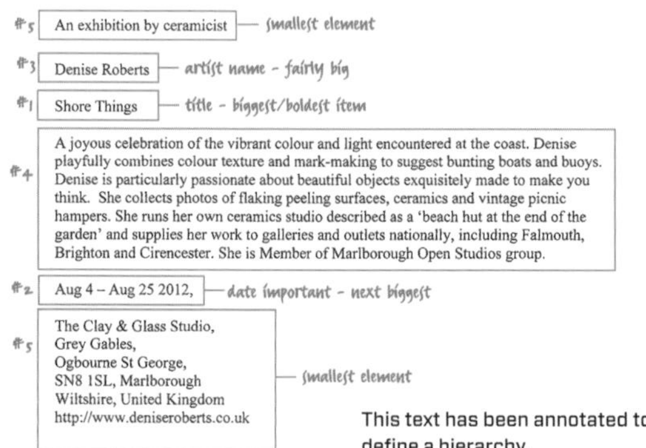

This text has been annotated to define a hierarchy.

Here the text is organized by scale.

Here the text is also organized by weight.

Here graphical elements have been introduced.

Examples of grids and hierarchy of information

"MEN WOULD RATHER HAVE THEIR FILL OF SLEEP, LOVE, AND SINGING AND DANCING THAN OF WAR," SAID HOMER. THE EDITORS OF AVANT-GARDE AGREE, AND DO HEREBY ISSUE A CALL FOR ENTRIES FOR AN INTERNATIONAL POSTER COMPETITION BASED ON THE THEME:

NO MORE WAR!

Judges: Richard Avedon, Leonard Baskin, Alexander Calder, Milton Glaser, Art Kane, Jack Levine, Herb Lubalin, Dwight Macdonald, Robert Motherwell, Robert Osborn, Larry Rivers, Ben Shahn, Edward Steichen & Sloan Wilson.

Posters designed by Herb Lubalin: *No More War*, for *Avant Garde* magazine, 1968 (**above**) and *Let Type Talk, Let's Talk Type*, 1959 (**right**).

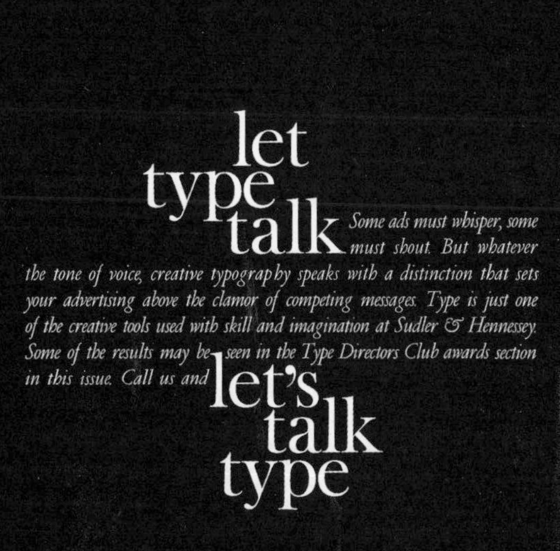

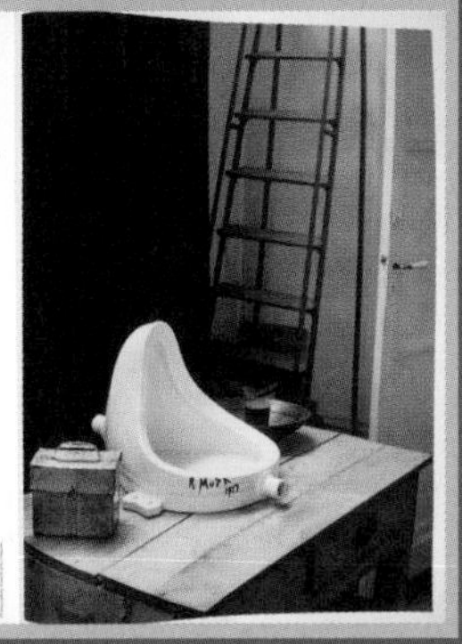

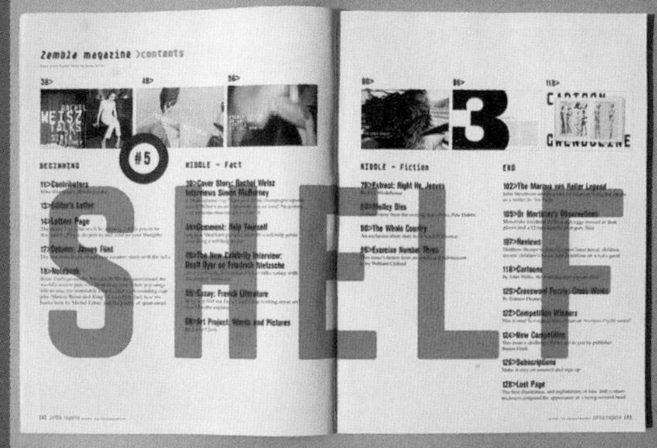

Above: Three spreads for *Zembla* magazine, designed by Vince Frost, demonstrate in turn: how graphic elements and scale of text are used to define a hierarchy (**top**), how hierarchy is created by a grid (**centre**) and the use of negative space (**bottom**).

Poster for the Holland Dance Festival designed by Gert Dumbar, 1995. This poster shows how text conforming to a grid in the centre of the image can be contrasted with text set at angles to produce a dynamic composition.

Dynamic composition and gesture

You have been introduced to the idea of structure, the grid and hierarchy. We will now look at how these can be used and applied to a piece of information design to create dynamic and engaging compositions. A designer can lead a viewer's eye around the page in a specific way. It is possible for a designer to make the viewer scan the page in an order that need not begin at the top left of a page and move to bottom right. The creative use of hierarchy and structure can allow the designer to construct a fluid movement around the page: a gesture if you will. The use of scale, placement and prominence of certain components can produce lively and attractive pages.

Think again of the page of information we talked about on p. 56. We have organized the content and established a hierarchy; you have decided the order in which it should be seen and read. If you were now to design that information, how would you begin? Would the first and most important piece of information sit at the top of the page and the least important at the bottom? In some cases this might be appropriate, but designing with structure, a grid and hierarchy does not mean that information cannot be presented to your audience in a dynamic and exciting way.

Having established a hierarchy and grid, we can begin to explore how we work with them visually and creatively. This will involve adding some of the ingredients we have mentioned before: scale, weight, colour, tone, space, graphical elements (shapes/lines), placement and, in some formats, sound and movement. The selection of typeface is also a key factor in the appearance, functionality and successful communication of information. Fonts are designed for specific functions (display, text) and many with a suggestion of a 'personality' or character attached to them. A typeface may have a large 'family', meaning it is produced in different 'cuts' (roman, italic, light, medium, bold, etc.), so a single font can offer the potential to create a clear hierarchy if utilized effectively.

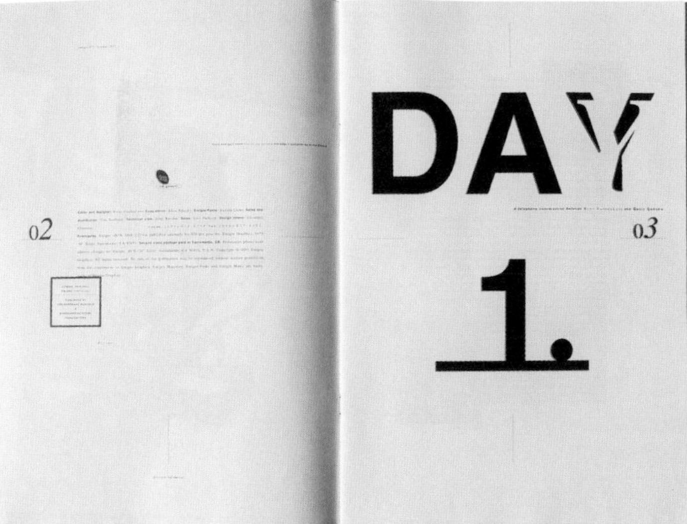

These 'ingredients' can be used to direct your viewer's eye to and around the information; they can create interaction and engagement or tension in order to bring information to life. Rather than looking at the top of a page, you may be drawn to the bottom, middle, left or right. In a print publication, a right-hand page is more visible than a left-hand page and as a designer you will need to be able to design a page that stands out on its own among many other pages.

The theme or content of your information will also influence how you use these ingredients; you should understand your audience and design with their expectations and experience in mind. A magazine aimed at 18- to 25-year-olds will take a different design approach to one targeting an older, more conservative, audience. An article on hip-hop music should feel different to one on classical music. This is where the designer will need to conduct appropriate research, so that they can base their designs on real facts rather than just intuition. The influences, feel and structure of the music and the audience demographic could inform how you design your page, based on what you uncover. The choice of typeface, how you use scale, colour, weight, etc., will all have an impact on the design and can create mood, pace and rhythm. They can instigate both an interest and a response from your audience to the information you are presenting. Remember that regular readers can willingly embrace any new structure, and it is important to consider first-time readers too.

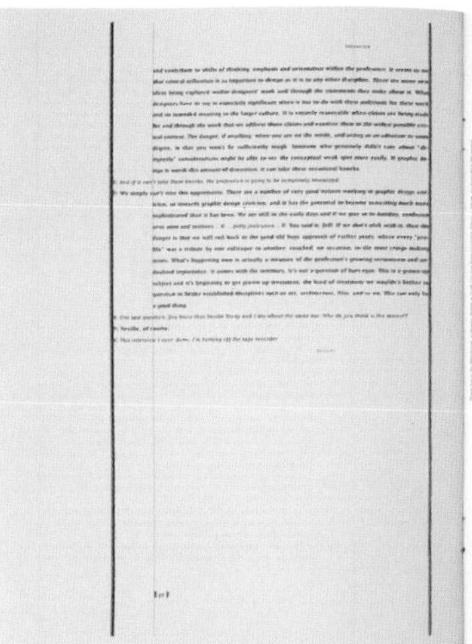

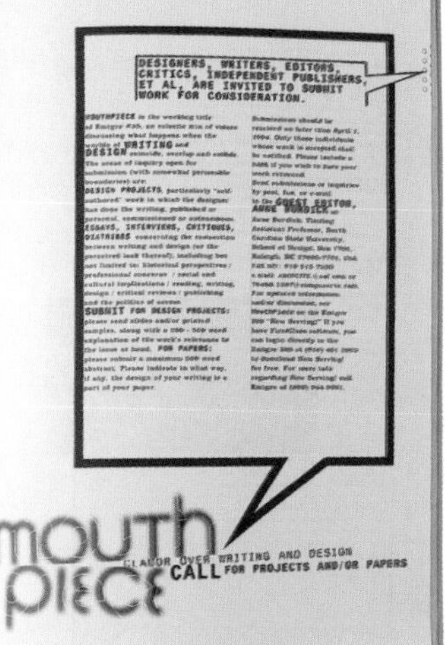

Three spreads from *Émigré* magazine by Rudy Vanderlans, 1994. This magazine was aimed specifically at graphic designers and as a result was able to 'push the boundaries' of layout, since it was designed to appeal to a visually sophisticated audience.

Top: Issue 32, pp. 12–13, 'In and Around'. This is a large-format (A2) spread that shows the grid in action on the right-hand page. Notice how the large hand-drawn type on the left-hand page balances the spread. Also, how the 'swoosh' under the word 'fury' draws your eye to the large block of copy on the facing page. The images within this block of text also break out of the grid to provide some tension within the composition.

Centre: Issue 27, pp. 2–3, 'Day 1'. Here the use of scale is exploited, with extremely large text placed facing very small text. This draws your eye to the title first, but also creates a focal point, which is balanced by the placement and handling of the small copy on the left-hand page.

Left: Issue 33, p. 41, 'mouthpiece'. This shows the use of columns of text of differing widths within a spread and the ability to be playful with the positioning of the title of the piece, using the speech bubble as the content of the 'mouthpiece'.

Examples of dynamic composition and gesture

To illustrate the successful implementation of dynamic composition, we are going to look at a piece of design work by the Swiss designer Josef Müller-Brockmann (1914–1996). Müller-Brockmann studied the history of art, architecture and design at the University of Zurich. He worked as an apprentice for the designer and advertising consultant Walter Diggelman before setting up his own studio in 1936, specializing in graphics, exhibition design and photography. He is considered to be one of the leading practitioners of the Swiss Style (sometimes called the International Typographic Style). This style is associated with minimalism and a strict grid structure, and features sans serif type and asymmetry to create dynamic, organized compositions. It employs simple methods to create order, variation, impact and surprise.

Müller-Brockmann began designing posters for Zurich Town Hall in 1950 and continued for more than 25 years. We use his *Beethoven* poster from 1955 to demonstrate the application of dynamic composition.

Look at the poster, and consider the tools the designer is using to attract our attention and move our eye around the piece. Where do you look first?

He attracts us with his bold composition, his use of contrast and strong graphic abstract shape. The type is in two sizes; 'beethoven' sits alone as the title or headline, while the details (date, time, location, etc.) follow. Is the first piece of information the designer presents to us the title, 'beethoven'? It is the first thing that we read, but it isn't the first thing that we see. The asymmetric arrangement of the curves, their scale, repetition and position on the poster capture our attention first and provide a focal point. It is these curves that sit at the top of the hierarchy; they attract and guide us to the information we need to see and read. They also evoke a feeling and mood; they are strong and powerful, there is movement and volume suggested, and they reflect something of the content – the music of Beethoven.

The arrangement of type is simple but well considered, with order created by using space and alignment effectively.

'Order was always wishful thinking for me. For 60 years I have produced disorder in files, correspondence and books. In my work, however, I have always aspired to a distinct arrangement of typographic and pictorial elements, the clear identification of priorities. The formal organization of the surface by means of a grid, a knowledge of the rules that govern legibility (line lengths, word and letter spacing and so on) and the meaningful use of colour are among the tools a designer must master in order to complete his or her task in a rational and economic manner.'

Josef Müller-Brockmann in an interview with Yvonne Schwemer-Scheddin
© *Eye* magazine, 2001

Beethoven, poster designed by Josef Müller-Brockmann, 1955.

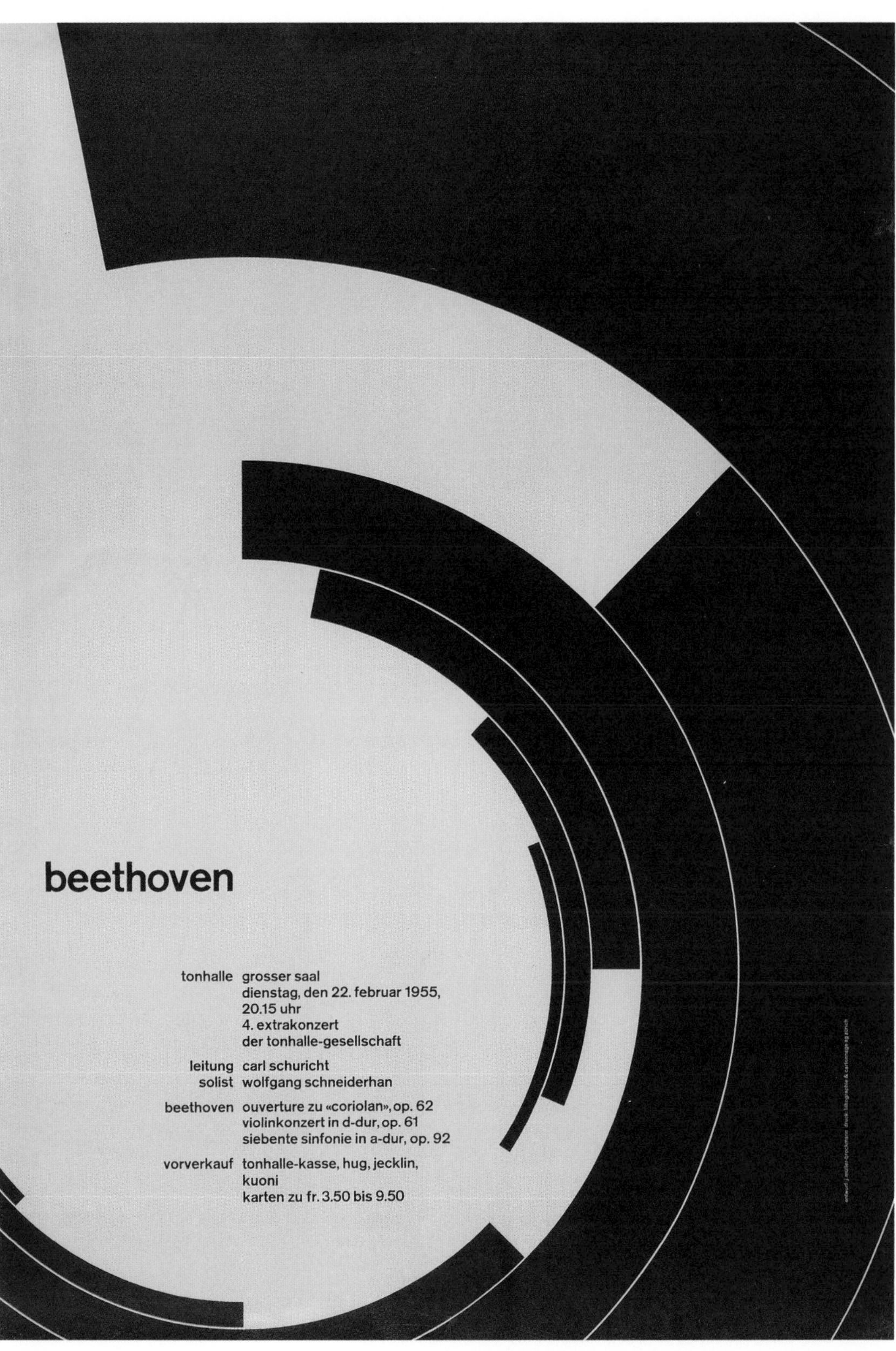
beethoven
tonhalle grosser saal
dienstag, den 22. februar 1955,
20.15 uhr
4. extrakonzert
der tonhalle-gesellschaft
leitung carl schuricht
solist wolfgang schneiderhan
beethoven ouverture zu «coriolan», op. 62
violinkonzert in d-dur, op. 61
siebente sinfonie in a-dur, op. 92
vorverkauf tonhalle-kasse, hug, jecklin,
kuoni
karten zu fr. 3.50 bis 9.50

Sequence of information

We have discussed the issues of structure, grid, hierarchy and composition, and how these are used to support effective, engaging information delivery to an audience. We know that we have to understand and organize the information we are working with, and we know we can take our audience on a journey around that information by using these tools. With all of the above we have been working towards creating a visual 'sequence' to communicate the varying levels of information. However, different platforms for information delivery (book, poster, wayfinding, web, apps, etc.) require other approaches to create an effective sequence. We need to understand how our audience will interact with these platforms in order to design effectively.

A poster presents all the information to its audience on its surface; a grid and hierarchy are used, but ultimately it is designed to attract interest and deliver content in an immediate way. With a book, there is a different set of considerations. A sequence, an order, is created on each page but also as we turn from page to page. A grid or grids will be used, as will all or some of the 'ingredients' we discussed when talking about hierarchy earlier in this chapter (see p. 58).

These elements are used to carry a reader through the book, moving comfortably from page to page. The grid and the hierarchy are used to create a framework for the design, an overall consistency and structure that supports the delivery of the content. This framework does not usually change from page to page, although the balance of ingredients may vary (for example, a new chapter could be signalled by using bold type, space or colour).

BBC Festivals Widget: interactive smartphone app designed by Phil McNeill.

1. Application menu.

2. Information on stage set times.

3. The location of the various stages: their scale is relative to the user's interest levels.

4/5. The location of your car/the toilets in relation to your current whereabouts.

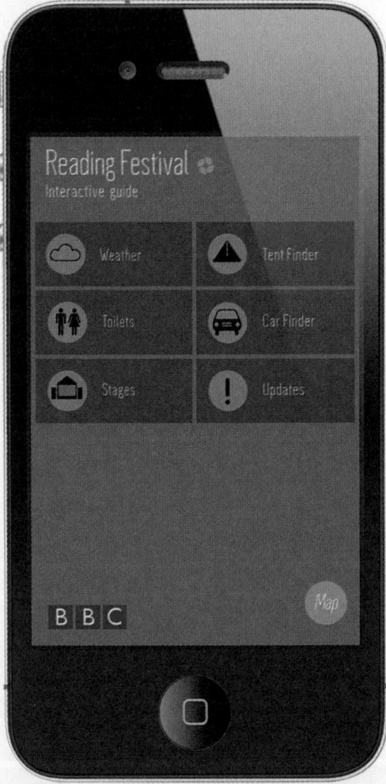

1

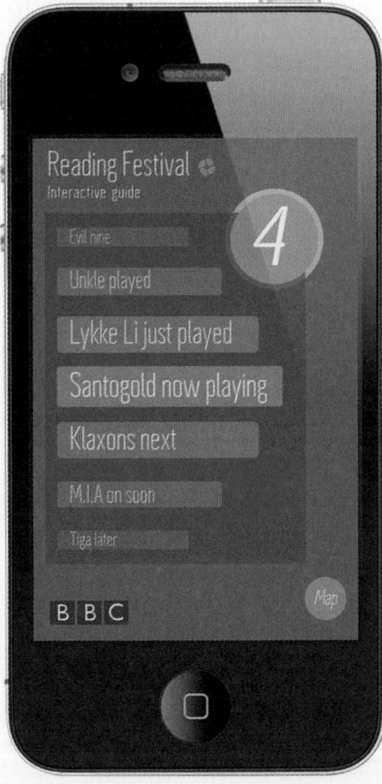

2

What happens when this page becomes a screen or a multi-touch screen? If you are familiar with these platforms, think about how you, as a user, interact with them. There is the potential to move through information in a very fluid manner; each user may select a different route through that information and require different things at different times, so there is no definitive sequence to the delivery.

In some instances, the choices that each individual user makes will be analyzed by the operating software; this can result in an active, ever-changing interface that can respond on an individual basis to its users. A website or app can make selections for an individual based on their input, as Phil McNeill demonstrated in his award-winning design for the BBC Festivals Widget, submitted to the D&AD competition.

There will be a clear structure and organization in evidence from a design perspective. This structure facilitates the user's navigation around the interface. A grid, hierarchy and all our ingredients will be utilized to guide users through possible routes. This medium also offers the potential to use movement and sound. We will look at information design for interactive and screen-based design in more detail in Chapter 7.

3

4

5

HINTS & TIPS

Organizing information

Organizing information should be the starting point when creating the initial structure of a design. The decisions you make at this stage, on what your audience needs to see and when, and how you use the tools we have described in this book so far, will facilitate the successful communication and understanding of your content.

Organizing information is a fundamental part of design. There is a wide range of factors you must consider as part of the overall design process, but rationalizing, understanding and organizing content forms the foundations of effective information delivery.

You may find it helpful to consider the following points when organizing information:

Read through the information/content you are designing.

What order does the information need to be presented in?

Establish what your audience needs to see first, second, third, and so on.

Decide how you are going to differentiate between the various levels of information, using the tools we have discussed in this chapter.

You could consider using scale, colour, a typeface with a variety of weights, white space and graphic elements to guide your audience around the information.

We will use the example of a college design brief to demonstrate the process of organizing and delivering content effectively. We have presented the text for our brief on a sheet of paper (opposite, top left). No consideration has been given to the design of the information. The copy is all one size and is in a single font. No special consideration has been given at this point to the structure of the information; a hierarchy has not been established; a grid has not been considered, the composition of the information is dull and doesn't help the reader find their way around the information. How do we improve this?

We begin to organize our information (top right).

In the main image opposite we have selected a typeface with a variety of weights that we have then applied to our information. We have also altered the point size of the copy; this clearly begins to differentiate which information should be read first, second and third. We are beginning to establish a basic hierarchy and organize our information.

It is at this point that we can begin to consider the most suitable grid structure to use to present our information.

School of Art and Design
2011/12:
Module GDES30055/57
gd3
Project Title: Bonington Gallery Promotion
Project Tutors: To be confirmed.
Project duration: 12 April – 14 May
Learning Outcomes
Demonstrate a personal intellectual engagement with the subject and show the ability to evaluate and synthesise secondary and primary sources.
Align Personal working processes with current professional thought and practice.Use appropriate visual language and media for specific design activities
Apply a professional attitude to independent learning, project management and make effective visual and verbal presentations.

Aims of the project
To develop a visual identity for a non profit making organisation
To develop ways of presenting information visually for a specified audience
To look at ways of directing an audience to a specific site

The Bonington Gallery has been the provider of a wide ranging programme of exhibitions and events, broadly encompassing both pure and applied contemporary creative practice; visual art, (all media), craft, design, performance and dance since 1989. It is one of the foremost spaces for contemporary art in Nottingham, located in the School of Art and Design at the Nottingham Trent University, in the heart of the city of. Emphasis is placed on programming work, which is challenging and innovative, with a commitment to encouraging the work of new, emerging artists as well as established practitioners. Exhibitors include national and international artists and designers, current students and staff from within the University and NTU alumni. The nature of the space itself makes it a particularly sympathetic venue for large-scale site-specific installation and multi-discipline events.

The Brief
The project is to produce a visual identity and promotional material for the Bonington Gallery space. Consider the look and feel of the 'marque' along with the kind of promotional material produced, such as leaflets, posters and flyers etc. Since the gallery is located within the university building you may also want to consider signage and possible wayfinding systems to guide visitors from the city centre to the gallery space as part of your submission.

Submission Requirements
These will be dependent on your solutions to the problem.
Mandatories are:A 'marque' and some guidelines on how it should be used.
3 promotional items (such as a poster, leaflet or catalogue

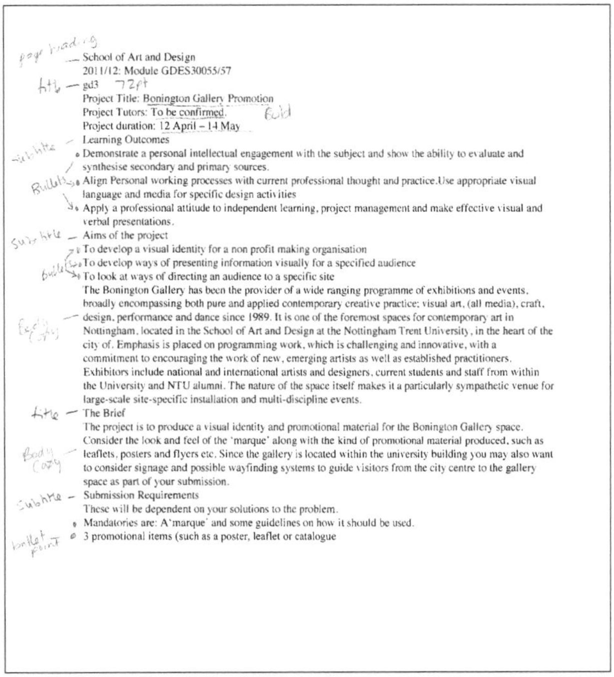

page heading — School of Art and Design
2011/12: Module GDES30055/57
title — gd3 72pt
Project Title: Bonington Gallery Promotion
Project Tutors: To be confirmed. Bold
Project duration: 12 April – 14 May
subtitle — Learning Outcomes
- Demonstrate a personal intellectual engagement with the subject and show the ability to evaluate and synthesise secondary and primary sources.
- Bullets Align Personal working processes with current professional thought and practice.Use appropriate visual language and media for specific design activities
- Apply a professional attitude to independent learning, project management and make effective visual and verbal presentations.

sub title — Aims of the project
- To develop a visual identity for a non profit making organisation
- bullets To develop ways of presenting information visually for a specified audience
- To look at ways of directing an audience to a specific site

Body copy — The Bonington Gallery has been the provider of a wide ranging programme of exhibitions and events, broadly encompassing both pure and applied contemporary creative practice; visual art, (all media), craft, design, performance and dance since 1989. It is one of the foremost spaces for contemporary art in Nottingham, located in the School of Art and Design at the Nottingham Trent University, in the heart of the city of. Emphasis is placed on programming work, which is challenging and innovative, with a commitment to encouraging the work of new, emerging artists as well as established practitioners. Exhibitors include national and international artists and designers, current students and staff from within the University and NTU alumni. The nature of the space itself makes it a particularly sympathetic venue for large-scale site-specific installation and multi-discipline events.

title — The Brief
Body copy — The project is to produce a visual identity and promotional material for the Bonington Gallery space. Consider the look and feel of the 'marque' along with the kind of promotional material produced, such as leaflets, posters and flyers etc. Since the gallery is located within the university building you may also want to consider signage and possible wayfinding systems to guide visitors from the city centre to the gallery space as part of your submission.

subtitle — Submission Requirements
These will be dependent on your solutions to the problem.
- Mandatories are: A 'marque' and some guidelines on how it should be used.
- bullet point 3 promotional items (such as a poster, leaflet or catalogue

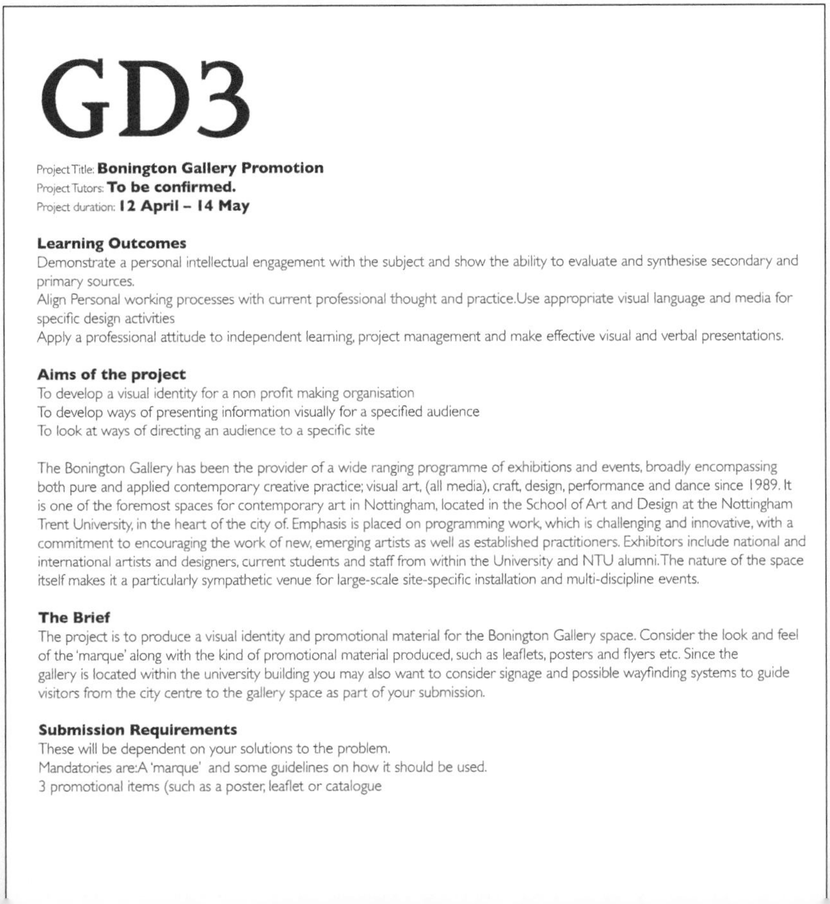

GD3

Project Title: **Bonington Gallery Promotion**
Project Tutors: **To be confirmed.**
Project duration: **12 April – 14 May**

Learning Outcomes
Demonstrate a personal intellectual engagement with the subject and show the ability to evaluate and synthesise secondary and primary sources.
Align Personal working processes with current professional thought and practice.Use appropriate visual language and media for specific design activities
Apply a professional attitude to independent learning, project management and make effective visual and verbal presentations.

Aims of the project
To develop a visual identity for a non profit making organisation
To develop ways of presenting information visually for a specified audience
To look at ways of directing an audience to a specific site

The Bonington Gallery has been the provider of a wide ranging programme of exhibitions and events, broadly encompassing both pure and applied contemporary creative practice; visual art, (all media), craft, design, performance and dance since 1989. It is one of the foremost spaces for contemporary art in Nottingham, located in the School of Art and Design at the Nottingham Trent University, in the heart of the city of. Emphasis is placed on programming work, which is challenging and innovative, with a commitment to encouraging the work of new, emerging artists as well as established practitioners. Exhibitors include national and international artists and designers, current students and staff from within the University and NTU alumni.The nature of the space itself makes it a particularly sympathetic venue for large-scale site-specific installation and multi-discipline events.

The Brief
The project is to produce a visual identity and promotional material for the Bonington Gallery space. Consider the look and feel of the 'marque' along with the kind of promotional material produced, such as leaflets, posters and flyers etc. Since the gallery is located within the university building you may also want to consider signage and possible wayfinding systems to guide visitors from the city centre to the gallery space as part of your submission.

Submission Requirements
These will be dependent on your solutions to the problem.
Mandatories are:A 'marque' and some guidelines on how it should be used.
3 promotional items (such as a poster, leaflet or catalogue

Above left: Page of text with no hierarchy applied.

Above right: The copy has been annotated by hand to establish a hierarchy.

Left: A basic hierarchy is applied to the information in the document.

Below: A selection of typefaces in different point sizes and weights.

72pt Eplica Bold
10 pt Gill Sans Bold
10 pt Gill Sans Light
8 pt Gill Sans Light Itallic

HINTS & TIPS

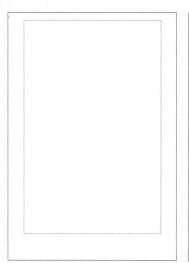

A single-column grid.

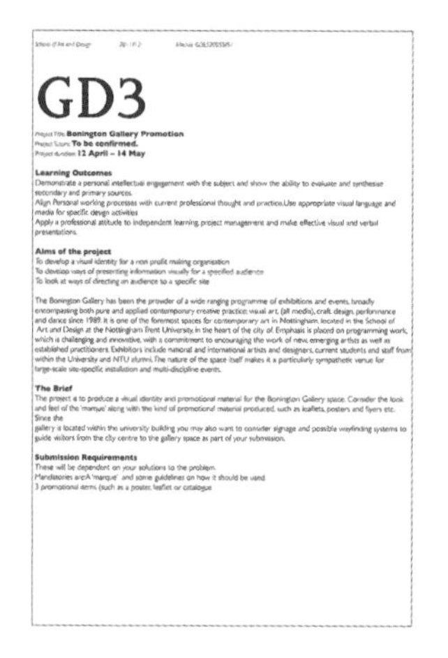

The single-column grid with type placed within it.

Using a grid

Once you have understood and organized your information, consider the type of grid. In this instance we need to create a grid that is relatively simple, as we are not dealing with huge amounts of complex content. We know the order of our information and have begun the process of creating a hierarchy. We are now looking for a grid to help anchor our information and to provide a framework for our content. This grid will eventually be turned into a template and used to present all subsequent briefs delivered to our students.

The illustrations here demonstrate two possible grids that we could use in this instance. There are many more possibilities, but with the particular type of content we are designing our focus is clear, direct communication, and a simple grid structure is our best option to support this.

A three-column grid.

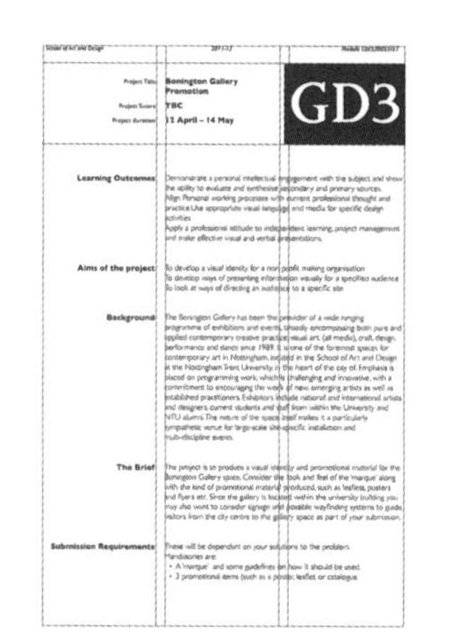

The three-column grid with text placed dynamically across the columns.

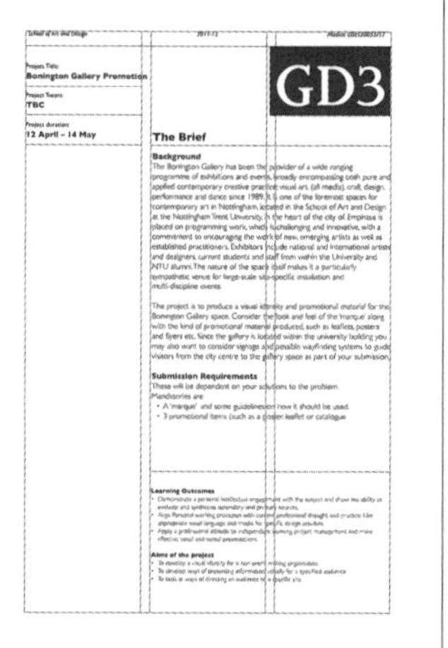

The three-column grid with type placed across two of the three columns.

First, a simple, conventional, single-column grid is applied to an A4 page (top left). We have created margins at the top, bottom and sides of the page; these areas will remain free of information and all copy will sit within these boundaries. The single column is our text area and is positioned centrally on the page. At top right we see this grid with content placed within it. There are several issues that are of concern with this grid. The line length (number of words on each line) of the body copy is quite long. This can be problematic, and will be discussed further in our next chapter on legibility. The single column means we have limited flexibility to use the grid creatively to order or break down our content. We are relying on the hierarchy we created when we began organizing our content, the use of different type sizes, weights and cuts of the font to guide our readers around the page. This is not the most exciting or dynamic design, but it does demonstrate the effectiveness of establishing a clear typographic hierarchy when designing information.

The illustration at bottom, far left shows a three-column grid on our A4 page. Again, we have created our margins at the top, bottom and sides of the page, but we have broken our text area into three equal columns. This grid offers us more options and flexibility with our layout, and the annotations highlight some of these. We can run information across all three columns; this allows us to run our title across the full width of the page, although we could also use a single column (one of three) or a double column (two of three) as part of our design. The illustrations at bottom centre and right demonstrate how this grid might be used with our content placed within it, and we have many more possibilities available to us; we can break down our information in different ways by using this structure. In conjunction with good organization and the application of typographic hierarchy, we have more opportunity to deliver our information effectively.

Some ideas on planning the grid

Define the order the copy should be read in.

Group relevant pieces of information together to allow the reader to navigate it clearly.

Decide on the size and format of your document.

Decide how much flexibility is required within your grid structure. Is one column enough or would multiple columns be more effective?

How do your images and text work together to draw attention to particular elements around the page?

Captions need to be considered as part of the composition.

Do you need to plan the composition to create a dynamic piece of design?

Have you used negative space effectively to draw attention to the information? (This could include asymmetric composition.)

When considering sequence, does the presentation of the information appear consistent between pages?

Don't be frightened of experimenting! Try out different grid structures, different ways of using and creating hierarchy, explore how space, colour, graphic elements etc. could be used within your overall layouts.

Deconstruct the work of other designers. What grids have they used? How have they created hierarchy? What visual tools do they use to create the successful design and communication of information?

HINTS & TIPS

Setting up the grid

In many instances, you will probably think about creating the grid for your designs on screen. However, there is no reason why you shouldn't draw up grids on paper before applying them to the digital realm. Working to scale enables you to get a real feel for the proportions you are dealing with, which isn't always possible on screen. Test out the suitability of the grid; play with your options before committing to screen. Try not to view the grid as being limiting; hopefully the examples we have shown in this book so far clearly demonstrate this is not the case. A grid supports the communication of information in a structured manner and should help, not hinder, the creative process.

Different types of grid

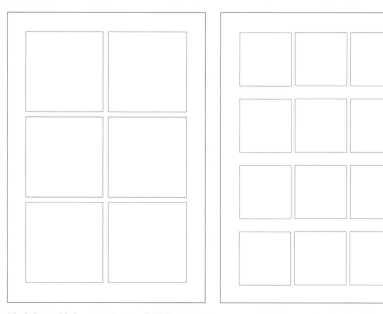

Modular grid (here with 6 and 12 fields).

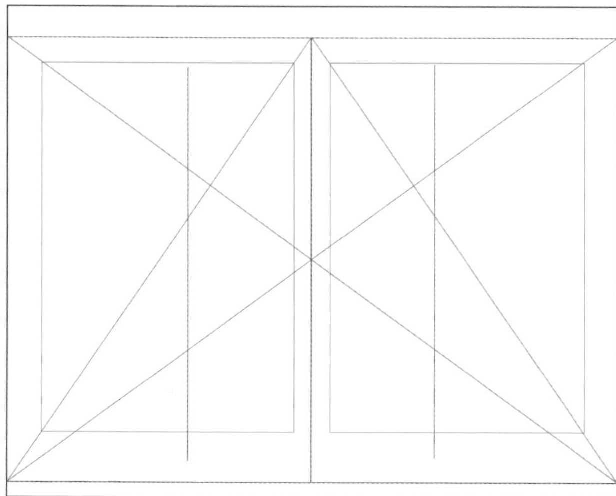
Manuscript grid

Some ideas on setting up the grid

Select the size of your document; this will vary according to the platform you are designing for.

Set/draw your margins at the top, bottom, left and right of the page.

Set/draw the number of columns you need on your grid.

Set/draw your gutter widths between columns.

Add in any other guides you need to define specific fields for information that need to be present when designing.

Column grid

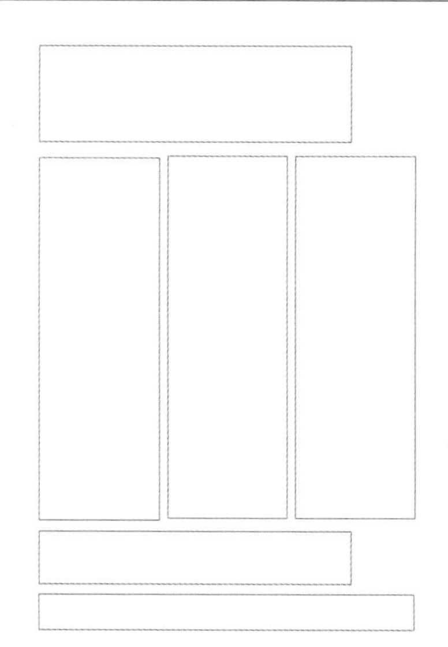
Hierarchical grid

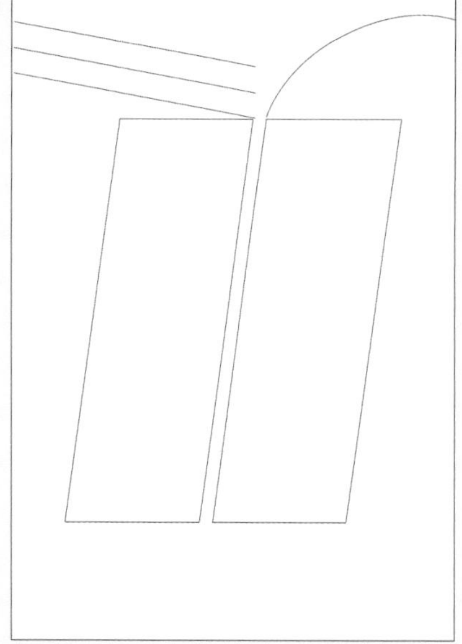
Deconstructed grid (using curved lines, expressive, etc.)

Grid structure and hierarchy

Project: The Finnish Institute in London Annual Review, 2010–2011

Design: Emmi Salonen of Studio EMMI, London

Photographs: Jere Salonen

Studio EMMI is a graphic design practice established by Finnish designer Emmi Salonen in 2005. The studio designs brand identities, websites, catalogues, books and other printed matter. Their clients come from the worlds of art, culture, commerce and academia.

Overview

For this case study, we discuss the approach that Emmi took to the grid structure and layout for an annual review that she designed for The Finnish Institute, a London-based private trust. Their mission is to identify emerging issues relevant to contemporary society and to act as a catalyst for positive social change through partnerships. They work with artists, researchers, experts and policy-makers in the UK, Finland and the Republic of Ireland to promote strong networks in the fields of culture and society.

Approach

The annual report needed to give an overall view of the organization and introduce the institute's director and the directors for the Arts & Culture and Society programmes. The information was divided into three parts in the booklet, starting with the introduction and general information, and followed by text and images of both the programmes.

The book's format is A5. It consists of 28 text pages, a 4-page insert with a short flap, and 4 pages for the covers. The cover has a die-cut corner on the spine that shows through the coloured sheet of the first page. The whole grid and structure is built around this idea. The second page of the book needed to be about the director's message and included her photograph, so could not be printed on coloured stock. Emmi then developed the idea into having just a short flap of the coloured paper so it would still show on the die-cut corner on the cover and bring an interesting detail to it. The flap has a logo printed on one side and the index on the other.

THE
FINNISH
INSTITUTE
IN LONDON
2010/2011
THE FINNISH INSTITUTE
IN LONDON
The Finnish Institute is a London-based private trust. Our mission is to identify emerging issues relevant to contemporary society and to act as catalyst for positive social change through partnerships. We work with artists, researchers, experts and policy makers in the United Kingdom, Finland and the Republic of Ireland to promote strong networks in the fields of culture and society. We encourage new and unexpected collaborations and support artistic interventions, research, the creative industries, foresight and social innovation.

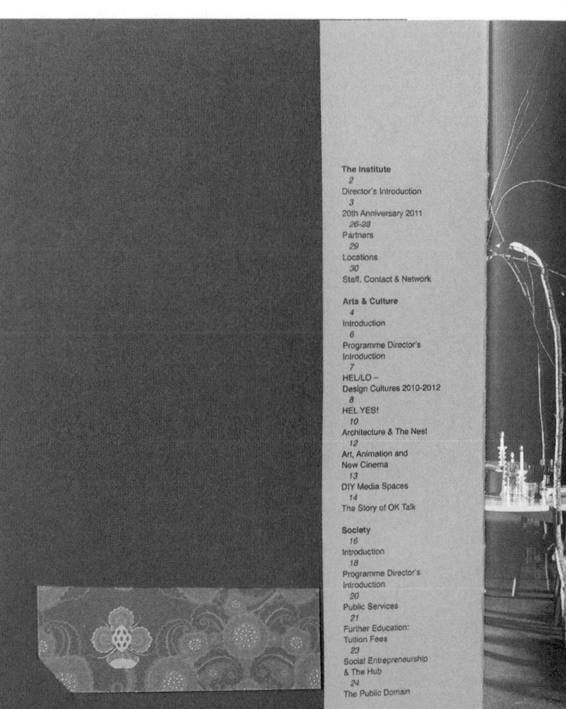
The Institute
2
Director's Introduction
3
20th Anniversary 2011
26-28
Partners
29
Locations
30
Staff, Contact & Network
Arts & Culture
4
Introduction
6
Programme Director's
Introduction
7
HEL/LO –
Design Cultures 2010-2012
8
HEL YES!
10
Architecture & The Nest
12
Art, Animation and
New Cinema
13
DIY Media Spaces
14
The Story of OK Talk
Society
16
Introduction
18
Programme Director's
Introduction
20
Public Services
21
Further Education:
Tuition Fees
23
Social Entrepreneurship
& The Hub
24
The Public Domain
2010/2011
THE FINNISH INSTITUTE
IN LONDON
The Finnish Institute is a London-based private trust. Our mission is to identify emerging issues relevant to contemporary society and to act as catalyst for positive social change through partnerships. We work with artists, researchers, experts and policy makers in the United Kingdom, Finland and the Republic of Ireland to promote strong networks in the fields of culture and society. We encourage new and unexpected collaborations and support artistic interventions, research, the creative industries, foresight and social innovation.

The rest of the layout follows the width of the flap on the inner margin. This area was then reserved for the numerous quotes the institute wanted to include in the booklet. Throughout the book that area remains tinted, or on some pages has a narrow image on it.

The booklet has a nine-column grid, and the inner paragraph is three columns wide. The body copy runs across the rest of the six columns.

Emmi used three typefaces to emphasize the hierarchy of the information. The pages start with headings in Georgia (11pt), followed by a page number and the name of the section: The Institute, Arts & Culture, or Society. The body copy is in Georgia (9pt) and the quotes are in Helvetica (7pt). The book also has a few short case studies that are set in the font American Typewriter (8pt) and tinted purple. To further differentiate them from the rest of the copy, the case studies are separated from the copy by horizontal lines at the beginning and end of the articles.

Top: These pages show the flexibility the grid has provided, using wide and narrow columns to distinguish body copy from captions.

Centre: The area designated for captions also provides a space in which to place imagery without it distracting too much from the content.

Right: The nine-column grid allows for large amounts of information to be dealt with in various ways. Here Partners are listed in three columns and placed next to a full-page diagram, with the cities listed in a single column of the grid structure.

Most of the images in the book are full-bleed A5. To have a nice rhythm throughout, Emmi varied the side of the page where these would go.

As an additional graphic element Emmi used a 6mm mint-coloured line in the gutter. This was quite risky; you have to trust your printer to trim the pages well in order for the lines to remain where intended.

Emmi then had the two-page coloured sheet at the back of the book, and it took some time to decide what best to put there. In the end she drew a map showing the locations that the Finnish Institute was involved in, and on the reverse she placed all the credits.

The cover is in dark aubergine-coloured paper stock and therefore doesn't have any images printed on it. The title is screen-printed in white and has a second die-cut, allowing a business card to be inserted in the front cover. This also shows the logo on the cover.

Outcome

The project shows that what appears to be a relatively simple-looking document has a strong rationale behind it. The grid structure is flexible enough, with the nine columns, to allow the designer to distinguish particular information on the page, while retaining aesthetically pleasing results. The reader has no difficulty in following the text, as the combination of font choice, colour-coding and column width make it clear which are the most important elements on the page.

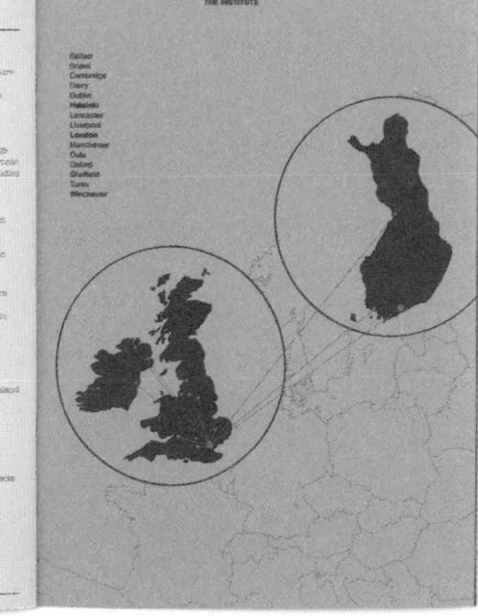

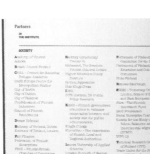

Chapter 4: Legibility and readability

This chapter looks at the fundamentals of communicating through type, image and graphic elements. It is important when producing a piece of information design to ensure that the message is communicated clearly without any ambiguity. The use of typography, colour and graphic elements is crucial to transmitting the necessary information in all design contexts, and every choice has an impact and significance.

Understanding legibility and readability

When referring to legibility and readability, most people think primarily about typography. The dictionary definition, however, refers to being able to read clearly. This means that legibility and readability can be applied to imagery as well as typography. For our purposes, these terms should refer to how recognizable and understandable a piece of communication is. Within information design many factors may be used to convey the data or message. These might include elements other than typography, such as diagrams, imagery, graphic elements and colour-coding. In order for the design to be user-friendly and coherent, these factors need to be carefully considered.

The terms 'legibility' and 'readability' can often be confused, so it is important to clarify their meanings. Legibility relates to letterforms and how easy it is to distinguish individual characters or alphabets in certain fonts. Readability refers to typeforms but also, more importantly, the sympathetic and logical placement of them within a composition. How clear and easy is it to read a piece of text? There are many factors that may affect this, such as the choice of font, size, colour, the use of space and the arrangement within that space. The way in which the text is presented can also affect its readability; for example, whether typography is viewed on screen, on a page, or within a dedicated exhibition space with ambient lighting.

'Most people think typography is about fonts. Most designers think typography is about fonts. Typography is more than that, it is expressing language through type.'
Mark Boulton, graphic designer, speaking at Typo-Berlin, 2007

Previous page: Letters on a letterpress.

Opposite: 'This is Dyslexia' by Wade Jeffree. These posters were designed as part of a student assessment brief from the International Society of Typographic Designers entitled 'Imbalance'. Wade designed a brand to raise awareness of the neglected condition of dyslexia. This project was awarded a distinction in the 2010 AGDA awards.

Legibility issues

When selecting fonts, two important characteristics of the letterforms affect the legibility of messages: the proportions of the counterspaces (enclosed spaces within letters), and the x-height of the lowercase letterforms. Fonts with large x-heights are thought to be more legible, as the individual characters are easily differentiated from each other. Similarly, fonts with large, open characters aid the distinction of different letterforms. This is important when considering how the typeface will be used. An audience may need to read text on signage from a distance or even from a moving car. Any ambiguity within the letterforms may cause confusion.

The position that type occupies on a page is just as important as the selection and treatment of the typography itself. For a message to be communicated clearly, all elements must work in unison to perform this operation successfully.

When considering how to use typography, it is important to assess the different functions that it performs. As well as the information contained within the words themselves, the way in which typography is laid out on the page can also help to convey a message or an idea. It acts as a signpost to attract attention and also explain or caption artwork. Traditionally, it was thought that serif fonts were more legible, but over the years it has been discovered that certain sans serif faces such as Verdana are more legible for people with dyslexia, because the characters are easily distinguished from each other.

Garamond**Helvetica**

You can see in the image above that, although the fonts Garamond and Helvetica appear the same size overall, Helvetica has a much larger x-height.

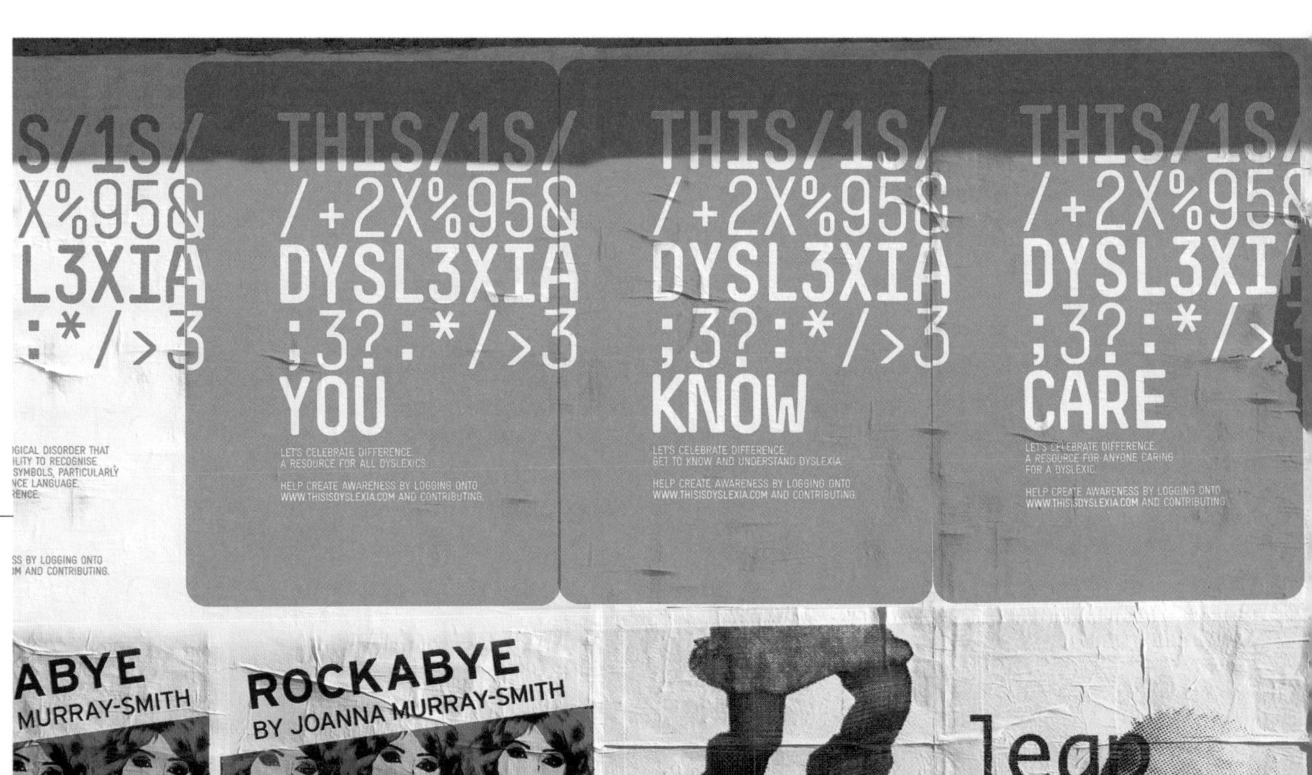

Right: Black and yellow warning tape.

Below: In nature the wasp's black and yellow colouring acts as a warning.

Readability: colour, tint and tone

Colour provides an immediate way to differentiate between typography and graphic elements. Think about traffic lights; it is not the positioning or sequence of the lights that is important but the colours – red for stop and green for go.

Colour has connotations attached to it. These can be instinctual or cultural. Colour is a powerful indicator within nature. Think about the brightly coloured marking of insects or animals; this is often a warning that they are dangerous in some way, usually poisonous! It is for these reasons that the yellow and black of our warning symbols acts as an intuitive signpost of impending danger.

Colours also have obvious meanings, for example, indicating temperature. Red is the colour of fire, suggesting heat; blue the colour of water and ice, suggesting cold. There are many different shades of red and blue and selecting particular intensities may convey other meanings.

'Colours speak all languages.'
Joseph Addison (1672–1719), poet

Using colour in design

Colour is an important element for any information designer; for that reason they must have a good understanding of colour and how it works. Most people are familiar with the rainbow spectrum classified by the English mathematician and physicist Sir Isaac Newton (1642–1727). This spectrum consists of red, orange, yellow, green, blue, indigo and violet. His experiments concluded that pairs of primary colours such as red, yellow and blue when combined produced the secondary colours purple, green and orange, while all three primaries combined together made black. The colour wheel has been simplified into six colours, as blue and indigo are very similar.

It is also important to note that when using projected light, these primary colours change from red, yellow and blue to red, green and blue. When projected, these colours combine to produce white, not black.

Colour is characterized into four elements: hue, shade, tint and tone. Hue is the variation in colour, for example red, blue or yellow. Shade is the colour with black added, tint is the colour with white added, and tone is created by adding both black and white (this is sometimes described as 'greying down'). When considering legibility, it is important that the designer understands these principles. If they are constructing signage using colour, there needs to be enough of a difference between the hues chosen but also between the lightness or darkness between the type and its background. There is no point using dark text on a dark background, even if they are different colours. Visibility is a priority with signage. Signs need to be read at a distance and there must be enough contrast for the message to be clearly recognized.

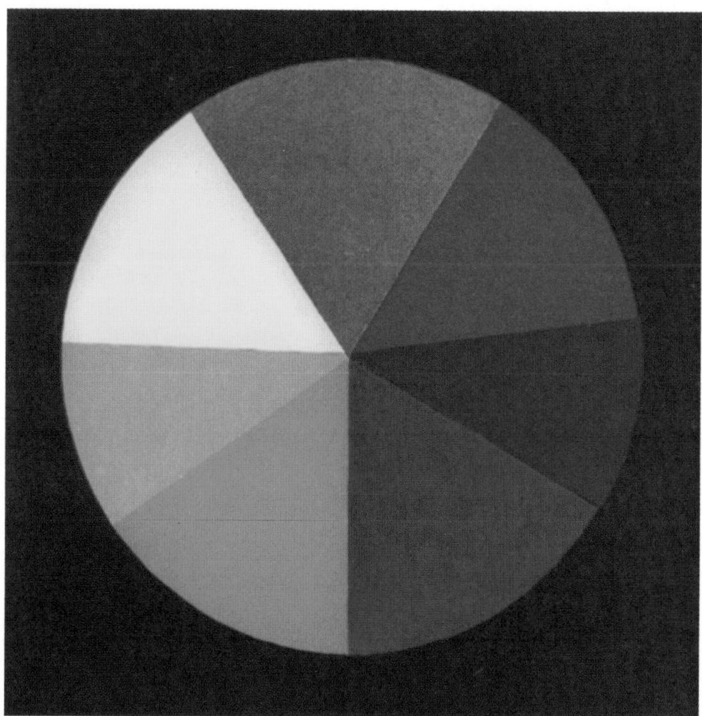

Sir Isaac Newton's colour wheel.

Colour-coding

Colour-coding is the process of attaching a specific colour to a category or group of content to make it instantly recognizable. It is used in various guises when it comes to conveying information. These can be abstract - for example, distinguishing between different routes on a subway system - or they can be direct; for example, designers have been known to use the colour green within packaging to suggest freshness or organic produce.

So, when faced with these choices, how does the designer choose colour combinations that remain readable? There are several factors to consider. It is important that the designer makes decisions about what they are trying to achieve through the colour-coding. If used effectively, colour can convey meaning; it can also show at a glance that elements are connected or separated.

When used with a large amount of visual information, colour-coding can help to locate the most important element. The reader finds it easier to distinguish between categories, and it can also make information memorable.

The New York subway map, reworked by Massimo Vignelli in 2008. Colour-coding is used to good effect to distinguish between the various subway lines.

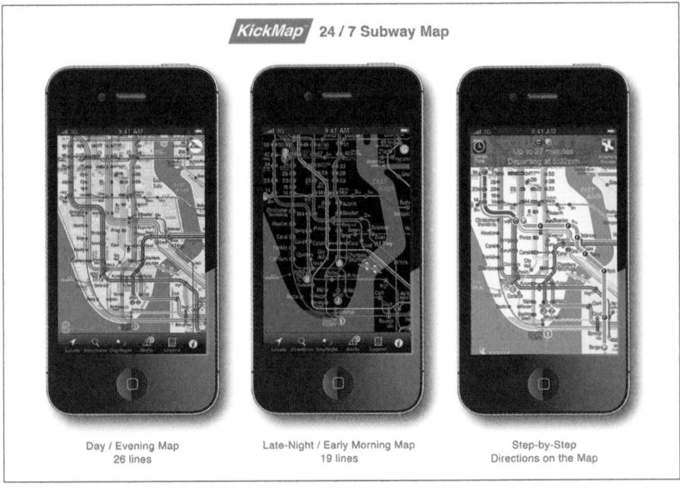

The KickMap 24/7 New York subway map app on a touch-screen mobile phone, designed by Kick Design. The use of night and day modes means colour-coding must be flexible enough to be distinguished on both a light and a dark background.

Colour as a navigational tool

The information designer can guide their readers through information by clever use of colour. By using a single colour for the same kinds of information, the reader is able to recognize and follow it. It unites the design and provides a landmark for the viewer to navigate. For example, you may set category headings in a catalogue in different colours. The colour remains consistent within those sections, allowing the user to find their position within the document easily. The eye is highly adapted to be able to make links between different elements of colour. Consistent use of colour gives pointers about the kind of information, perhaps separating a category title from a headline on the same page. Connecting colours is a subtle non-verbal way to reinforce the connection between the two groups of information.

When choosing colours there are two factors that should be taken into account:

1) How close they are to each other on the colour wheel. By choosing colours at least one or two shades apart from each other, you will make it easier for the reader to tell them apart because there is more contrast.

2) Think about the background on which the colour is placed. If this is a page, what colour will contrast with it? If in an environment, how will the lighting, either daylight or artificial, affect the colour choice during the day or night?

Above and top: Different levels of Brookfield Multiplex's World Square car park in Sydney are differentiated by colour in a wayfinding system designed by BrandCulture.

Above and right: Colour-coding on *The Guardian* newspaper's iPad app. The colour bar at the top of the page acts as a reminder as to which category of the application you are currently viewing.

Legibility, readability and contrast

Colour can be a significant factor when designing with large amounts of information or when the message needs to be identified quickly. The contrast between the typography or graphic elements and their background is essential in order for the viewer to recognize the message clearly. There needs to be a significant difference in tone between one component and another for clear distinction. As discussed and illustrated on p. 44, poor contrast can be problematic for any members of the audience with visual impairments. They may not be able to differentiate between colours with the same tonal quality. It can also be difficult to distinguish from a distance or in adverse weather conditions if used on environmental information design. A basic piece of advice would be to achieve maximum contrast between the foreground and the background. Use light type on a dark background and vice versa for clear, legible and readable information.

As we have discussed, readability refers to how understandable a piece of text is. Legibility refers to the construction of the letterforms themselves. Readability studies suggest that we read along the tops of letters rather than their entire shapes. British author and designer Cal Swann has described the top half of letters as being made up of characteristic shapes that provide the reader with visual clues as to the whole shape of a word. He proposed that when the letters of the alphabet are put together they make up a word shape; subsequently, it is this word shape and not the individual letters that we recognize.

It is for this reason that letters arranged vertically top to bottom are difficult to read. Word space is also an essential factor when considering legibility. The space around and between letterforms is as important to readability as pauses are to timings in music as wordsruntogetherwithoutspace.

Text cropped to show only the tops of letters.

Text alongside the outline of the word shape.

Lorem ipsum dolor sit amet. Con minimim venami quis nostrud laboris nisi ut aliquip ex ea com dolor in reprehenderit in voluptate nonumi. Mimimum veniami ex ea con dolor nisi ut aliquip. Consequat Duis autem vel eum iruire dolor in endrerit, voluptate velit est. Sit amet, consectetuer adipiscing elit, sed diam nonummi.

Lorem ipsum dolor sit amet. Con minimim venami quis nostrud laboris nisi ut aliquip ex ea com dolor in reprehenderit in voluptate nonumi. Mimimum veniami ex ea con dolor nisi ut aliquip. Consequat Duis autem vel eum iruire dolor in endrerit, voluptate velit est. Sit amet, consectetuer adipiscing elit, sed diam nonummi.

Paragraph of text set in light and bold typefaces.

Lorem ipsum dolor sit amet. Con minimim venami quis nostrud laboris nisi ut aliquip ex ea com dolor in reprehenderit in voluptate nonumi. Mimimum veniami ex ea con dolor nisi ut aliquip. Consequat Duis autem vel eum iruire dolor in endrerit, voluptate velit est. Sit amet, consectetuer adipiscing elit, sed diam nonummi.

Paragraph set in condensed type.

LOREM IPSUM DOLOR SIT AMET. CON MINIMIM VENAMI QUIS NOSTRUD LABORIS NISI UT ALIQUIP EX EA COM DOLOR IN REPREHENDERIT IN VOLUPTATE NONUMI. MIMIMUM VENIAMI EX EA CON DOLOR NISI UT ALIQUIP. CONSEQUAT DUIS AUTEM VEL EUM IRUIRE DOLOR IN ENDRERIT, VOLUPTATE VELIT EST. SIT AMET, CONSECTETUER ADIPISCING ELIT, SED DIAM NONUMMI.

Paragraph set in all caps.

For large amounts of text for continuous reading, sometimes referred to as 'text type', avoid using typefaces that are too heavy or too light. A font that is too light cannot be easily distinguished from its background. Conversely, a font that is too heavy is less legible, as the thickness of the stroke diminishes the size of the counterspaces, making the letterform less recognizable. Some typefaces have what is termed a book weight. This is a medium-weight font that attempts to strike a balance between the extremes of bold and light and is more suited to large amounts of copy, both printed and on screen.

Avoid using condensed or extended faces for body copy. For the letterforms to be easily recognized, the space in and around the letters is crucial at small sizes. Distorting letters by altering the proportions means they do not appear familiar to us and so retards reading. Type families may include extended or condensed fonts whose proportions fall within the accepted range, but it is best to avoid these if possible for large amounts of body text.

A skilled information designer follows a logical process to select an appropriate typeface, scale letterforms and place them sympathetically in a layout. The ability to prioritize information into understandable hierarchies based on the rules of good typographic practice results in clear and concise design that the audience can recognize and interpret immediately.

For optimum legibility, do not set body text in all capital letters as this hinders the speed at which you can read. A combination of upper- and lowercase letters produces a more readable piece of typography, since we recognize word shapes not individual letters. The pattern of ascenders and descenders provides an easier way of recognizing the words and so aids legibility. TEXT SET IN ALL CAPITALS DOESN'T HAVE THE SAME RHYTHM, AS ALL THE LETTERFORMS ARE THE SAME HEIGHT. For this reason, it is harder to recognize word shapes in large amounts of text. It is possible to set short passages of text in uppercase successfully. However, when text is set in uppercase the characters may look 'squashed'. In these instances, it may require some extra word spacing or tracking to make it more visually appealing and readable.

Weight, size and scale

Typefaces are produced in many different weights. A quality font family will range in weight from extra-light or hairline, through roman, medium and bold into extra-bold and black versions. Fonts designed for screen-based use are also available in a variety of weights. Establishing the correct weight, size and scale of typographic elements for messages is key to good information design. It is beneficial to exercise restraint in the design of typographic information. Overcomplicating only confuses the reader and degrades the information presented.

Once the designer has selected a typeface, they must then decide its size and weight. The context in which the typography is used is critical in determining an appropriate type size. As a society we associate size with importance. It is for these reasons that designers may use scale to emphasize a component within a design.

It may be useful to think of where the design will be viewed; for example, reading, walking or driving. This may help to scale elements. Reading letters are small enough to be used for text and captions with print- or screen-based information design. Walking letters are of a size suitable for directional messages that guide pedestrians on city streets or in interior public spaces. Driving letters are large enough to be seen by drivers looking for directions or information.

When we talk about reading we are referring to books, newspapers and other text that is read from an average distance of 30–36cm (12–14in), often described as 'body copy' or 'text type'. For printed matter, it is best to use text sizes that range between 8 and 12 points, as studies suggest it will be more legible and comfortable for the reader. Screen-based fonts need slightly larger sizes of 10 to 14 points, as different screens cannot render type as accurately as print. Generally in print, any type above 12 point is known as display or headline type. These are normally used for titles, headlines and signage, or any text that may want to grab attention at large sizes.

Signage for parking at 13–17 East 54th Street, New York, designed by Paula Scher and Pentagram.

To establish clear hierarchy within typography, avoid using too many different type sizes and weights at the same time. It is easier for the reader to follow if there is clear differentiation, but too many sizes creates a cluttered and confusing design. Exercise restraint and keep to two or three font sizes to maintain functional and aesthetically attractive designs.

Several factors affect these scale and weight decisions, such as the viewer's distance from the piece. Speed may be an issue when type is used for information for drivers. Environmental letterforms are scaled for maximum effect in busy urban streetscapes or on roads.

Weight can create hierarchy and generates a darker tone in the design, acting as a focal point and drawing the eye to particular elements. In typography, the placement and spacing of black type on white background creates the illusion of a block of grey tone. As different typefaces have various stroke widths and x-heights, fonts set in the same size, with the same leading and tracking, may appear to produce different tones on the page. The white of the paper acts as the tinting factor that determines the illusion of grey, along with the type's style. The type will also appear to be darker if the spacing between letterforms is reduced.

This can be used to maximum effect to draw attention to particular elements. An example of this is the graphic design by Paula Scher and Pentagram for parking at 13–17 East 54th Street in New York. Here, large type is used to great effect to provide wayfinding and information about the car park for drivers.
The main features are the use of bold reversed-out text for directional signs and light informational text for other features that act as an aide-memoire for where the driver has parked their car.

The tone of typography can also be used in a subtle fashion. Long typographic lists such as tables in annual reports or lists of names and addresses in telephone books can be very difficult to navigate. A skilled information designer can vary the weight of the font by a small amount between lines of copy. This prevents the viewer losing their position within the information and creates visual rhythm and pace.

It is essential to consider your design context when selecting the size and weight of your typeface. A screen-based medium such as the Kindle (right) will require a different choice to a wayfinding sign in an urban streetscape such as Applied's 'Legible London' freestanding map, designed by Tim Fendley (below).

Typographic elements

Your consideration of typographic elements such as choice of typeface and the setting of paragraphs will have great impact on the legibility and readability of your information design. If you are unfamiliar with some of the terminology relating to typography, see pp. 90–91 for a glossary of terms.

Typeface

The selection of a typeface for any project is an important decision. Typefaces are like people: they have individual personalities. For example, Garamond is traditional and conservative, Dax is sleek and youthful, Bello is cheeky and nostalgic, and Helvetica is serious and workmanlike.

We choose to use certain fonts because of the values they communicate. They can be strong, bold, forthright, whimsical, distressed, futuristic, common or utilitarian. Serif faces have more in common with traditional or luxury values, having a sense of history and integrity to them. Sans serifs are modern and uniform and so lend themselves to more functional purposes.

With the advent of digital technology, the number of fonts available is huge, so a designer must consider carefully how a font will be used for a project. Is it to be used at a large scale on signage, small scale in a newspaper, or does it appear as a three-dimensional object? With information design it is imperative that the font chosen is legible in that its characters are recognized and readable.

Kerning

Kerning is the term that denotes the space between two letterforms. Particular combinations of letters may become difficult to read if they have too much or too little space between them. The best example of this is the combination of r and n. This can sometimes be mistaken for an m in particular typefaces. Kerning attempts to balance the spacing and make it even across the whole word.

Most designers find that they have to kern typography at display sizes. The bigger the type, the more attention to detail is required as any imperfections are exaggerated.

Garamond
Dax
Bello
Helvetica

Fonts with personality.

kerning
kerning

Examples of good and poor kerning. Poor kerning results in letterforms touching, and thus resembling other letters and words, which can cause confusion.

CRANBERRY AVENUE
C R A N B E R R Y A V E N U E

Examples of good and poor tracking. Notice the inconsistent spacing in the lower version, especially between the A and the V.

Tracking

Tracking is defined as the amount of space between letters in a whole word. This can be adjusted to increase or reduce the space to make letterforms more discernible. Reducing the amount of tracking allows the designer to fit more text onto a single line when using a large amount of copy. If this space is reduced too much, however, the letters begin to collide into one another, reducing legibility.

Leading

Leading is described as the space between lines of typography within a paragraph or block. It is a historical term derived from the process of using metal type characters for printing. Strips of lead were used as horizontal spacers between the lines of metal text. It is important not to have too much or too little leading between lines. Too little means ascenders and descenders on consecutive lines may collide, whereas too much means that the lines are overly spread out, causing the eye to become distracted when moving between different lines of copy.

Paragraphs

It is thought that legibility is better if you use align-left, ragged-right type alignment. Force-justified text causes the spacing between words to be altered to fit the copy and so results in unpleasant 'rivers' of white space running through the text.

When using aligned-left text, aim for consistent and rhythmic line endings. Avoid the strange and awkward-looking shapes that occur when the default settings of a desktop publishing program are used. For best results, a long, short, long rag shape aids legibility. This can be achieved by using line breaks within the text (Shift + Return) to shuffle the text around without creating unwanted paragraph breaks.

It is best to indicate paragraphs clearly, but take care not to upset the visual consistency of the copy. Indenting is the most common way to do this, along with adding space between paragraphs within a piece of text. The normal rule is to indent the text to the same measure as the point size; for example, 12-point text would require an indent of 12 points.

Strive to achieve text without widows or orphans, as they create inconsistent text blocks and interfere with the flow of reading. They produce pages that look ugly and ill-considered. By definition, a widow is a single word or a very short line at the end of a paragraph, while an orphan is a line detached from the rest of its paragraph; this could be the first line of a paragraph at the bottom of a column of text or the final line of a paragraph at the top of a new column of text (it is a line of text left alone, separated from the paragraph it belongs to). The best way to avoid these is to either shuffle the text around by looking at line endings and adding line breaks or to subtly change the tracking across the text by a minute amount. This will rectify the problem without affecting the appearance of the text.

Lorem ipsum dolor sit amet. Con minimim venami
quis nostrud laboris nisi ut aliquip ex ea com
dolor in reprehenderit in voluptate nonumi.
Mimimum veniami ex ea con dolor nisi ut aliquip.
Consequat Duis autem vel eum iruire dolor in
endrerit, voluptate velit est. Sit amet, consectetuer
adipiscing elit, sediam nonummi. Euismod tincidunt
ut laroeet dolore magna aliquam erat voluptat. Ut wisi
enin ad minim. Quis nostrud ad nostris pro amat.

Lorem ipsum dolor sit amet. Con minimim venami
quis nostrud laboris nisi ut aliquip ex ea com dolor in
reprehenderit in voluptate nonumi. Mimimum veniami
ex ea con dolor nisi ut aliquip. Consequat Duis autem
vel eum iruire dolor in endrerit, voluptate velit est. Sit
amet, consectetuer adipiscing elit, sed diam nonummi.
Euismod tincidunt ut laroeet dolore magna aliquam
erat voluptat. Ut wisi enin ad minim. Quis nostrud ad
nostris pro amat.

Paragraphs with align-left, ragged-right type. Note that in the lower paragraph the line endings have a more consistent 'rag', where the designer has taken care that no distracting shapes are created from the negative space.

Glossary of typographical terms

Ascender: The portion of the lowercase letter that appears above the x-height.

Baseline: The imaginary line upon which the letters sit.

Word annotated to show baseline, x-height, cap height, ascender and descender height.

Body text: Body text or body copy is the text that forms the main part of the work. It is usually between 8 and 14 points in size.

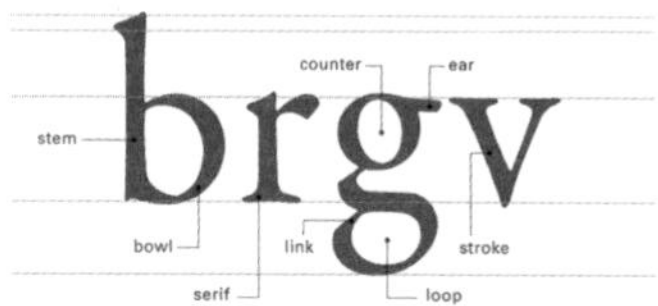

Single letterform annotated to show stem, stroke, counter and bowl.

Bowl: The stroke that surrounds and contains a counter.

Capital letters: Uppercase letters, sometimes called majuscules.

Counter: The negative space within the body of a letterform.

Descender: The portion of the lowercase letter that appears below the baseline.

Display type: Large and/or distinctive type intended to attract the eye. Specifically designed to be viewed from a distance.

Em: Typographic unit of measurement derived from the set width of the square body of the uppercase M. An em equals the size of a given type; i.e., the em of 10-point type is 10 points. An en is half an em.

Font: The physical attributes needed to make a typeface.

Kerning: The adjustment of space between two individual letters to ensure overall visual balance across a single word.

Leading: The space between lines of type measured from baseline to baseline. It is expressed in points and is derived from metal type printing when strips of lead were placed between lines of type to provide line spacing.

Legibility: The ability to distinguish one letter from another due to characteristics inherent in the typeface design.

Lowercase: Small uneven letters derived from handwritten forms that evolved between the eighth and fifteenth centuries. sometimes called 'minuscules'. The term 'case' comes from type cases used in the printing industry, which held the metal type.

Measure: The lengths of a line of text expressed in picas.

Pica: The measurement for specifying line lengths. One pica is 12 points or 4.22mm. There are 6 picas to an inch.

Point system: The measurement for specifying typographical dimensions. The British and American point system is 1/72 of an inch, or 0.35mm. The European Didot system provides similar size values. The point size of a font is based on the height of a printing block, not on the size of the lettering (this originally refers back to metal type but now refers to the bounding box on digital type).

Readability: The overall visual representation of the text or narrative. This includes typographic, illustrative, photographic and other elements that are part of the overall design.

Roman: The basic letterform.

Sans serif: A font without decorative serifs. Typically with little variation within stroke thickness, a larger x-height and no stress in rounded strokes.

Script: A typeface designed to imitate handwriting.

Semi serif: A font with serifs on only certain parts of the letterform.

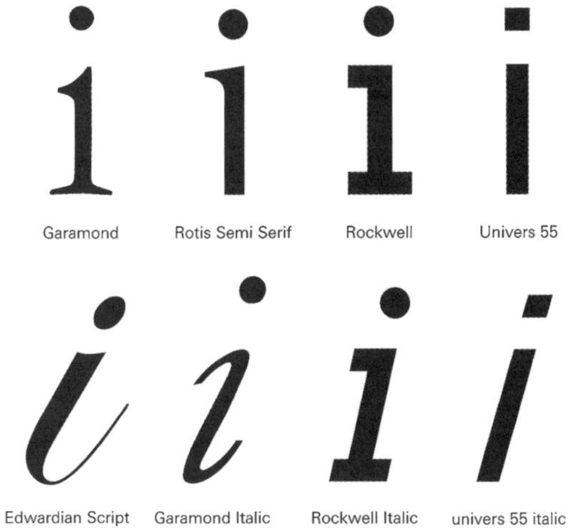

Garamond | Rotis Semi Serif | Rockwell | Univers 55

Edwardian Script | Garamond Italic | Rockwell Italic | univers 55 italic

Several lowercase letter 'i's to distinguish between sans serif, serif, slab serif, roman, italic and script.

Serif: A small stroke at the end of a main vertical or horizontal stroke. Also used as a classification for typefaces that contain such decorative rounded or pointed square finishing strokes.

Slab serif: A font with heavy, squared finishing strokes, low contrast and few curves.

Stem: The main vertical or diagonal stroke of a letter.

Stroke: The diagonal portion of letterforms such as N, M and Y. Stems, bars, arms and bowl are collectively referred to as strokes.

Tracking: The adjustment of the overall amount of space between letters of a word, across a line or whole block of text (not to be confused with kerning, which involves the adjustment of the space between individual letters).

Helvetica Ultra Light Condensed	Helvetica Ultra Light Condensed Italic	Helvetica Ultra Light	Helvetica Ultra Light Italic	Helvetica Ultra Light Extended
Helvetica Light Condensed	Helvetica Light Condensed Italic	Helvetica Light	Helvetica Light Italic	Helvetica Light Extended
Helvetica Condensed	Helvetica Condensed Italic	Helvetica	Helvetica Italic	Helvetica Extended
Helvetica Bold Condensed	Helvetica Bold Condensed Italic	Helvetica Bold	Helvetica Bold Italic	Helvetica Bold Extended
Helvetica Black Condensed	Helvetica Black Condensed Italic	Helvetica Black	Helvetica Black Italic	Helvetica Black Extended

A typeface family, showing light, regular, bold, extra-bold, condensed and extended fonts.

Typeface: The letters, numbers and punctuation marks of a type design.

Typeface family: A series of typefaces sharing common characteristics but with different sizes and weights.

X-height: The height of a lowercase 'x' of a given typeface measured from the baseline to the meanline. Different fonts can be the same point size but have a different x-height (see p. 79).

Graphic elements

When viewing a design, a user will normally scan the graphic looking for the most important areas. This can be difficult to ascertain in a complicated design. The designer can use graphic elements to provide visual signals for a user; this will draw their attention and allow them to locate essential information quickly. There are several methods of accomplishing this task. They are often achieved through the use of rules, dots, lines and arrows.

Rules

Rules are lines that designate areas within a design. They can be used to divide, frame and emphasize elements within a space. They break up information visually and signify how information is related. Think about magazines or newspapers where two or more stories may occupy one page. If colour isn't used to separate information, rules can be employed to section off different groups. They can be used to indicate columns and rows or within tabular information to be used to separate titles from data sets.

Dots

One way to draw attention to specific details within a design is to use dots or bullet points. The area of tone created by the point draws the eye to it and helps establish hierarchy. Dots act as a signpost to important sections of information by highlighting them within the main design. Short bulleted lists help to give meaning and make the information clear.

Lines

Lines can be used in several ways, with or without arrowheads, and signify connections between components of the graphic. They are directional pathways that lead the eye to a specific endpoint. Dashed lines are often used to signify movement, or even invisible forms of energy, such as the transmission of data from earth to a satellite and back. Curved lines can also be used to create form.

Massimo Vignelli's 1964 poster for the Piccolo Teatro in Milan demonstrates how the designer has used rules to divide, frame and emphasize elements.

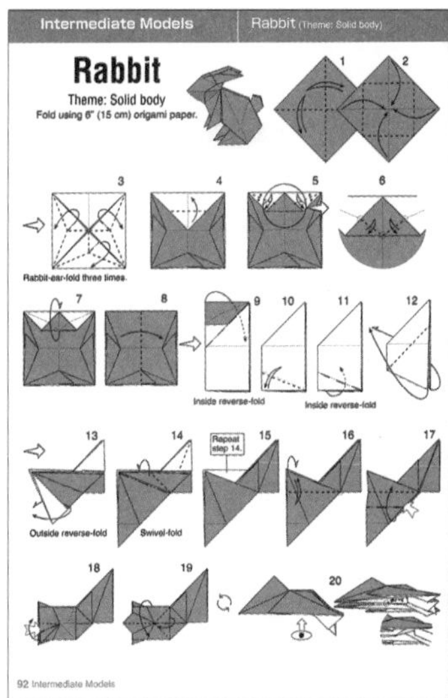

Intermediate Models | Rabbit (Theme: Solid body)

Rabbit

Theme: Solid body

Fold using 6" (15 cm) origami paper.

Rabbit-ear-fold three times.

Inside reverse-fold

Inside reverse-fold

Outside reverse-fold

Swivel-fold

Repeat step 14.

92 Intermediate Models

Above: Origami instruction diagram using dotted lines and arrows.

Right and below left: The arrow is a useful graphic device that directs the attention of the viewer. The bold wayfinding design used at the Zmik Spacial Design Artshop09 attracts the gaze to a particular path or route that leads to a specific location.

Arrows

The arrow is used in many forms of information design, such as diagrams, wayfinding and explanatory graphics. It is a useful graphic device that directs the attention of the viewer. It moves their gaze to a particular path or route and leads to a specific location. Using an arrow allows the viewer to concentrate only on the information that is necessary, filtering out everything that is not required. Since it is a graphic and not text-based, it is a universal symbol and so acts as one of the first steps in the comprehension of information. When designing with arrows, take care to make it forceful enough to capture the audience's attention, but not to overpower the overall design.

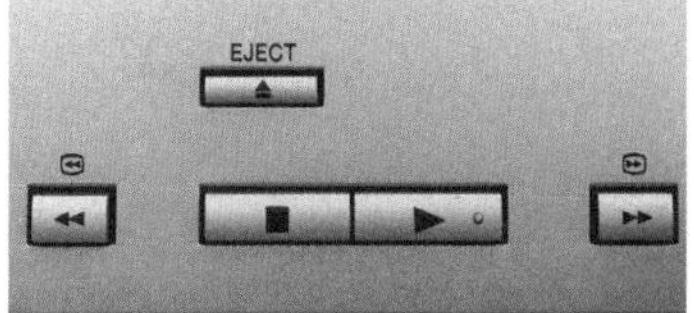

Above, top: One-way arrow on brick wall.

Above: Play and rewind/fast-forward buttons, which show directions literally.

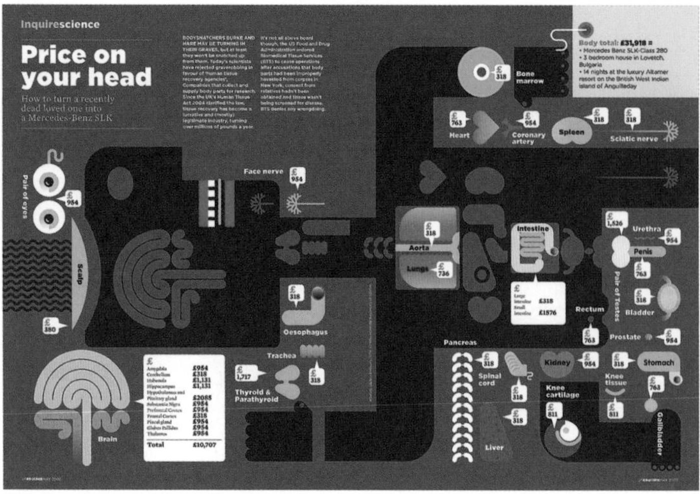

Above: 'Price on your head', by Peter Grundy for *Esquire* magazine. In this infographic Grundy uses illustration playfully to demonstrate what the sale of parts of the human body can earn you. Since this is a gruesome subject matter, the illustrative diagram communicates the ideas quickly and humorously. According to the piece the proceeds of the sale of all of your organs is equal to the price of a Mercedes-Benz.

Below: EFFP's *View* magazine, designed by Purpose Design. EFFP is a business consultancy specializing in the agricultural-food industry. The publication *View* was sent out to their existing and potential clients and outlined their strategic insight and knowledge. The document created for them by Purpose was a large-format black and white newspaper. It uses bold graphic elements, photography and diagrams to reflect the company's ethos to communicate in a clear and straightforward manner.

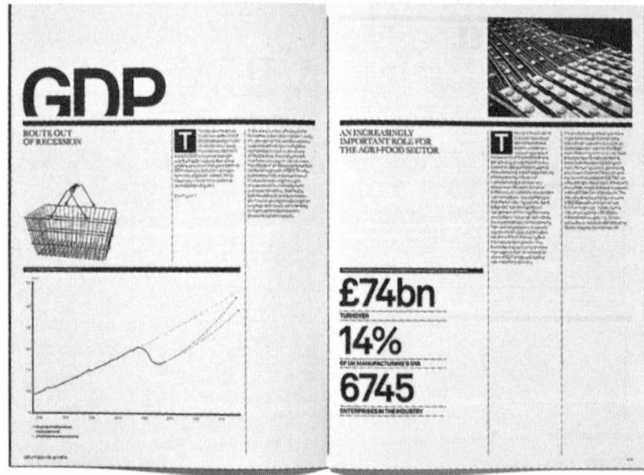
GDP

ROUTE OUT OF RECESSION

AN INCREASINGLY IMPORTANT ROLE FOR THE AGRI-FOOD SECTOR

£74bn

14%

6745

77%

23%

The spending cuts will be the deepest and longest since 1948. A 22% reduction in DEFRA's budget by 2014/15 could have a materially detrimental impact on the agri-food sector.

Imagery

Illustration

Illustration can be used within a piece of information design in a number of ways. It is a powerful tool to consider when designing: it can help to convey a story to an audience, it can provide a narrative that runs across a series of pages, and it can engage and maintain the interest of an audience across a variety of platforms. Illustration does not have to be static. With the platforms available to us for information delivery we may consider using animated illustrative elements to help communicate our content; however, the overall principles we need to consider will apply across the full range of options we have at our disposal, so we should understand how illustration can be used before we introduce it into a design.

Well-considered illustration is able to add colour, both physically and metaphorically, and suggest personality, mood and tone. Used effectively it can attract attention, create movement and provide contrast. It also helps to anchor a layout: using a large illustration provides a focal point, as the layout of a page can be built around the placement of an illustration. It is important to consider the proximity of elements within a design and ensure there is a relationship between the elements you are using. The rules of hierarchy still apply when using illustration. Consider what your viewer needs to see first, second and third. How and where does illustration fit within the mix? What do you want your audience to engage with or 'read' first? If the illustration is the most important element, the designer must ensure that it takes centre stage within the overall composition of elements by being the main focal point.

Illustration can also play a valuable supporting role. Drop-in illustrations can be utilized to break up dense information, they can highlight key points within text, and they can be used as a device to take an audience through or around a design. This could be within a printed page, on a web interface, or as part of a wayfinding system; illustration can help a viewer navigate through and around complex information. The use of a successful illustration should also suggest and capture the mood and tone of the content it relates to. This, in turn, will ensure that the design appeals to the selected target audience.

Photography

Photography can be used in a variety of ways to support the communication of information. It may be used to indicate and represent content in a literal manner; for example, on food packaging. It may be used along with other graphic elements and text as part of an overall communication, in some instances providing a focal point, an anchor around which the other elements work. As with illustration, it can also play a significant supporting role. It can be used to punctuate and break up information; for example, photographs relating to content may be placed in large amounts of text. This supports the overall readability of the information, breaking up large amounts of content into digestible chunks, dividing information and supporting navigation through it.

Photographs shot with the same visual style provide continuity in a design; this can help readers identify related content and create consistency across a series of pages in a book, newspaper, series of posters or on a website. Photography can be used to create shape or to break a grid structure to provide dynamic composition. Its placement within a design can imply energy and movement and suggest or support the required mood and tone of an overall piece of design.

Cropping photographs may help to create interest, while scale can be used to make a dynamic, engaging layout and provide contrast and imply hierarchy within information. A large image may draw a viewer's eye to the most important piece of information, whereas a smaller, cropped image may be used to direct them where to go next. Photographs can be the principle feature of the narrative, or support surrounding elements in conveying their message.

As with all information design, understanding and organizing your content is key. It will influence how photography is used, and help the designer to decide whether its inclusion is appropriate. Depending on the platform for delivery, the role of photography is crucial. For example, within a newspaper, photography is one of the most important elements of the overall editorial design and communication of information; it is key to effective capture and delivery of content to an audience and is used as the first means of communication. Over the last decade, digital photography has transformed news reportage. Think of the front page of a newspaper: the image is carefully selected to communicate a message in an instant to a reader; the image is read before the text. In this instance, an image may be considered to be more powerful than a thousand words. Newspapers, magazines and certain types of books acknowledge and utilize this within their designs.

Above: Posters from the Museum of London's 'You are Here' poster campaign, designed by NB Studio, shown in situ on the London Underground and in Trafalgar Square. The idea behind the campaign was the thrill of being on the same physical spot as someone or something historic, which was encompassed in the campaign's 'You are Here' tagline. NB Studio sourced images from the museum's archive and then placed them on site to produce a bold and thought-provoking piece of design.

1 euro // Terça-feira, 13 Outubro 2009 // Ano 1 // Número 137 // www.ionline.pt
Director: Martim Avillez Figueiredo // Director-adjunto: André Macedo

i

RANKING NACIONAL 16 PAGS.

Saiba qual é a escola ideal para o seu filho

- 01 As escolas mais bem classificadas
- 02 Ensino privado continua à frente do ensino público
- 03 As melhores escolas de cada distrito
- 04 As melhores em Matemática
- 05 As melhores em Português

Roseta: "Não vejo Sócrates com o diálogo de Costa"

Bailarino sofre. O i numa audição de Olga Roriz

A coreógrafa procura os melhores intérpretes para a "Sagração da Primavera", que estreia em Maio no CCB

Economistas distinguidos com o Nobel graças à crise

O Sporting está mesmo a salvo de um qualquer Abramovich?

Left: Cover of the Portuguese newspaper *I*: issue 137, 13 October 2009. I was voted the world's best-designed newspaper by the Society for News Design in 2011. The paper delivers traditional newspaper content by taking a magazine-like approach to engage the readers. It uses photography and imagery particularly well, for example in the cropping of cover images to add intrigue, as shown here.

Pictographs, icons and symbols

Information designers can use pictographs and symbols as simple representations. They are mainly used when more complicated illustrations or photographs are unsuitable, such as within signage and wayfinding. It is important to understand the difference between them. Pictographs are defined as stylized images that directly resemble an object or concept. They can be categorized into three groups. A resemblance icon directly portrays the object it refers to, such as a steaming cup to indicate a café. Icons signify a more abstract depiction than the object shown, for example the recycling symbol which uses arrows to suggest the concept of reuse. A symbol is an icon that has no relationship or resemblance to the object or concept it represents; an example of this would be the icon for biological hazard or biohazard used to signify a health risk.

Pictographs and icons are useful because they communicate information quickly. It is important to note that some symbolic icons may be dependent on cultural reference and so could be misunderstood in certain countries. An example is the trefoil symbol that indicates radioactivity, which has been mistaken for a propeller.

Right, top to bottom: resemblance icon: steaming coffee cup; symbolic icon: recycling symbols; the symbols for radioactivity **(left)** and biohazard **(right)**.

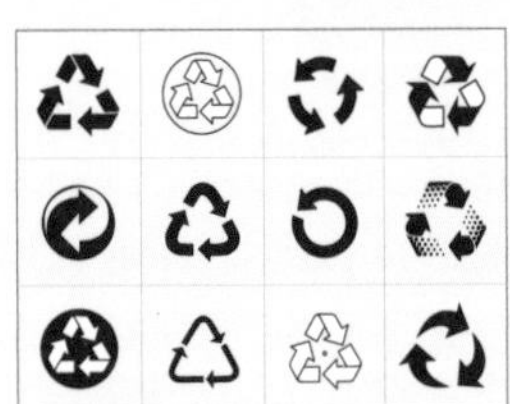

Diagrams

Diagrams are plans, sketches or drawings that are designed to demonstrate or explain how something works. They can be used as instructions or visual aids to communicate complex pieces of information. They are often used to convey or clarify the relationships between the different parts of a whole. These are early versions of what we would now call 'infographics'. The information designer may choose to use diagrams to communicate a message without the need for text or minimal captions. When designing for an international audience or one with varying levels of literacy, a diagrammatic approach may be of more use. The lack of text negates the need for translation.

Diagrams are often used to communicate step-by-step instructions. They are more effective than photographs, as the designer can focus the viewer's attention on particular elements by editing out unnecessary details and backgrounds. Simplified representations are conveyed through plain line drawings. The number of steps used will depend on how complicated the information is. The designer can highlight and enlarge details to draw attention to them; this can provide clarity that may not be available with the use of photography. An example of this would be the use of instructions to construct flat-pack furniture. The instructions would rely on the use of simplified sequential drawings with numerical steps that show the construction of various components at certain stages.

Below: Step-by-step diagrammatic instructions for the assembly of an Airfix model Messerschmidt aeroplane.

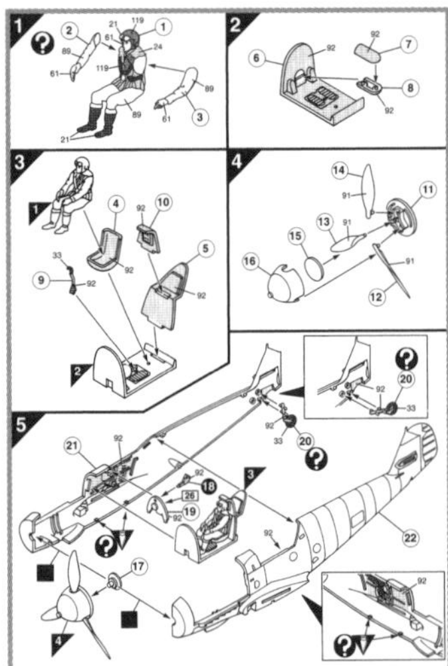

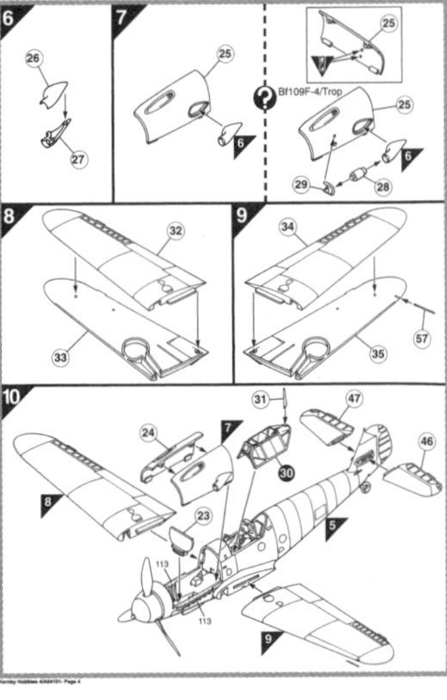

Various kinds of information conveyed through diagrams:

Right: 'Tree of Skills' by Peter Grundy. This diagram on the subject of lifelong learning was commissioned for *The Guardian* newspaper. It shows which organizations provide teaching, advice, funding and training to the teaching workforce. It uses decorative illustration to guide the user through the variety of training providers available.

Centre: 'David McCandless vs Neville Brody', designed by Toby Bradbury. This uses illustration and simple graphs to depict the differences between the two designers, based on a BBC *Newsnight* broadcast in August 2010.

Below: 'Left vs Right', political spectrum diagram by David McCandless and Stefanie Posavec, uses a combination of mapping and illustration to show two opposing views or contradictions at the same time. The illustration makes it easy to compare the differences and similarities.

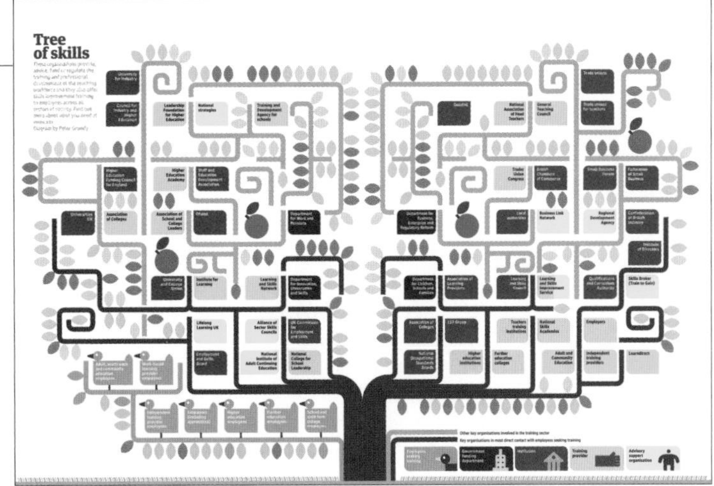

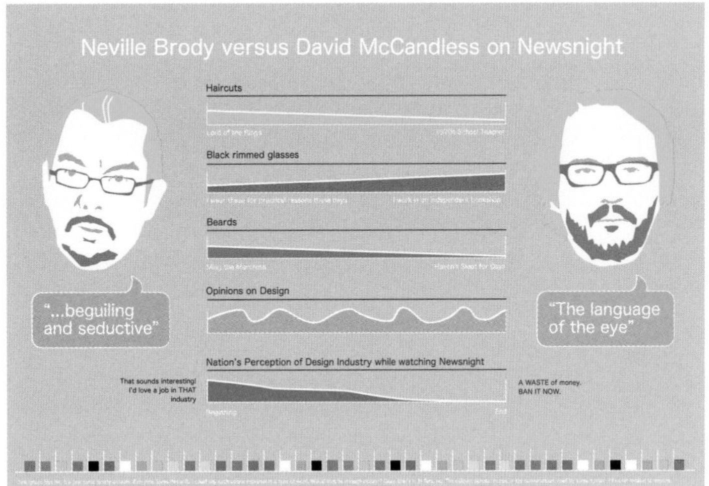

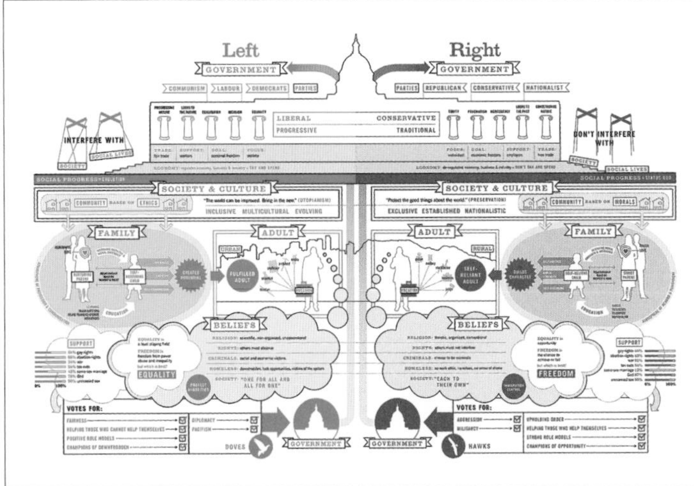

Instructions can also take the form of exploded drawings. These drawings are arranged around an axis and appear as if they have been deconstructed or dismantled, with the individual pieces arranged in the areas to which they belong. This kind of diagram helps the viewer with naming the various components and provides an overview of how pieces link together as part of a whole unit.

When communicating conceptual information, the designer may choose to use a diagrammatic representation to visualize a relationship. An example of this would be a tree diagram, such as those used to describe a family tree. These explore the links and relationships between family members over the generations. Venn diagrams are also used to explain relationships between groups, although these are of a more abstract representation. The circle is widely used to represent a single group, although ellipses or any other kind of geometric shape can be employed. The area where the shapes overlap contains information that is common to both groups.

HINTS & TIPS

Visibility and contrast

When designing with large amounts of information, it is important to consider how visible elements are within the design. We discussed in Chapter 2 the importance of designing for a specific audience and how visual impairment may be a factor that needs to be addressed. In terms of legibility, it is not only those with sight problems who may have difficulty reading a piece of typography or seeing an image. The context in which the piece is presented may have an impact on how readable it is. Think about text used within wayfinding systems. The fonts used should be bold enough to be read from a distance. The style of font, weight and colour will all be determining factors in how legible and readable a piece of information is. Contrast is important because, if the difference in tone is not great enough, the audience will have difficulties in distinguishing it. Lighting can drastically affect the readability of text. Typography seen in direct sunlight may be visible, but consider the cash machine or ATM where text on screen is employed. In dull light, the type on screen seems legible and clear. However, in direct sunlight the glare on the screen can render the type indistinguishable from its background.

Colour-coding

Colour can help the viewer remember information, but any more than three or four colours becomes difficult to recall. Imagine you colour-code the letters of the alphabet and apply them to words. A 26-colour code relies on retaining a lot of information in your short-term memory. The result is that you make the piece colourful but unreadable.

Nameable colours are more memorable

In order for colour to be memorable the viewer should be able to name them with ease. Stick to the basic six-colour palette and there will be no ambiguity as to whether a colour is lime-green, grass-green or yellow-green. The more distinction between various colours, the less chance of confusion.

Make colour codes equally strong

Design systems that have colours of equal strength and contrast. This ensures that one colour is not viewed as more important than another. Strong colours will have more emphasis when viewed with pale ones. Colours that have equivalent strength also have comparable legibility, even at a distance.

Bakerloo
Central
Circle
District
Hammersmith & City
Jubilee
Northern
Waterloo & City
Victoria
Piccadilly
Metropolitan
DLR
Emirates Air Line
Overground

Above: Names and identifying colours of the London Underground lines. The combination of name and colour aids recognition more than colour-coding alone. There is less chance of colours being confused, and makes it easier for the user to commit each line to memory.

Above left and left: Front and back cover design by Peter Saville Associates for New Order's album *Power, Corruption and Lies*. The artwork uses colour-coding to depict the album title, each letterform having been assigned a specific colour.

Choice of typeface, weight and scale

It is important when using typography to consider the purpose of the text or images. Ensure that the typefaces chosen are appropriate for their function. For example, don't use display typefaces that are too bold or have unusual characteristics for body copy. Similarly, ensure that the 'tone of voice' of the font matches the subject matter. If you intend the text to be 'transparent' and unassuming, make sure you don't use too many typefaces as they may distract.

When elements are to be seen from a distance, they require maximum visibility. It is for this reason that the designer must choose fonts carefully. Simple bold sans serif fonts may be more useful in this instance.

Similarly, various requirements need to be taken into consideration when designing for screen. Since it is impossible to foresee how the design will be viewed, such as at what screen resolution or whether it is on an HD screen or Cathode Ray Tube (CRT), the designer must work within certain parameters to make sure that the design can be seen by the maximum number of viewers. Typefaces should be chosen that have been designed with the limitation of the screen resolution in mind, such as Verdana and Georgia.

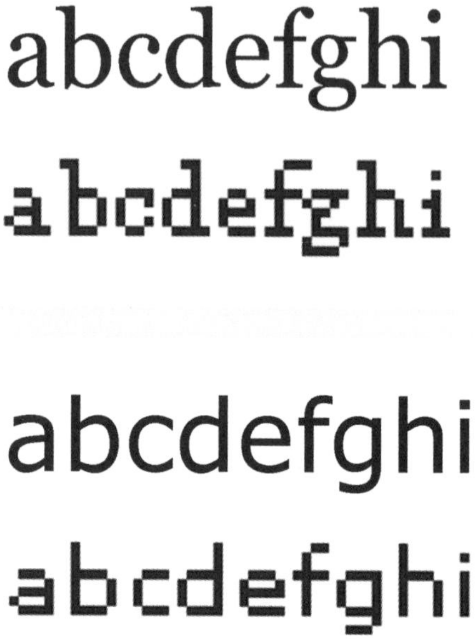

abcdefghi

abcdefghi

abcdefghi

abcdefghi

Typefaces for screen use – Georgia (top) and Verdana. Note how the letterforms are still recognizable as the font at 8pt (72dpi).

abcdefghi

Bodoni typeface at screen resolution. This font was designed for print not screen. Seen here at 8pt (72dpi), the lower letterforms are hardly recognizable in some cases.

When attempting to create emphasis within text, use italic type or a contrasting font, not both, as that could lead to misunderstandings. Too many weights may also confuse. The weight of the face creates a tone on the page. The heavier the weight of the font, the darker the tone generated. This acts as a signpost to the viewer and draws their attention.

Most guidelines for signage suggest that type size should increase by 72 points or 1 inch for every 25ft (7.6m) from which the user views it. The Royal National Institute for the Blind in the UK states: 'The lettering height is measured by the x-height of the character set, which is the height of a lowercase x. The x-height is dependent on the sight distance and is determined in millimetres by multiplying the sight distance in metres by 57, but the x-height should not be less than 20mm.'

Many designers aim to use a limited range of weight and scale to provide a hierarchy within the copy. It is considered unnecessary to increase both the size and weight of type to create emphasis when one alone will suffice.

When using more than one typeface, aim to employ maximum differentiation between the fonts. A serif and sans serif teamed up will be more efficient than using two serifs, as the audience may not be able to distinguish between them as easily as a designer can.

When establishing hierarchy through type it may be helpful to use at least two points of difference between the text; for example, headings in large bold type and subheadings in smaller, italic type.

Bodoni	**Futura**
Clarendon	Univers
Mrs Eaves	Verdana

Serif (left-hand column) and sans serif fonts (right-hand column).

Project: Animals in the House, for the Transparency section of *GOOD* magazine, September/October 2008

Design: Barbara Glauber and Erika Nishizato of Heavy Meta, New York

View the project online: www.good.is/post/animals-in-the-house

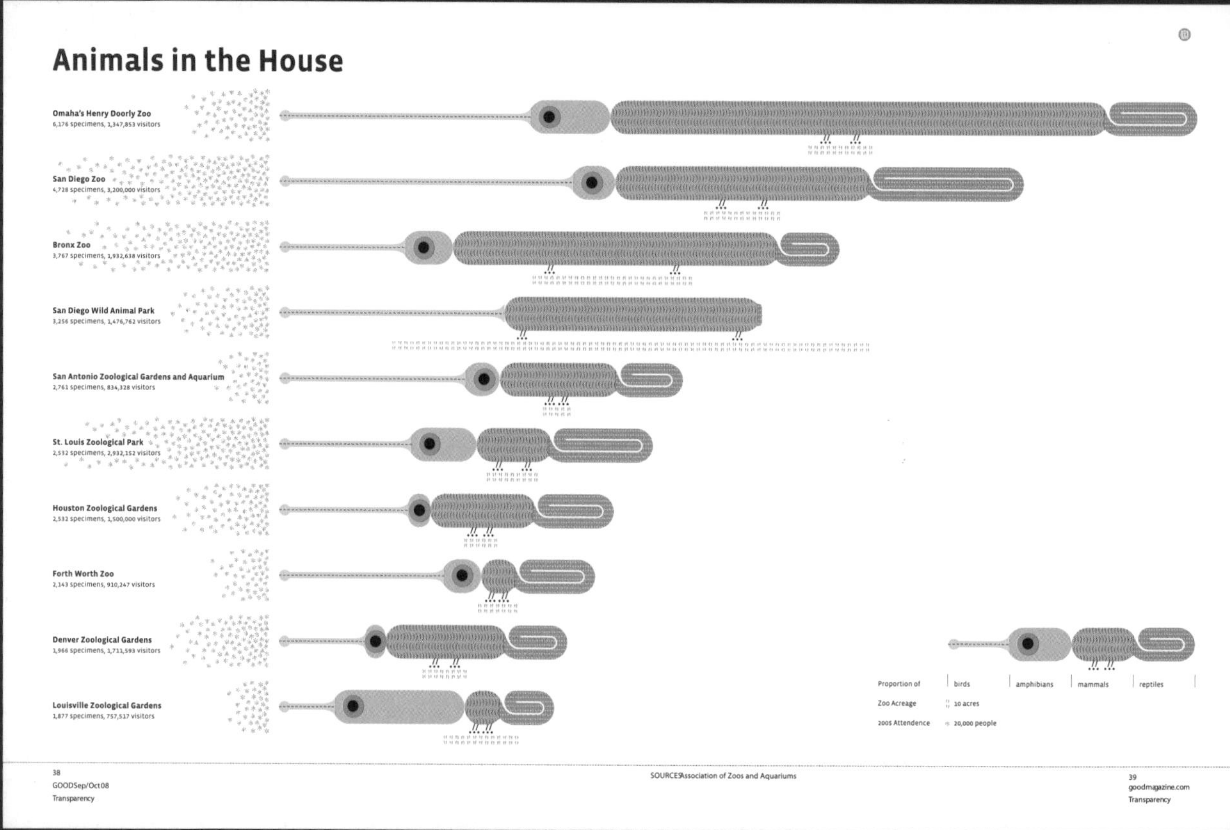

The finished graphic.

Run by principal Barbara Glauber, Heavy Meta is a design studio in New York that focuses on the design of publications, exhibition and information graphics. Barbara's work is in the collection of the Cooper-Hewitt National Design Museum and has won numerous awards. Here we describe how she created information graphics for the Transparency section of *GOOD* magazine, a quarterly print publication reflecting the activity and work of the GOOD global online community and presenting content about social issues and culture. This piece has also appeared online at visualize.us.

Overview

GOOD Magazine's regular Transparency section features infographics designed to visualize some of the social issues of concern to its readership and the online community. Selecting graphics for inclusion is an unusual process. Editors begin by sending the designer a slew of potential data sets to peruse. It is not immediately apparent from these raw files which chunk of what information will be interesting when visualized, or whethe it will need additional data in order to make a point.

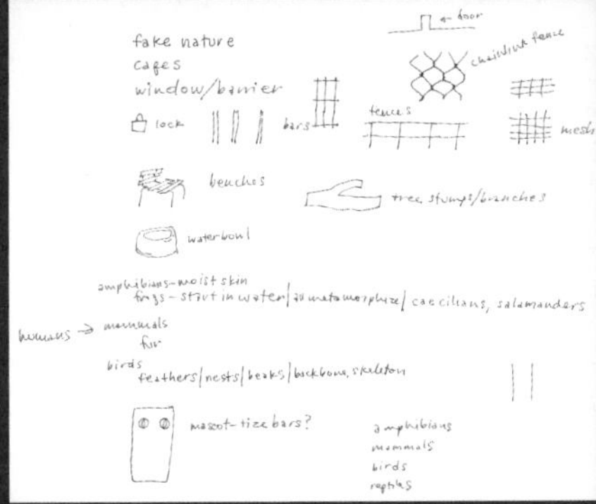

Clockwise from top left: Handwritten list of animal types in certain zoos.

Quick sketch of items associated with zoos.

Quick sketch of body parts associated with particular animal classifications.

Quick sketch of hybrid animal based on body parts and relative size based on a number of animals.

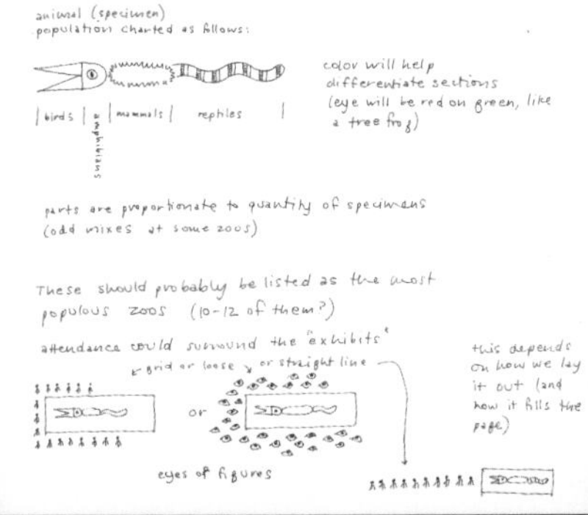

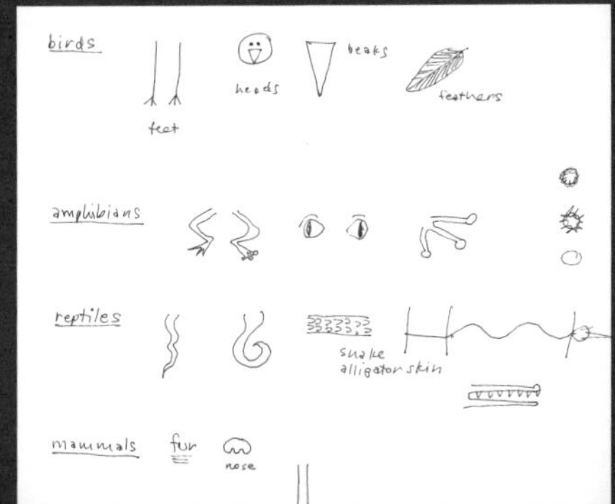

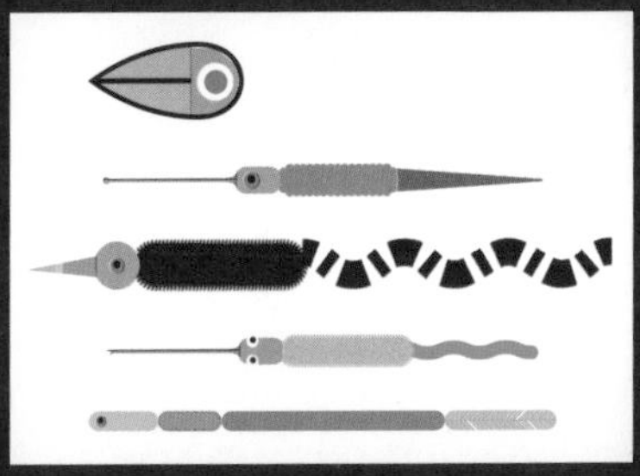

Computer graphic of hybrid animal shapes.

Approach

The designer is asked to choose five of the data sets, and Barbara thought that the subject of zoo population had great potential. The data consisted of lists of specimens, divided into four types of animals: birds, amphibians, mammals and reptiles.
She thought this would best be visualized by creating a hybrid creature whose four segments could be scaled proportionately. It was difficult to find the right representational method; it needed to be creature-like, yet rational. For inspiration, Barbara looked at the work of American illustrator Charley Harper (1922–2007). His drawings can be wonderfully abstract, and his ability to translate complex natural forms into rational, geometric shapes was remarkable. Barbara made sketches noting the different methods Charley used to define various animal parts, creating a kind of taxonomy of creature parts. She then tried to figure out which body parts best represented each type. She ended up using beaks for birds, heads for amphibians, thoraxes for mammals, and tails for reptiles. She struggled with the rendering style, moving away from being too illustrative but without becoming too abstract. Connecting lozenge shapes that recall chromosomes worked best.

To relate to the other graphics the design team had created for the section, some of which contained typographic elements, they incorporated pieces of letters into the animals, using parentheses for mammalian fur, colons for reptile scales, and inch marks for grass. Throughout the series, asterisks represent people – in this case, zoo visitors.

Outcome

This case study shows a level of innovation in that it uses a traditional bar-chart approach, but presents the bars in an illustrative form. The creation of the hybrid animals makes the design engaging but also simple to decode. It is an educational piece that shows in an instant the ratio of mammals to amphibians and birds, along with the number of visitors and the concentration of animals in the space. The design represents the childlike quality that most people associate with the subject of zoos. The project was very well received and Barbara's interest in information design has subsequently blossomed. Since this project, she has taught workshops in information design at California Institute of the Arts and a class at The Cooper Union School of Art in New York.

Graphics in information design

Project: Health and safety programme for Fletcher Construction on behalf of the Victoria Park Alliance, Auckland, New Zealand
Design: Grant Alexander, Sam Trustrum, Richard Unsworth, Ed Prinsep and Felicity Douglas of Studio Alexander, Auckland, New Zealand
Portrait photography: Kristian Frires
Location photography: Dave Olsen

Graphics on side of container.

Container graphics in situ.

Graphics in the canteen area.

The Victoria Park Alliance comprises the New Zealand Transport Agency, Fletcher Construction, Beca, Higgins and Parsons Brinkerhoff. The Alliance worked on constructing the Victoria Park Tunnel on State Highway 1, which is one of New Zealand Transport Agency's Roads of National Significance. This is comprised of a 450-m (1,480-ft) cut-and-cover tunnel for three lanes of northbound traffic and the associated carriageway including realignments and widening works. At the height of construction, 600 personnel were active on the project.

Overview

In 2010, the Victoria Park Alliance identified the need to develop a positive internal safety culture to meet the growing needs of today's construction site. Safety psychologists advised the Victoria Park Alliance that a positive safety culture could be achieved by winning the hearts and minds of personnel who were typically familiar with hazardous environments and performing difficult and dangerous tasks to achieve progress. An effective message of personal relevance was required to encourage safe behaviour and to avoid incidents and accidents.

Approach

In February 2010, the Victoria Park Alliance held several small workshops with key personnel to develop ideas and formulate an engaging solution. The result was the development of a large-scale initiative to engage with workers by encouraging personnel to question safety issues in their working environment and to consider the impact of an accident on their personal life and families. The key to engagement was to make the message personally relevant to the broad audience at hand. A simple visual innovation needed to be developed to communicate the importance of safety awareness and teamwork initiatives towards safety on-site. Specific areas that were identified as paramount included: the importance of checking personal protective equipment before commencing work; and to think twice about safety consequences before entering the worksite.

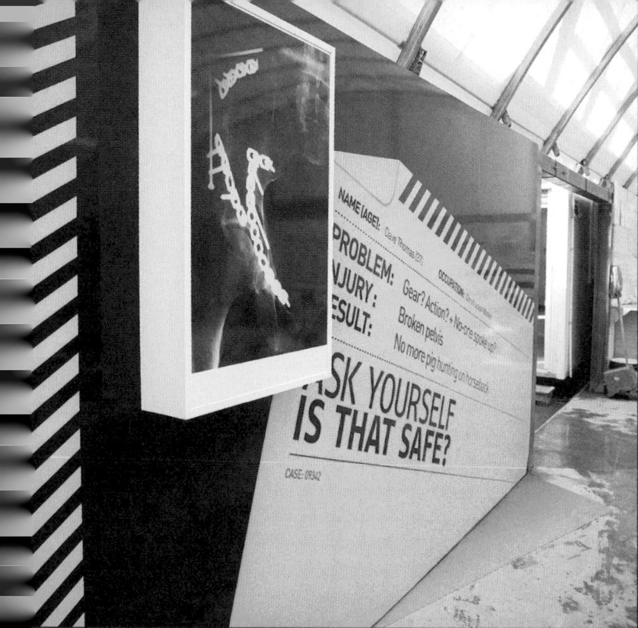

Close-up of 'Lightbox Stories' graphics in the canteen area. This shows the real-life story of Dave Thomas, who sustained a broken pelvis in an accident with an excavator arm. The graphics show the x-ray detailing the extent of his injuries.

Establishing a visual initiative

The first awareness initiative developed was of the bright yellow 'tagging out' label to be used as the common thread of the visual campaign. The use of a striking, stylized, well-recognized safety image on large-scale displays gave the campaign a loud visual feel. This was supported by the direct key message: 'Ask yourself is that safe?', representing exactly the behaviour to be encouraged; i.e., that everyone has the right to challenge and question how work is conducted.

Lightbox stories

The second series of graphics featured X-rays and stories of how worker's lives have been affected by real-life accidents. To make the messages more personal and specific to the workforce, the designers integrated personal stories of Alliance team members who had suffered serious work-related injuries in the past. An employee who had suffered a serious injury during the early days of the Victoria Park Tunnel project was approached for his support. Dave had sustained a broken pelvis as a result of being crushed by an excavator arm while in the rear of a tipper truck. His message was very raw and emotive to many employees. A lightbox with a copy of a stylized X-rayed pelvis was displayed next to a yellow label stating the action 'Gear? Action? + No-one spoke up'; the physical consequence, 'Broken pelvis'; plus the personal consequence, 'No more pig-hunting on horseback'. These engaging graphics were positioned in social areas to encourage conversations on safety, personal protection equipment and speaking up, as well as discussions on personal priorities.

Reality portraits

The idea of utilizing real-life stories was expanded. An employee was approached who had strong family links within the organizations and whose cousin had sustained a work-related injury on a previous project. It was felt that he would be readily recognized by personnel and strengthen the emotive link with the workforce. The graphic was designed to encourage a wider sense of family; 'It's not just you, it's the people you could leave behind'. A series of moody portraits was commissioned, focusing on the emotional mayhem felt by family members as a result of an injury. These oversized, larger-than-life portraits were placed on the sides of site containers and dropped on site in high-impact vantage points. Combined with the large captive audience, this resulted in a direct reality check.

Check yourself before you wreck yourself

The final piece in this environmental campaign was positioned at the end of a tunnel at the entrance to the worksite. It featured a centre-piece mirror and a checklist of vital personal protection equipment (PPE), forcing workers to check their PPE reflection as they enter the worksite.

Outcome

Employees across the board were seen to engage with the larger-than-life visual reminders, to check themselves and consider their families and lifestyle before neglecting safety practices to save time or cut costs. This has been a successful step towards changing attitudes and humanizing the reality of preventable accidents on-site.

Graphics: 'Is that safe?'

Drifting
down
of rare earths
listening,
yours

Chapter 5: Realizing the design through appropriate media

This chapter looks at the various media available to designers and how to realize solutions using different kinds of formats, software and materials. It examines how the choice of media and materials has an impact on how the design is perceived within specific environments. We look at designing for multiple platforms, especially in the light of the recent rise of mobile phone and tablet applications, and how designers have used software such as Processing to display data visually.

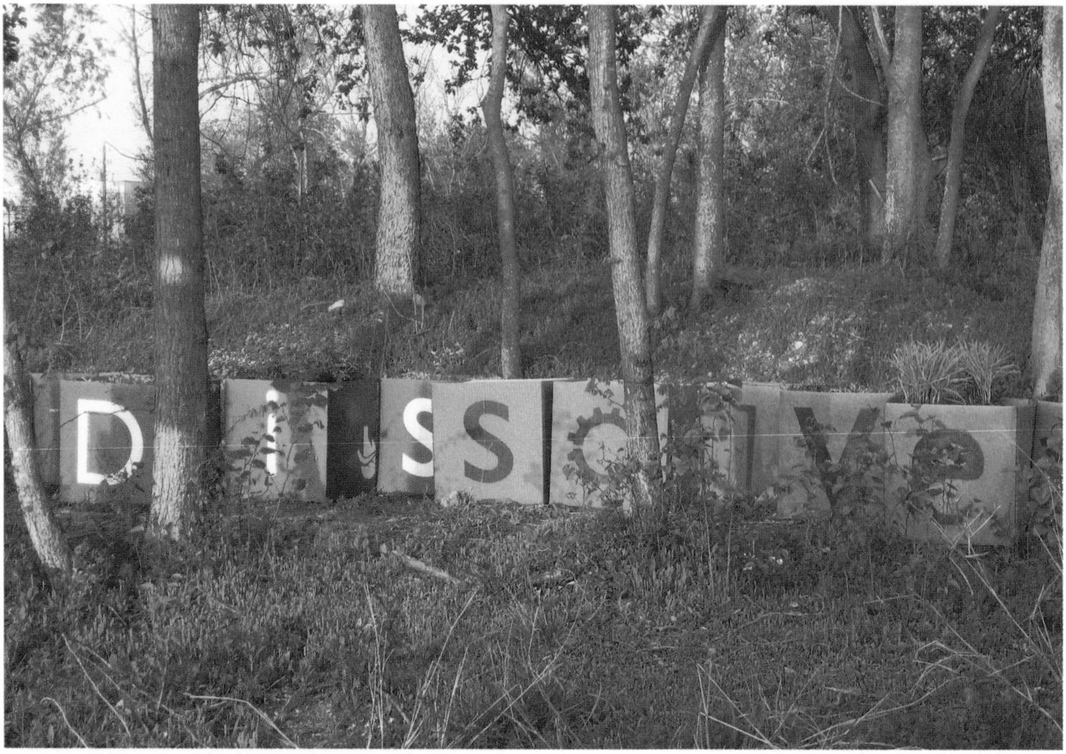

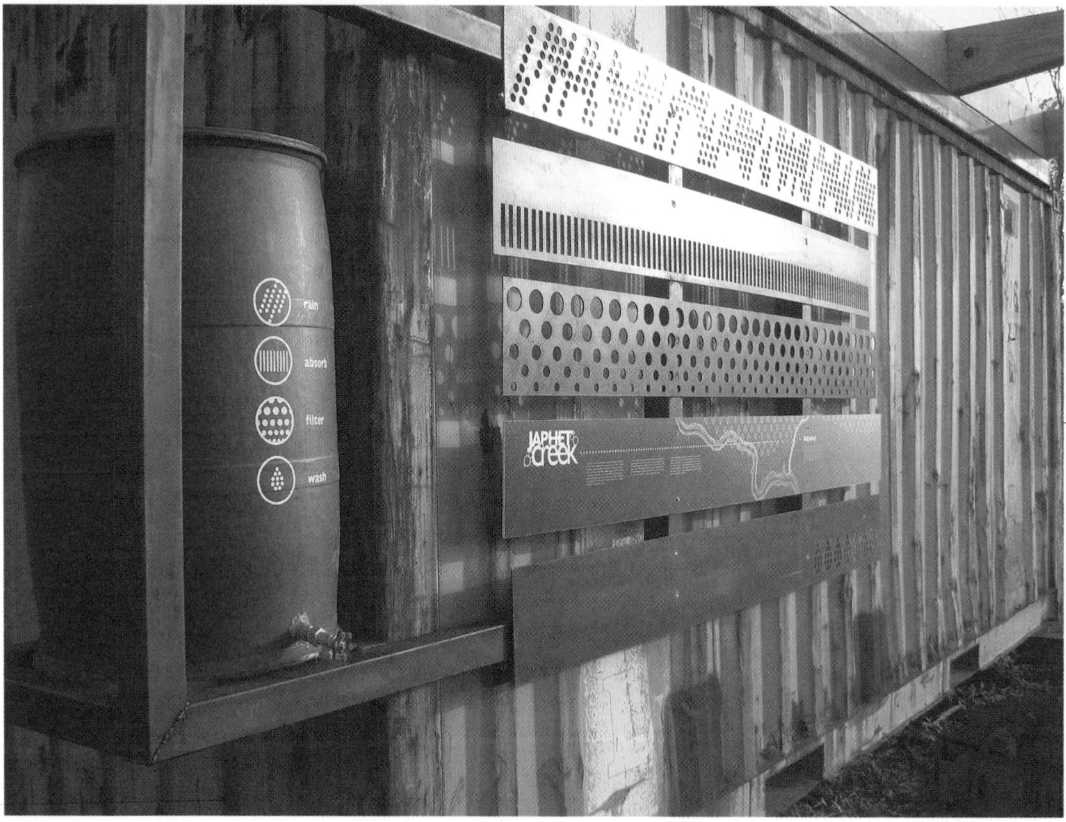
rain
absorb
filter
wash
JAPHET creek

Explanation of media

The choice of media for any project is an important one. It should be sympathetic to the subject matter and be part of the communication process. Media can be broken down into three basic categories. These are not by any means set, but for our purposes they are: print, screen and environmental (which includes three-dimensional).

The media chosen is intrinsic to the design and should not be an afterthought. From the paper on which an image is printed to the acrylic or metal used as signage in wayfinding, the information designer has much to consider. Certain materials may be beyond the realms of the designer. If contributing a design for an existing magazine, for example, the choice of paper might be beyond your control. There are particular reasons why designers choose certain materials or media. There are several factors that may influence their choice. Information design is a vast subject that covers print, environmental and screen-based design. Each of these areas demands sensitivity to their different requirements.

The material chosen could be used to reinforce the concept of the design; it may be selected because the design needs to be durable, practical and long-lasting or it may be because the design has to incorporate movement or include some sort of animation.
This chapter explores various media, and discusses the reasons why they might be selected for a range of projects.

Previous page, opposite and above:
The Dis(solve) Natural Signs project, a studio collaboration by the School of Art Graphic Communications Program and the Gerald D. Hines College of Architecture at the University of Houston, demonstrates how a wide variety of materials can be used in information design to communicate a message. The project was developed to create a series of park amenities for Japhet Creek in Houston, an area of natural beauty. The aim was to inform and educate visitors, but also to convey an important environmental message. By using recycled or repurposed materials, several of which are biodegradable, the designers imbued the project's narrative with meaning.

Choosing appropriate media

Knowing which media to select is a very important factor when designing. It is not just a case of choosing what you like; often the media can be designated for you. However, depending on the project, information may have to be conveyed across several platforms and through various media, and in this case, you may have to provide numerous ways of delivering the data through many different materials.

As an example of this, we have chosen the signage for Metropolitan Wharf in London by Mind Design. The building is an iconic eight-storey Grade II-listed Victorian riverside warehouse. It has recently been restored and now provides accommodation for offices. Mind Design produced the signage and a customized font for the project. Since the development is located on the embankment of the River Thames, studio founder Holger Jacobs and his team came up with the idea of using driftwood for the tenants' board. The project was technically quite challenging. Driftwood had to be found in the right dimensions, then cleaned and dried. The question of how to apply the lettering had to be carefully considered. Most of it was done with sandblasting, but some of it had to be manually enhanced with wood dye. Each piece had to be drilled from the back and fitted with studs that clamped onto large copper rails. This way, each sign can be removed individually and exchanged if new tenants move in. When the tenants' board was completed, only around half of the units were occupied;

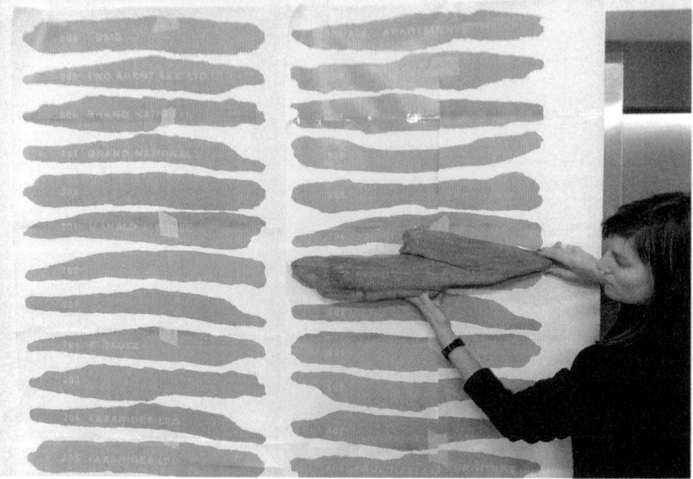

Creating signage for Metropolitan Wharf, London, by Mind Design:

Top: Driftwood is collected from the River Thames.

Centre: The pieces of driftwood are sorted and selected for use, taking into consideration the length of the information to be displayed.

Right: The sequence of the pieces in the display is chosen to be both practical and aesthetically pleasing.

Left: Names are sandblasted onto the driftwood and then painted to ensure maximum legibility.

Below: The finished signage.

this meant certain pieces of driftwood had to be left blank so names could be added later. The typeface was designed in collaboration with Neal Fletcher and matches the historic lettering on the outside of the building. In order for the font to work practically, two versions were completed with subtle differences – one for sandblasting and one for printing.

It is important to note that the materials chosen for the design were dictated by the overall concept and budget. The choice of driftwood is sympathetic to the building's heritage and location. Had the building not been by the riverside, the materials selected could have been very different. The overall finished product is both beautiful and functional. It is produced in such a way that it can be updated over time with minimal effort.

The difference between print and digital

When designing for a particular medium it is important to know its possibilities and limitations. Designing for print and digital is very different. It is not simply a case of transferring the printed medium onto a screen; the navigation, quality and size of rendering, along with considerations of interactivity, should be considered.

An example of this can be seen in the recent introduction of *Wired* magazine's iPad application. *Wired* invested a lot of time, effort and research into broadening its distribution through this new digital format. This magazine serves as a good example as to the difference between the printed and screen-based mode of delivery. In an interview with *Print* magazine in April 2011, Scott Dadich, executive director of digital magazine development for the US magazine publisher Condé Nast, stated, 'The physicality of the printed magazine is one of its greatest features. It is very easy to understand where you are, front, middle or back. In a digital reading environment, we lose these navigation cues; it's easy to get disoriented and not understand "where" one is in the issue.'

Wired UK's art director, Andrew Diprose, acknowledges how Scott's work with Adobe shaped how *Wired* originally approached design for digital format. Here, we show how the design for the *Wired* iPad interface has developed alongside the successful UK print edition of the magazine.

This type of technology opens up lots of storytelling opportunities using a variety of new tools such as video, audio, flipbooks, slideshows, image pans, 360-degree panoramas and hyperlinking text within the copy. This provides an immersive and highly engaging experience that the printed version cannot offer.

However, there are limitations to this kind of experience. Many designers approach the layout on screen the same way they do for print-based media. It is easy to forget that the practice of reading on screen is very different. The size of the screen is often smaller than the page, and the quality of the rendering of typography is not as high. For example, you could not render ultra-bold text next to ultra-light on screen, whereas you could in print. Also, the user does not have to be contained by a page; in the digital realm they can scroll around information, or even change its orientation from portrait to landscape.

Navigation in print is as simple as flipping a page. The user can scan through quickly at full size and decide what to read based on what grabs their attention. On screen this becomes more challenging. Navigational elements have to be clear and obvious, so there is no misunderstanding. A smaller screen can mean smaller text and narrower columns, which can prove difficult to read. Readability tests suggest that columns should have around seven to ten words per line, or 50 to 70 characters. This is the reason many websites use a single column of text that has scroll bars.

When designing with print, fewer clues have to be given as to how to navigate the information. Although the principle on screen is similar, these clues have to be more specific and visually stronger.

Designing for different digital platforms

When designing screen-based information, there are several digital platforms that may have to be taken into account. These range from traditional screen delivery platforms such as websites or television to mobile technology such as tablets and smartphones. All are of varying sizes and resolutions and will have particular limitations that may require amendments during the design process.

All digital technology uses a screen to display the information. In the same way that computer monitors are calibrated for optimal viewing, the display screens on mobile phones and other digital devices are calibrated for brightness, contrast, colour depth and resolution. This can cause problems when rendering typography, as it will not appear as crisp as it would in print, and also with colour, as different screens are calibrated in different ways.

Navigation can also be challenging, as the user needs to be guided as to where and how to follow the path between pages or screens. This section highlights some of the differences and considerations needed when designing for these platforms.

One of the biggest problems information designers face is how to retain quality and parity when designing for multiple platforms. Most designers will design with limitations in mind and adapt the content in line with the capabilities of the software. To illustrate this, we have chosen the BBC News app for the iPad (pp. 114–15) and the BBC iPlayer mobile app for iPhone and Android (pp. 116–17).

Opposite, top: The cover of *Wired UK*'s print edition.

Opposite, bottom: Cover of the same edition designed for the iPad version. You will notice that there is less textual information on display on this version. Also, serif or script typefaces have been replaced by sans serif fonts for maximum legibility on screen.

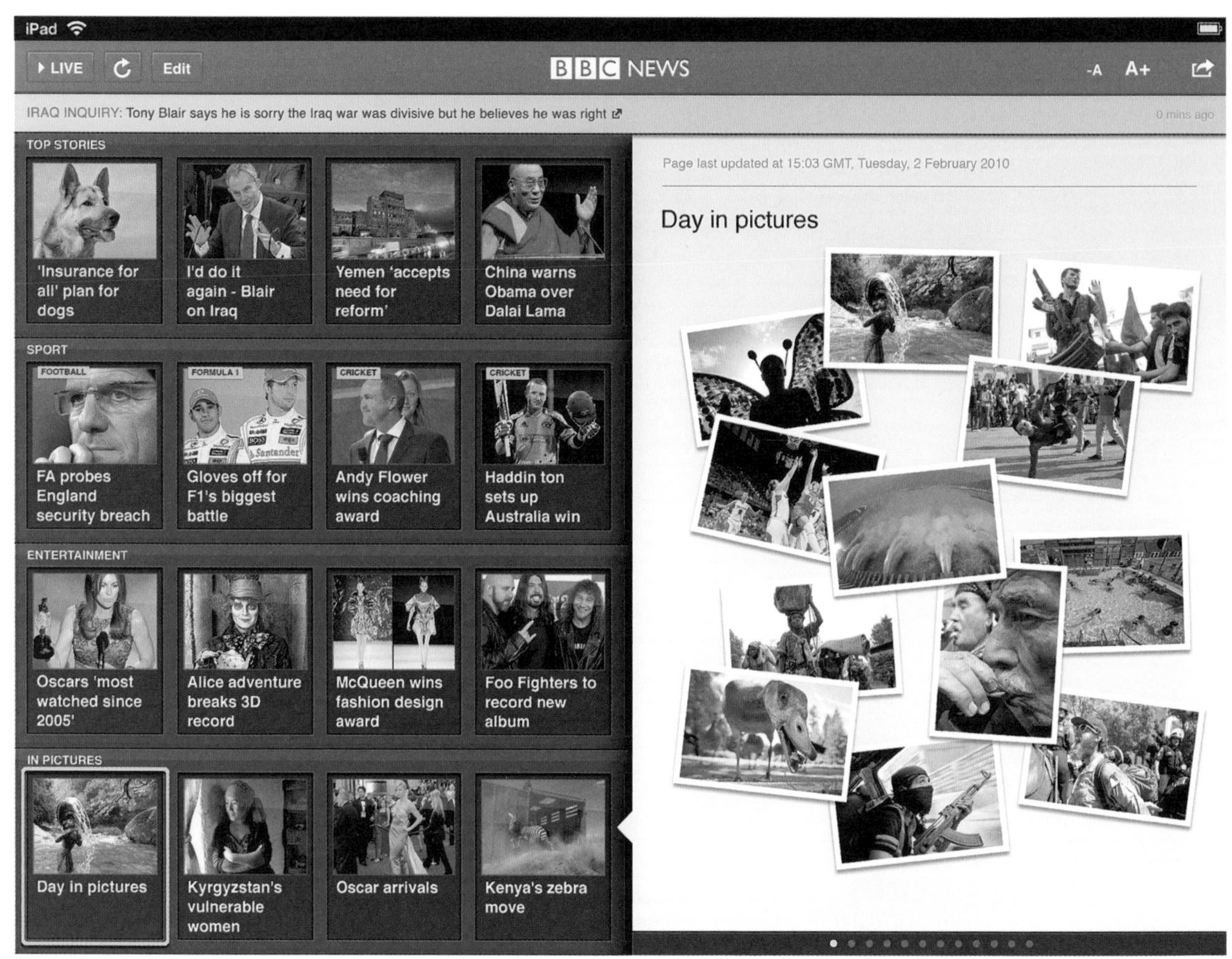

BBC News iPad app, designed by
The Noble Union.

Designing for the iPad

How do you present textual news information on a limited screen size and allow someone the ability to select from various news stories at will? News on screen is not delivered the same way it is in print. Users have become information grazers, and rely on visual cues on screen-based technology to guide them through the content. Having a limited view means information has to be heavily edited and made engaging for the viewer.

The BBC approached this problem when developing their news application for the iPad. Their goal was to produce an app that presented a new way to navigate and deliver media and text content in a friendly, intuitive and usable way.

The team identified two keywords – skim and dip – from which to design. A simple method was developed to allow users to navigate the news stories and be able to swap between them with ease. A scrolling carousel navigation system was designed to enable the user to 'skim and dip'. One way of helping users to navigate the carousel was to include thumbnail images for each story to make the overall browsing experience a visual one. The screen has also been split to show the chosen story alongside others presented in a carousel. This allows users to tap stories on the home screen and have them appear instantly in the reading pane.

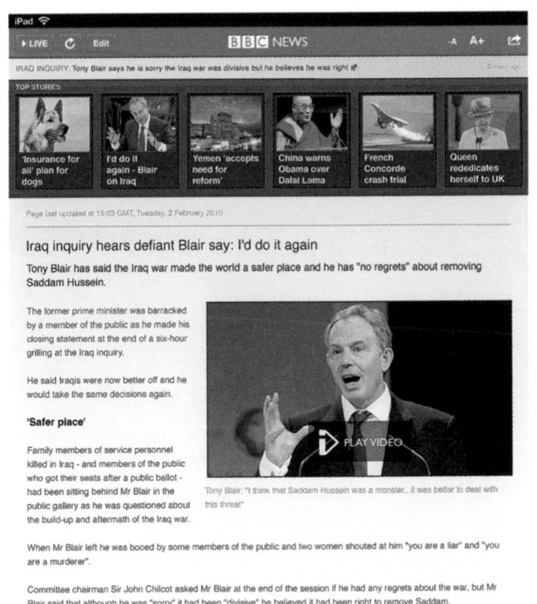

BBC News iPad app: live page in portrait format.

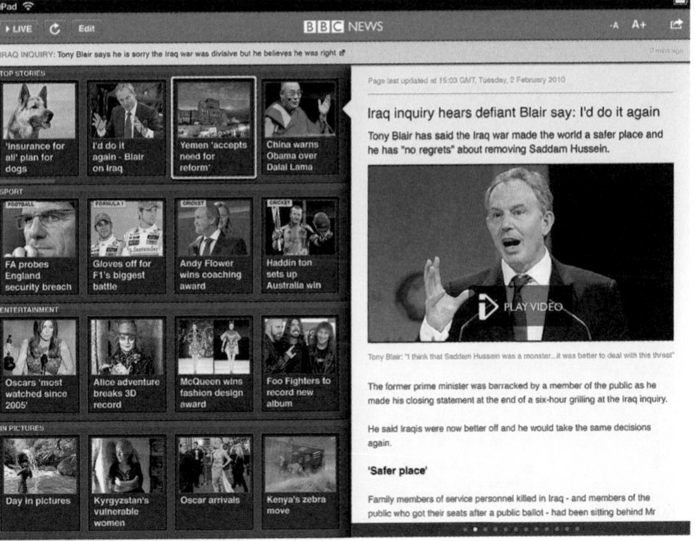

BBC News iPad app: live page in landscape format. Here the carousel navigation is much larger, allowing more choices to be included on the page for the user.

Designing for mobile phones

Designing for a mobile phone screen can also be challenging, as the space available is even more limited. How do you encourage an audience to watch TV programmes on their mobile device?

In 2012 the BBC released its BBC iPlayer mobile app, having realized that more and more people were choosing to watch television or listen to the radio on their mobile devices. The team tasked with designing this app, headed by senior designer Chris Elphick, identified several goals when developing the platform. These were: to let the audience plan their daily viewing; to encourage the audience to explore more programmes; and to consider the restrictions such as portrait and landscape orientations, screen size and gestural interaction. Since the iPlayer already existed online, it was important to retain the identity and usability of the original platform.

One of the challenges was to understand the differences between the mobile platforms for Android and iPhone. Although both use gestures as navigation tools they can be different. The team chose to keep the gestures simple and universal. The team explored several possibilities regarding landscape and portrait orientation, trying to present as much information as possible in a single view. Research suggested that certain users preferred the simplicity of a menu with fewer options. In the landscape orientation, the view is changed to scroll through like a picture gallery to try to overcome this problem. The team looked to how users interact with TV to improve the live experience. By looking at 'channel hopping', a system was devised to allow users to browse channels while watching live TV, without leaving the playback; that way users could peruse other content related to the programme. This presents several channel windows within the interface with important information that users can scroll through.

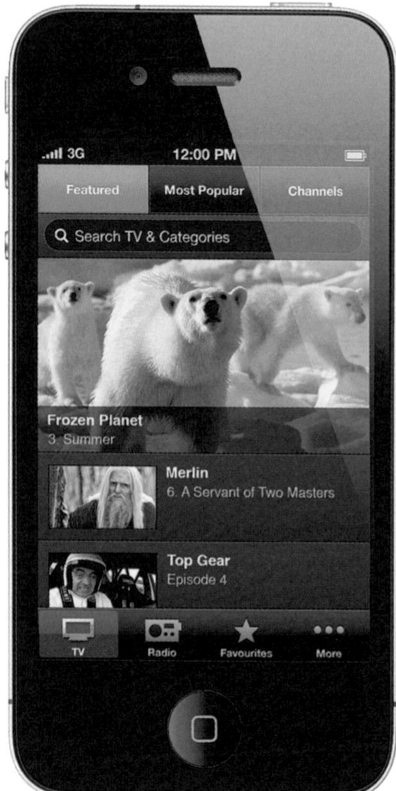

BBC iPlayer mobile app, designed by a team headed by Chris Elphick.

Left and above: Portrait and landscape views on the iPhone.

Right: Developing the live hopping function using Post-it notes (BBC1, BBC2, BBC3).

Far right: Developing the swipe and tap functions using Post-it notes.

Below right: The live channels switcher.

Developing the viewing of information in overlay.

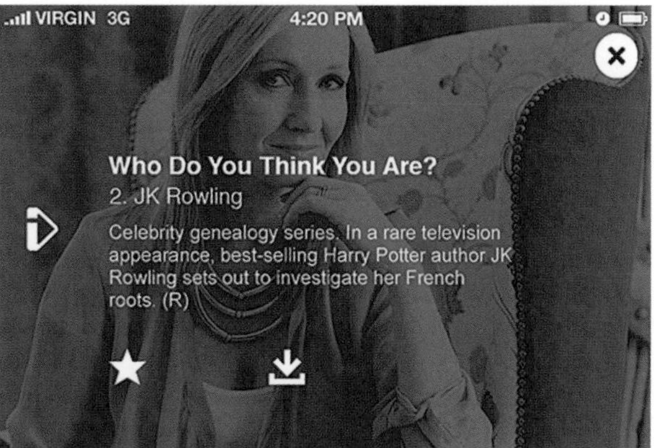

Landscape view of information in overlay.

Computer data visualization

The use of specialized software has given designers access to tools that allow visualization of data in ways that were previously very difficult.

There are several ways to visualize data; we are familiar with various categories such as charts, diagrams, graphs, tables and maps. The way in which a piece of data is presented depends on the data itself and what it is meant to convey to an audience. Many software tools such as Microsoft Word, Excel and Adobe Illustrator have automated these functions. These techniques are not always appropriate when presenting information, though, and many information designers seek to interpret data in new and challenging ways. As a result, some designers have begun to write specialist software to find new ways to represent visualizing data.

Processing is one such piece of open-source software, originally developed by Casey Reas and Ben Fry. The idea was to serve as a 'software sketchbook' and to teach computer programming within a visual environment. It has grown into a tool for creating visual images, animation and interactions. The software works by writing single lines of code, adding them one line at a time. By writing a line of code you may have a shape appear on screen; another line may control its colour or movement or how it changes depending on the interaction with a mouse.

Several designers have used Processing to display data visually, which has resulted in both screen-based and print outcomes.

Data visualizer: Jer Thorp

Jer Thorp is from Vancouver, Canada, and currently lives in New York. His award-winning software-based practice explores the boundaries between art and science. In 2011 Thorp was commissioned by *Popular Science* magazine to produce an image that visualized the archive of their publication. The resulting graphic explored the use of different technical and cultural terms that have been used since the magazine's introduction 140 years ago.

The image uses a molecular chain to act as a focal point, using the decades to cluster information. Within each cluster, an atom represents an issue and the number of words in each issue determines the size of the atoms. Around each atom histograms are placed that show the frequency of terms used in each issue. Jer used a custom tool built in the Processing software to plot the frequency of the words and identify the ones that would be the most interesting to use. The software allowed him to generate artwork from the acquired data and turn that into visuals that have been printed.

Data visualization of the *Popular Science* magazine archive by Jer Thorp, 2011. The graphics visualize how different technical and cultural terms have come in and out of use in the magazine since its inception.

The finished piece in *Popular Science* magazine.

In early versions Jer picked out interesting words from all the available choices and arranged them by year to suggest a molecular structure.

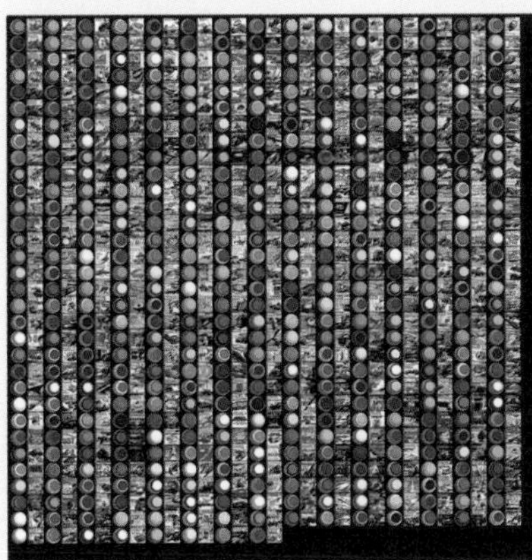

Here, molecular structures have been generated based on cover imagery and word frequency and arranged in a regimented grid structure.

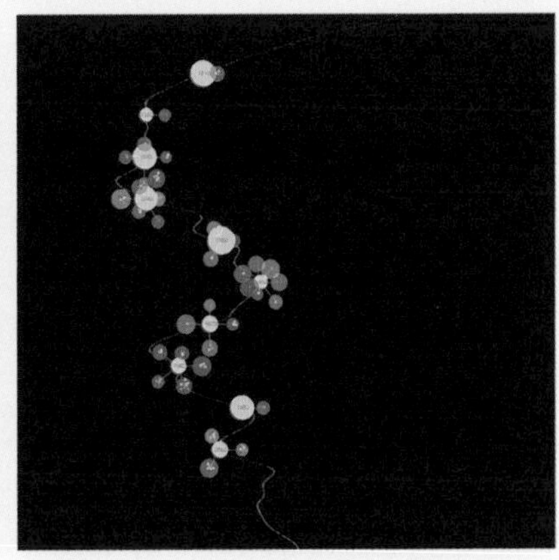

Jer begins to arrange the elements to mimic a molecular DNA structure.

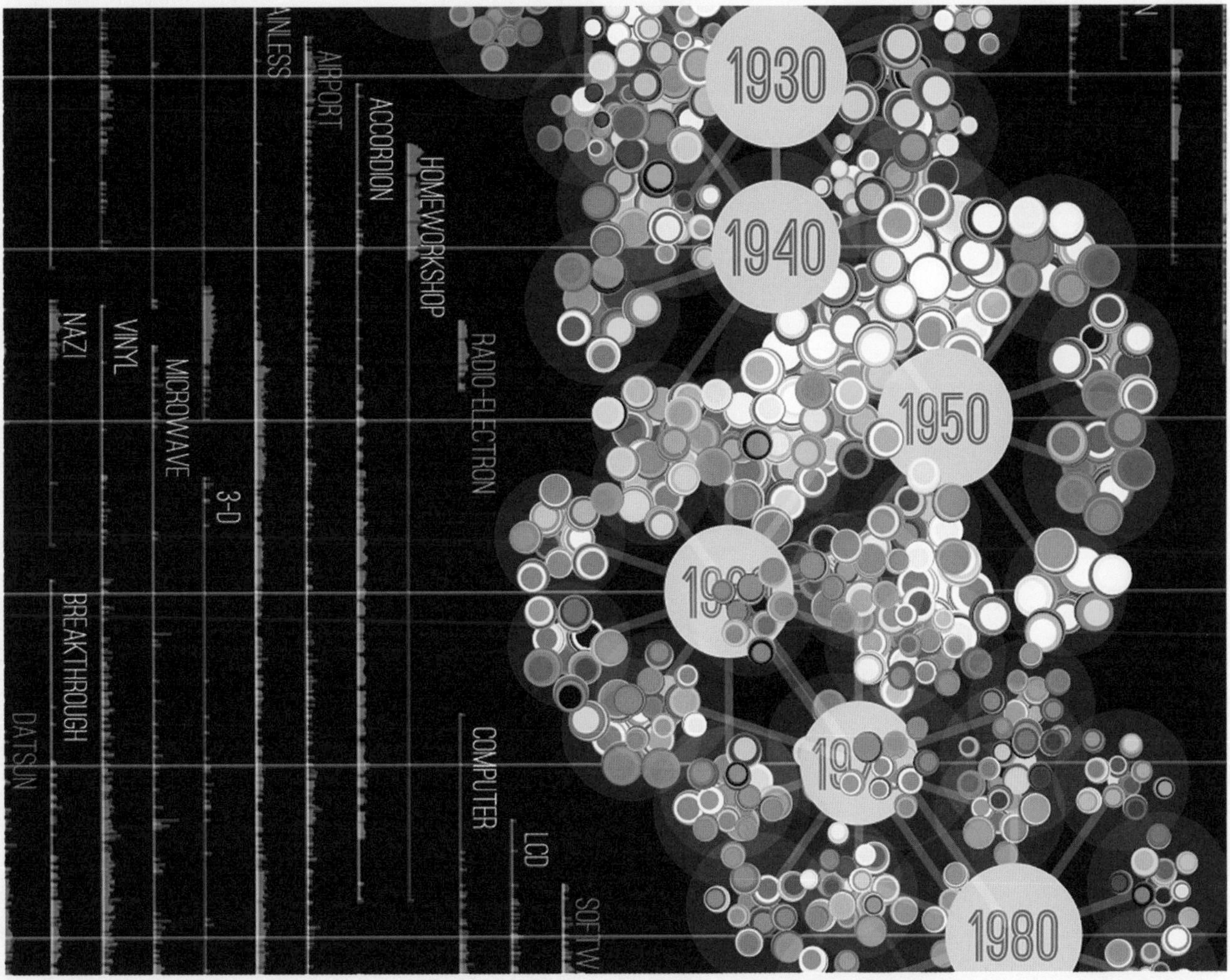

You can see the progression of the design with the elements now resembling what would become the final outcome. Here the various cultural terms have been added along with more detailed structure and decade markers. Jer says his working process is 'riddled with dead ends, messy errors and bad decisions – the 'final' product usually sits on top of a mountain of iterations that rarely see the light of day.' In this instance there were 134 images that came out of the development of this visualization: we have chosen just a few.

Data visualization: Aaron Koblin

Aaron Koblin is creative director of the Data Arts Team at the Google Creative Lab. His work primarily concerns telling stories with data. He studied with Casey Reas, the co-creator of the Processing software that he uses to create experiences from data. He engages the viewer with the information aesthetically and explores the relationships among data sets. Aaron's work takes real-world and community-generated data and uses it to reflect on cultural trends and the changing relationship between humans and technology.

To demonstrate the use of software to visualize data we have chosen a project Aaron produced in conjunction with his colleagues Gabriel Dunne and Scott Hessels. This work was originally developed in 2006 as a series of experiments for the project Celestial Mechanics at UCLA. Aaron later continued the project with *Wired* magazine.

There can be 30,000 manmade objects in the sky above us at any one time, including planes, helicopters, weather balloons and other technology. Aaron used Processing to plot Federal Aviation Administration data to produce a piece of animated information showing the paths of air traffic over North America.

The piece shows a 24-hour period where the animated path of each plane is shown as a coloured line. Within the piece there are 573 aeroplanes, each represented by a unique colour. The software plots each plane's journey from origin to destination. It serves to demonstrate the complex nature of the flight paths high above the ground. The animation shows the time differences across the continent with air traffic ebbing and flowing as one side of the country goes to sleep and the other wakes up. The viewer can filter the information to view aircraft by model or type, low altitude or high altitude, or ascending or descending paths. This allows the viewer to see patterns emerge around population centres and the complexity of directing air traffic at major cities.

Digital data visualization allows the designer to present information in real time and to interpret a database that can constantly be updated. The Processing software enables amendments to be made comparatively swiftly and easily without having to reproduce the visual by hand. The designer sets the parameters and the code provides the visuals.

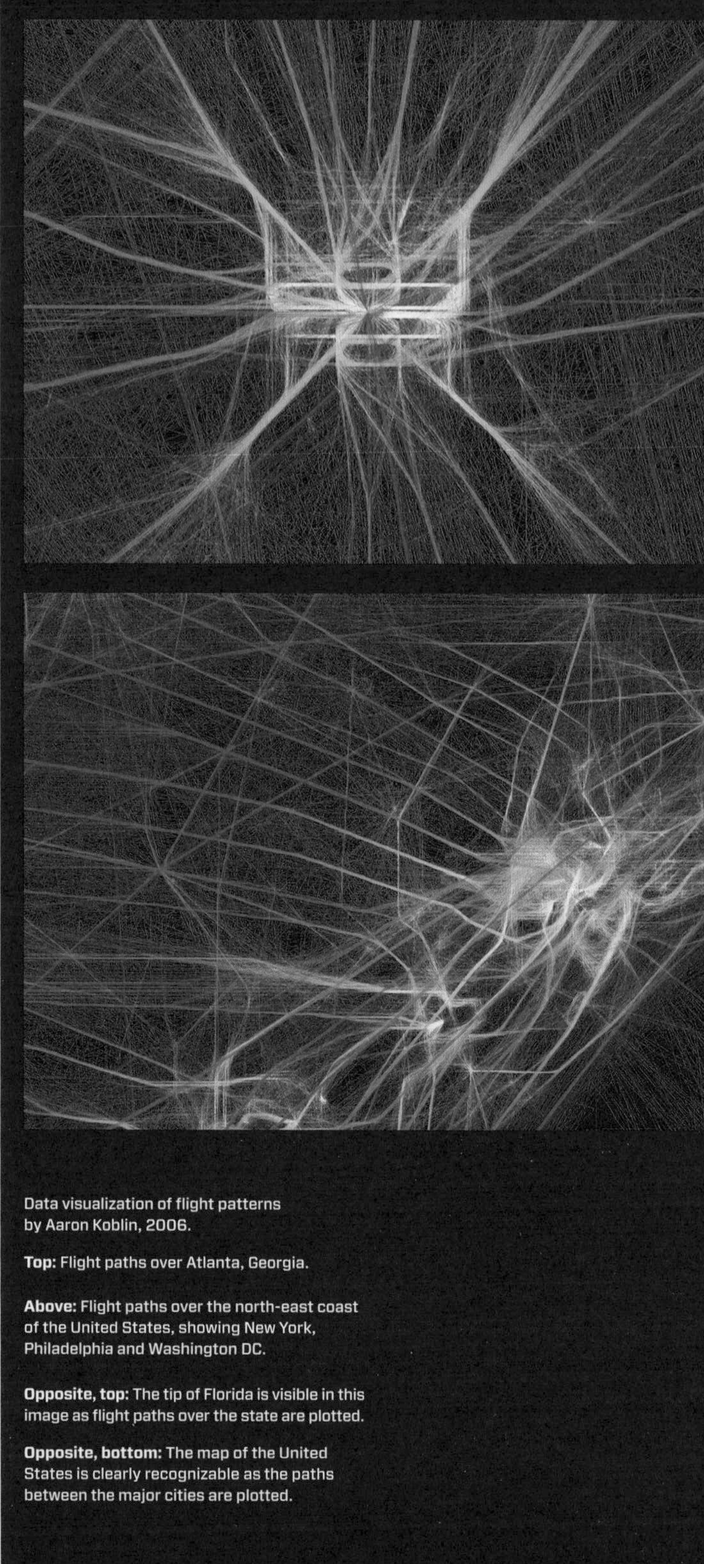

Data visualization of flight patterns by Aaron Koblin, 2006.

Top: Flight paths over Atlanta, Georgia.

Above: Flight paths over the north-east coast of the United States, showing New York, Philadelphia and Washington DC.

Opposite, top: The tip of Florida is visible in this image as flight paths over the state are plotted.

Opposite, bottom: The map of the United States is clearly recognizable as the paths between the major cities are plotted.

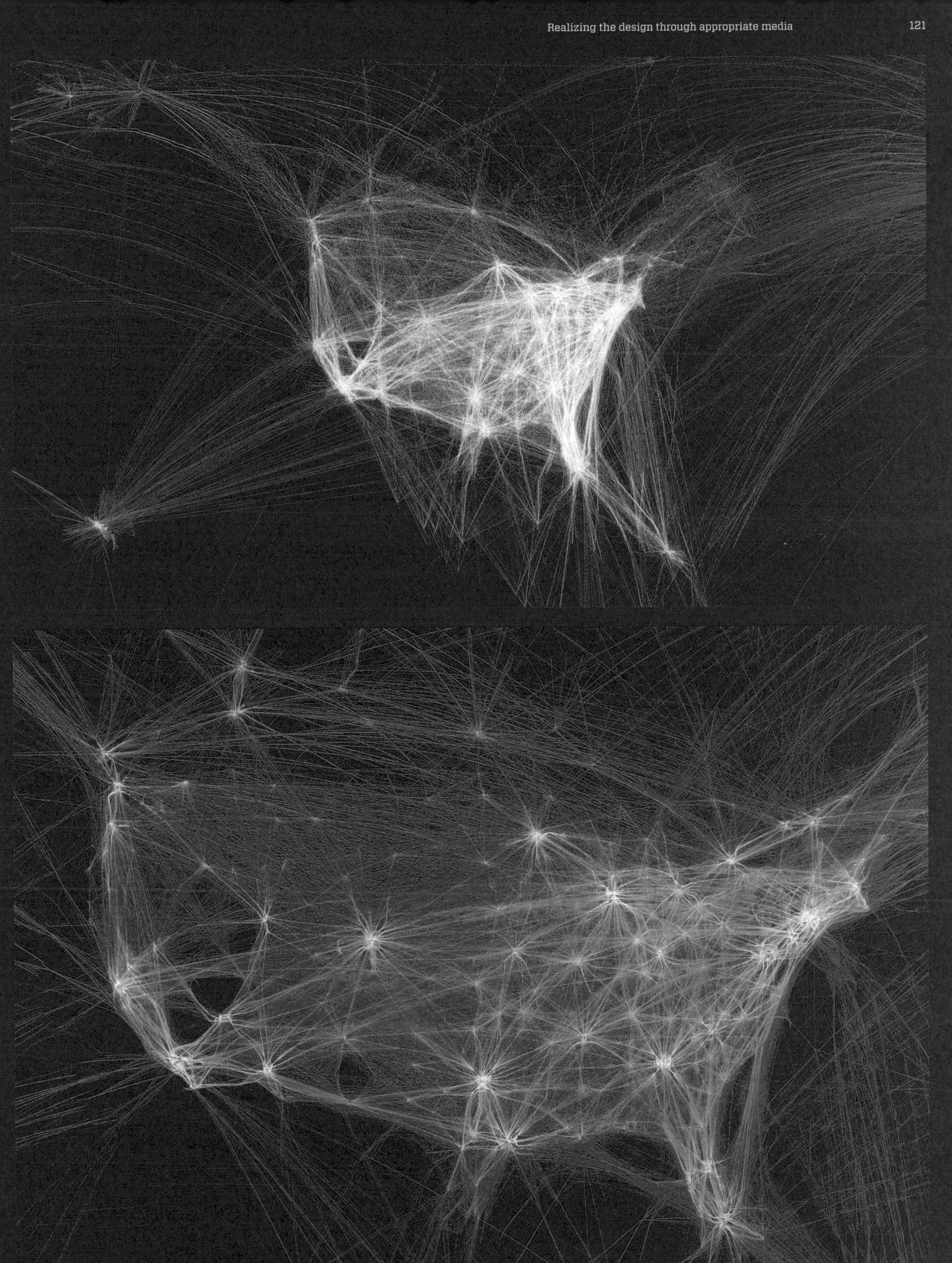

Exhibition design and design for the environment

There are many challenges to overcome when designing exhibitions. Storytelling is central to the successful communication of content and ideas. A story is constructed using four elements: a narrative, a narrator, a path and a context. When these elements are considered and combined successfully, your 'story' is complete. Breaking down a project into these four areas is very helpful; designing an exhibition can feel daunting, and these elements provide a framework and structure for delivery.

When an exhibition is being planned, the commissioning body will have an idea of what message or information they want to communicate to an audience, although at this point there is no narrative. A narrative is created when the information is considered and constructed by a designer and is given a beginning, a middle and an end. This is the basic structure of a story; a narrator is then needed to tell the story.

The narrator is the medium the designer selects to communicate the content of the story. This may be text-based, using motion graphics, interactive, 2D or 3D; most exhibitions utilize combinations of different media to communicate to their audience. There are some highly creative examples of the use of media to support the delivery of content within exhibition design; one of the projects we are featuring (Science Storms; see opposite) is a good example of this.

The path of an exhibition is essentially its physical structure when translated into a three-dimensional space; it is the design of the space. The path would be used to determine what an audience would see/experience and when; it is the sequence in which the audience will experience the story.

In most exhibitions you will not see the whole exhibit at once. Content will be delivered in sections, and the exhibition designer will consider what, how, and when you see the information. Exhibits may be presented in a timeline, with a physical hierarchy to direct the audience from one place to another, or as themes, but whichever method is used, the space must be logically and consistently organized so that the story makes sense and is read in the right order. Revealing information in stages, using a hierarchy method, ensures that the audience is not overloaded with content. As with a story, the first stage should set the scene and entice the audience to continue and discover what happens next. Offering information in this way is a key factor in the prolonged engagement of an audience within an exhibition space.

When considering all of these aspects of storytelling, it is important not to forget the context. Think about the context as the environment or space that surrounds the exhibition, the introduction of the audience to the exhibit. How can this space help prepare the audience or introduce them to what they are about to experience? This can set the mood and tone for the exhibition. It could provide snippets of information from the exhibition to engage the audience, or it may be lit in the same way as the exhibition space itself; there are many ways one could do this and it is important to consider how the viewer approaches the space.

A good exhibition designer will use space, scale, hierarchy, media, materials and various technologies to tell the story of a particular exhibit in a particular way. The content, the information being presented, in conjunction with the target audience, will shape how that story is told. Different stories require different treatments; a good exhibition designer will create and design an experience appropriate to that story. They will consider their audience and the overall goals of the exhibition; these may be to inform, educate or inspire, for instance. They will explore how best to achieve their goals using the tools at their disposal. They will consider what the space or spaces they are dealing with are like, what materials they will use, how durable the exhibits have to be, how much audience interaction is involved, what technologies (and budget) are available, and how they can be used to help them achieve their goal.

Science Storms, exhibition designed by Evidence Design for the Museum of Science and Industry, Chicago.

Exhibition design: Science Storms

The example we are featuring here is the Science Storms exhibition created by Evidence Design for the Museum of Science and Industry (MSI) in Chicago. This exhibition is a great example of successful storytelling, with the message being driven and communicated through creative and appropriate use of media, delivered in an inspiring, well-designed environment to a specific audience.

The challenge put to Evidence Design was to create an exhibition to inspire middle-school children to embrace the potential and excitement of the sciences. How could an exhibition of physics and chemistry be brought to life so that the audience is immersed, engaged, curious, excited and educated by the experience?

The subject matter of physics and chemistry is quite often a turn-off for many people, so the way the story was told within the exhibition had to be inventive. The space the designers were dealing with was also important and offered considerable opportunities; it was 2,415 square metres (26,000 square feet) with a gallery height of 20m (65ft). This space allowed the designers to create exhibits at a large scale. These were both dynamic and functional, acting as signposts to different areas of the exhibition, breaking up the space and creating focal points that draw the audience into the exhibits. They attracted attention first, then offered the opportunity for interaction, discovery and exploration.

The exhibition places the audience at the centre of the experience. It offers the opportunity for hands-on experimentation, investigating the science behind the phenomena through state-of-the-art interactive media used within the exhibition. Evidence Design explain that, 'By doing as well as seeing, visitors find themselves immersed in the adventure of experimental science and in the imaginative and creative processes of scientists. Science Storms aims to inspire a new generation of scientists through the synthesis of compelling interactive exhibits, environmental media and strong contextual storytelling.'

Creating Science Storms

Challenge
To re-envision the existing presentation of physics and chemistry to achieve MSI's core mission: to inspire and motivate our children to achieve their full potential in the fields of science, technology, medicine and engineering.

Solution
To transform the heart of the museum into a wondrous laboratory where visitors interact with dynamic, large-scale experiments that explore earth's most powerful phenomena – tornadoes, lightning, fire, tsunamis, sunlight, avalanches and atoms in motion – and then, through hands-on experimentation and interactive media, investigate the science behind nature's forces.

Approach
In 2003 the design team led a multidisciplinary task force to explore new ways to communicate 'essential science' to the public, define MSI's role in science education, and describe a compelling visitor experience. The group moved past driving the exhibit concept from a position of 'facts we should know' towards a much more compelling place: inspiration and the process of science.

Development
The collective goals of Science Storms depended on the buy-in of all core collaborators throughout every stage of the project. In the ensuing six years, the design team nurtured a deep partnership with MSI to achieve an ambitious program while leading a vast array of technical and creative consultants, producers, artists, writers, scientists and fabricators.

Concept
The design team developed an audacious concept: to leverage the power of natural phenomena to serve as a portal into the adventure of experimental science and the creative processes of scientists.

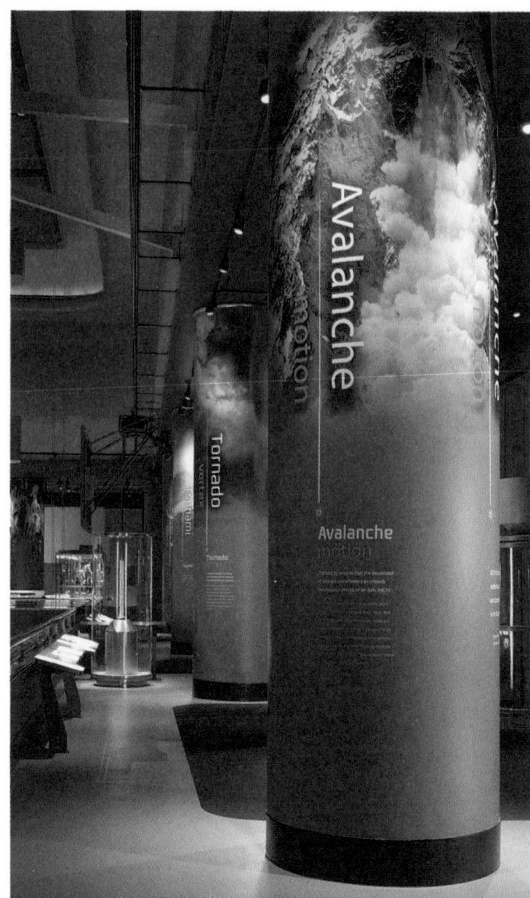

Large-scale pillars displaying information on avalanches and tornadoes at the Science Storms exhibition.

Design challenges
- To provide a visually and thematically cohesive experience.
- To allow close engagement to control, observe and measure each phenomenon.
- To develop an integrated interpretive program to convey instructions, information and context.
- To overcome the lighting and acoustic challenges inherent in the 2,415 square-metre (26,000 square-foot) space.
- To design elegantly detailed, rugged exhibits, casework and furniture to withstand intense public use.

HINTS & TIPS

Knowing the possibilities of media

When considering which media or material to use, it is important to bear in mind the context in which the design will exist. Which audiences are interacting with or viewing this piece? Is it in print, which requires crisp, precise typography, or illustration? Does it need to be able to withstand the elements if it is placed outdoors? Will it be legible in low light in the evening without specialist lighting? If technology is to be used, will it require any specialist equipment to view the design? The client and audience will answer many of these questions, but several will have to be decided by the information designer.

To illustrate how context is important within information design, over the next two pages we examine the design consultancy Bibliothèque's design for the exhibition Less is More: The Design Ethos of Dieter Rams, held at the Design Museum in London in 2009–2010. The exhibition presented the work of Dieter Rams, head of design at the German consumer electronics manufacturer Braun from 1961 to 1995. Rams's industrial design was hailed for the elegant, legible, yet rigorous visual language used within its products.

Used within the exhibition were 244 objects across five sections and spanning six decades. Jonathan Jeffrey, founding member of Bibliothèque, explains: 'We didn't devise a graphic identity for the exhibition; it was more about extrapolating key visual elements from a selection of the products (speaker grilles, calculator layouts, hi-fi interfaces, etc.). We used these to help organize the exhibition space and illustrate stories behind the development of the products – these worked as backdrops and introductions to sections. Rams's quite clearly delineated design ethos only made our job easier, as there was such a vast array of beautiful objects to choose from. The layouts on many of the Braun products are excellent examples of three-dimensional information design. This is not just from the use of controlled typography, but also in the pragmatic use of colour, geometry, positioning and alignment of dials, switches, buttons, jackplugs and even screws.'

Mason Wells of Bibliothèque comments: 'As well as the graphics we also designed the spatial aspect – here we tried to keep the gallery as open as possible to reflect the linear development of many of the products. Simple open tables allow the objects to be viewed from all sides, where very often the back is just as well considered as the front.'

The design solution used a range of graphic manifestations, each appropriate to a specific area of the exhibition content. For example, a flexible typographic system had to be devised to accommodate the 244 objects incorporated. The entrance to the exhibition was an internal façade using the 606 compression shelving system designed by Rams for Vitsoe in 1960; it extended the entire 15m (50ft) width of the upper gallery. E-flute semi-transparent material was used in conjunction with Vitsoe X-posts to define the gallery space in a light and airy way. Key graphic elements using visual language from selected products and interface graphics were incorporated on the façade to set the tone.

Left: General view of the exhibition.

Below: Wall graphics in the exhibition.

Less is More: The Design Ethos of Dieter Rams, exhibition designed by Bibliothèque.

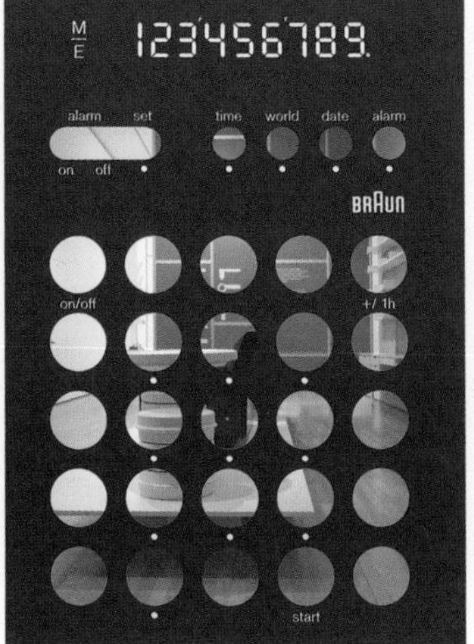

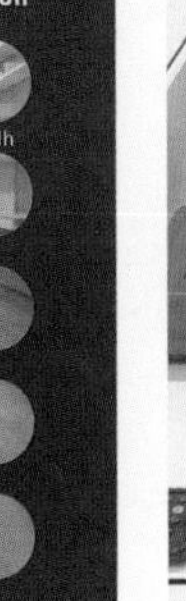

One of the room partitions.

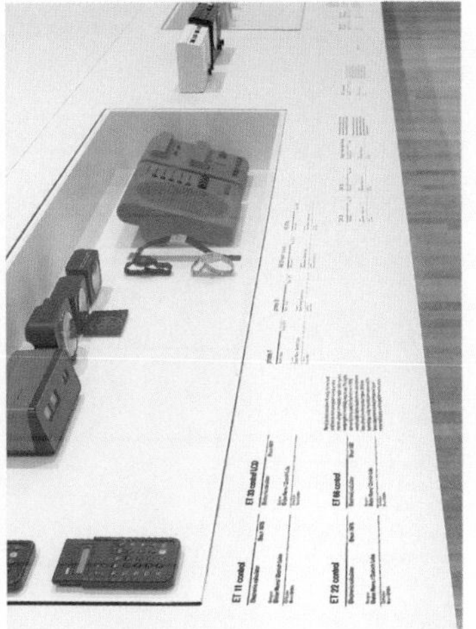

The captioning system.

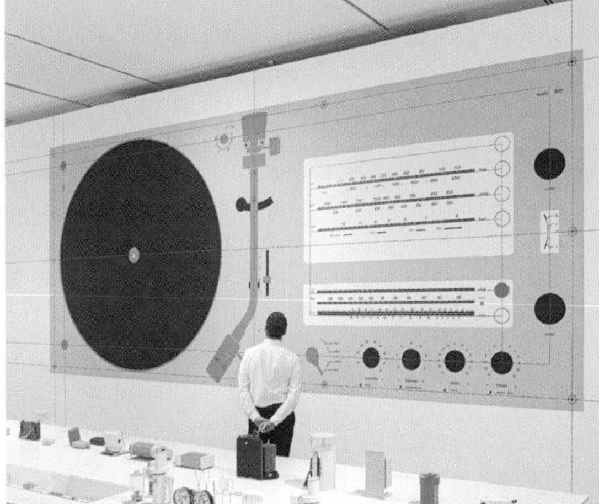

The 7m-wide (23ft) mural.

Each section was defined by partitions to create the five different areas of the exhibition. The screens used product elements such as speaker grilles, calculator layouts and hi-fi interfaces. These were to distinguish the relevant areas and to help tell the story of the products. 'The aim was to suggest the product had been deconstructed and rescaled beyond the intended proportions,' Tim Beard, a partner in Bibliothèque, explained. 'Within each partition elements were removed by routing away geometric shapes of the products; the negative space left acted as a window into a different section.'

A 7m-wide (23ft) mural of the Audio 300 stereo system on the back wall was painted, as opposed to using vinyl or a digital print. This was superimposed with a grid to reinforce the rational approach to product layout. This was supplemented with technical illustrations that utilized photographic elements and line artwork, also used for the exhibition marketing.

The completed exhibition perfectly complemented the design of the manufactured objects. The materials chosen, such as the shelving system, minimal white tables and plinths, and the semi-transparent graphic partitions, used the same simple graphic language as the original items, thereby making the display sympathetic and appropriate to the subject matter.

No technology was used to augment the display, as this was deemed inappropriate. The focal point was on the design of the objects, not the technology delivering the information.

The key aspect to bear in mind when choosing materials and media is to know how appropriate they are in delivering the information quickly and clearly.

A particular material or technology should not be used for the sake of it, but because it enhances the message or data being delivered, either through three-dimensional pieces, flat artwork or computer-generated animation.

There are plenty of formats to select from and they can be tricky for the information designer to navigate, so choose wisely.

Remember that the content is the most important feature, and this should drive all decision-making.

You may be restricted by budget: specialist materials such as wood, glass and metal, along with digital equipment, can be costly and require expert craftsmen and technicians.

The Guardian*'s visual identity in print format*

Project: Redesign of *The Guardian* newspaper in 2005

Design: *The Guardian*'s in-house design team

Hadley Freeman Stephen Mangan Catherine Bennett Viv Groskop Amartya Sen

Wednesday 04.07.12
Published in London and Manchester
£1.20

The US versus Britain in Afghanistan
Exclusive extract from a brilliant new book on the war within the war, in g2

Murray surges into last eight
Kevin Mitchell in Sport

Diamond cuts up rough

Bob Diamond could be in line for a golden goodbye of up to £22m. He has been paid some £100m by Barclays in the past six years Photograph: Dan Kitwood/Getty Images

Barclays boss forced out as he prepares riposte over role in Libor scandal

Jill Treanor
Patrick Wintour
Heather Stewart

Bob Diamond, the boss of Barclays who resigned from the embattled bank yesterday, will come out fighting for his reputation today when he appears before a powerful committee of MPs.

The high-profile and outspoken banker is expected to unleash a wave of explosive revelations about the role of City watchdogs and senior Whitehall figures in the manipulation of crucial interest rates that landed the bank with a record £290m fine last week.

The Bank of England's deputy governor, Paul Tucker, is expected to be in the spotlight at today's committee meeting, after Barclays released an email written by Diamond recording a conversation with Tucker in October 2008 regarding the inter-bank lending rates.

Yesterday the chancellor, George Osborne, who had been putting Diamond under intense pressure to quit, said his sudden resignation was "the right decision for Barclays - and for the country". "I think Bob Diamond's resignation is the first step towards the new age of responsibility we need to see."

After an extraordinary 24 hours during which the bank's chairman, Marcus Agius, quit only to be temporarily reinstated after Diamond's departure, the role of Bank of England officials in the rate-rigging scandal is likely to take centre stage in today's hearing with MPs.

With Barclays in turmoil, Diamond is fighting for his own reputation, which politicians have used to symbolise the culture of greed in City banking. Diamond, under pressure from the banking regulator and the governor of the Bank of England, Sir Mervyn King, quit after he decided he would be the lightning rod for the scandal at the hearing.

The American-born banker, who could be in line for a payoff of £22m, is facing pressure to walk away with nothing after being paid £100m by the bank in the past six years. There are also calls by shareholders for the bank to look at ways of clawing back bonuses paid in the past.

In a statement yesterday, Diamond said: "I am deeply disappointed that the impression created by the events announced last week about what Barclays and its people stand for could not be further from the truth."

At his appearance before the Treasury select committee of MPs - chaired by the Conservative MP Andrew Tyrie, who the government has also appointed to lead a parliamentary inquiry into banking - Diamond will try to explain the bank's actions for the period between 2005 and 2009, when the attempts to manipulate Libor took place.

The sequence of events unleashed by the email in the darkest days of the banking crisis also forced the departure of Jerry del Missier, who was Diamond's closest colleague at the bank.

Del Missier, a Canadian, was promoted to chief operating officer a fortnight ago, but was named as the top executive who instructed more junior staff to lower the bank's submissions to the key benchmark rate, the London interbank offered

4-6 »

Continued on page 2 »

When the penny dropped that he was the problem, Britain's highest-profile banker quit in a late-night call, writes **Jill Treanor**

On Monday afternoon, Bob Diamond rehearsed for his planned appearance today before the Commons Treasury select committee. As his public relations team ran him through question after question that the MPs were likely to fire at him, the American-born banker saw that he - and his brash personality - was the main problem facing Barclays bank.

Diamond, 16 years at the bank, but only 18 months into his dream job as chief executive, spoke to a few close colleagues before setting off for home, knowing that David Cameron had used the revelations about Barclays' attempts to manipulate the London interbank offered rate (Libor) to call an inquiry into the wider banking industry.

Though regulators admit that Barclays is only one of up to 20 banks caught up in the scandal, Diamond epitomised it.

Diamond rang Barclays chairman Marcus Agius and told him it was time for him to go. It was a stunning change in stance from the defiant email to staff he had sent a few hours earlier, telling them he "loved Barclays" and was committed to putting right the wrongs exposed by regulators.

Behind the scenes, bigger forces were at work. The regulators had watched the political temperature rising during the day and the Bank of England governor, Sir Mervyn King, and Lord Turner of the Financial Services Authority secretly met Agius, who had himself resigned only hours before, in the late afternoon.

King would not comment yesterday, but Turner said: "There were major challenges for Barclays in making sure they could convince people there had been a fundamental cultural change

Continued on page 5 »

Police raid Sarkozy's home and offices in funding inquiry

Angelique Chrisafis Paris

French police yesterday raided the home and offices of the former French president Nicolas Sarkozy as part of an investigation into illegal campaign financing and alleged cash payments from L'Oreal heiress Liliane Bettencourt, France's wealthiest woman.

Early yesterday morning, police searched the mansion rented by Carla Bruni in a chic gated community in the west of Paris, where she and Sarkozy live.

Officers also searched the office of the legal firm where Sarkozy is a partner and the new office he moved into after losing the presidential election to François Hollande in May.

The Sarkozys were away, having left for a Quebec chalet holiday on Monday, Sarkozy's lawyer said.

As president, Sarkozy had judicial immunity, which protected him from legal action, but this expired on 16 June.

A judge in Bordeaux is currently investigating whether Sarkozy's rightwing UMP party benefited from cash gifts from the mentally fragile Bettencourt, 89, during Sarkozy's successful 2007 election campaign. The investigating magistrate is trying to establish whether Sarkozy's campaign might have received €800,000 (£640,000) in illegal funding.

In February, Eric Woerth, the former French budget minister and UMP treasurer, was placed under judicial investigation over cash he was alleged to have received from Bettencourt to fund the 2007 campaign. He denies any wrongdoing.

The investigation is part of the wider Bettencourt saga, which has gripped France for years.

Sarkozy's lawyer, Thierry Herzog, said the raids would show nothing and that he had already supplied information to investigators that debunked suspicions of secret meetings with Bettencourt. "These raids ... will as expected prove futile," he said in a statement. Herzog said magistrates looking into whether Sarkozy had received funds from Bettencourt had been supplied with diary details of all his appointments in 2007. These, he said, "prove that the purported 'secret meetings' with Mme Liliane Bettencourt were impossible".

Sarkozy, 57, could come under the spotlight in a number of legal cases now he is no longer head of state. He could become a focus of the separate investigation into whether or not there was a shady "cabinet noir" at the highest reaches of the French government which used the secret services to spy on journalists at Le Monde to uncover their sources for stories about the Bettencourt affair. Sarkozy has denied any links to the case.

16 »

Sarkozy is being investigated over allegations that he illegally received funds from L'Oreal heiress Liliane Bettencourt

Current front page of *The Guardian* newspaper in print format.

As technologies and behaviours change, how do established brands deal with the challenge of delivering their content, in this case news, across a variety of platforms? How do you maintain the visual identity, capture the quality, intention and integrity of the original, but translate it effectively into an experience appropriate to both the product and the platform?

This is one challenge that many publications have found themselves facing with the rapid expansion and creation of digital technologies.

The Guardian is a British newspaper first published in 1821. Its current design was launched in 2005, when the paper adopted the Berliner mid-size format (the first UK newspaper to do so). It was also the UK's first full-colour national newspaper. *The Guardian* is considered to be a high-quality independent newspaper with a strong design aesthetic. It has a distinct graphic language, a strong typographic style and excellent use of colour throughout to define different sections and support navigation through the paper.

How has this paper managed to create a coherent visual style that translates successfully across a variety of platforms? In an interview with *Creative Review* that discusses 'Brand Guardian', Mark Porter, the newspaper's creative director, talks about how the redesign of the paper had 'almost accidentally ... laid the foundations for a strong branding programme'. (*Creative Review*, February 2009, p. 32). The strong visual language that had been created for the paper, the typeface and use of colour on a white background became the distinct elements that appear across the range of *The Guardian*'s communications.

The Guardian*'s visual identity in signage*

Project: Wayfinding design for *The Guardian*'s offices in King's Cross, London

Design: Cartlidge Levene, London

This established visual language was carried across into the wayfinding designed by Cartlidge Levene for *The Guardian*'s offices in Kings Place, King's Cross, London. The agency had the challenge of designing a solution with a low environmental impact. The directional signage is manufactured entirely from cardboard. This was made into a series of boxes that were then screen-printed with colour (from the newspaper's colour palette), utilizing the newspaper's Egyptian font.

Wayfinding system for *The Guardian*'s offices, designed by Cartlidge Levene.

Cardboard wayfinding signage suspended from the ceiling.

Vinyl graphics applied to walls and glass partitions.

The Guardian's *visual identity on the iPad*

Project: Design for *The Guardian*'s iPad app

Design: Andy Brockie, senior digital designer of *The Guardian*'s digital design team

This visual identity has also been adapted and applied to the advertising communications produced by *The Guardian* and to the apps created for the iPhone and, more recently, the iPad (launched in October 2011). The designs for each platform require careful consideration. What is possible? What are the limitations? How do people use their iPhone to receive news and information and is that different to the way an iPad is used? Andy Brockie from *The Guardian*'s digital design team offers some insights into the process of designing *The Guardian*'s app for the iPad.

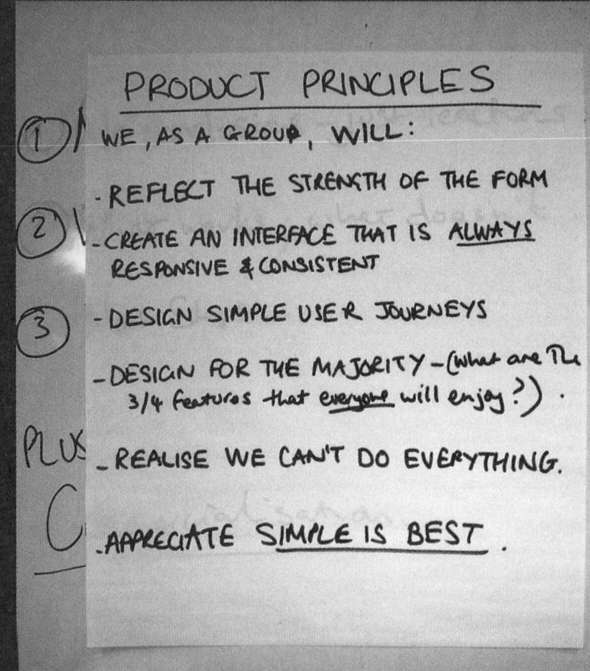

The principles of the brief as set out by the team.

Overview

The original brief was to make the optimum experience of reading a newspaper possible on an iPad. Some members of the team had already made two successful iOS *Guardian* apps; an iPad app (Eyewitness) and *The Guardian* iPhone app. From these projects the team had learned a few things that they turned into product principles:

1. Reflect the strength of the form

- Don't recreate elements for the sake of it.
- Make it appropriate to your brand.
- Make it work in either orientation (designing for two orientations was probably one of the hardest things to get right).
- Aim for an immersive experience.

2. Create an interface that is always responsive and consistent
Borrow as you can from Apple, and know that your app will be compared to the experience of using Apple's other apps. It has to match up to them in terms of design and build.

3. Design simple user journeys
Get users to the content as quickly as possible. Do all you can to make the interface melt away, so it's no longer thought about.

4. Design for the majority
Understand how the majority will use this app; complexities can still be offered but must not create barriers for most users.

5. Realize we can't do everything

- Cut features in favour of quality.
- Do one thing well and add as you go.

6. Appreciate that simple is best
In favourable app store reviews, the word 'simple' comes up more than any other.

n early version of the application showing different navigational nodels. The team tried to combine lists and sliding panels. However, he feeling was they were a little too complex. The team were keen to ave the interface dissolve, to put the content directly under the ingertips, rather than having separate navigational and content modes.

Approach

The team looked around the app market at what other iewspapers and magazines were doing, as well as other RSS eader and social networking apps. From these they started to ealize what they didn't want to do and began to build a picture of what they thought was missing and frustrating to use from other print publications' iPad translations.

he team had to ask how information delivery changes when ou deliver content with a different tool. As the paper was the tarting point, they began by breaking down what they had earned from decades of desktop publishing development in that irea. They wanted to pass on those principles, and the iPad roject gave them the opportunity to do so for the first time in a igital space. They were looking at a more sophisticated design anguage than they had previously used; a lot of this was down o the space afforded and the screen resolution allowing for nore finessed typography (the first time they had been able to ise print typefaces from the newspaper).

n addition, they tried to recreate new, interesting methods of ierarchy through scale, allowing people to discover and read iews through serendipity. They put the emphasis back on the editors and asked the user to trust them to deliver a finite package of broad news that a user could skim through as effortlessly as flicking through the pages of the newspaper.

he iPad device changes how news content is consumed; with he iPhone app and website, consumption is brief and top-level, whereas the iPad is much more likely to be used around the iome, in bed or on long journeys with more deliberation. This illowed the team to provide the user with something more than list to get to know, and the layout of the app was deliberately esigned to surprise; its rhythm is irregular to better reflect the

Directions

Early designs closely reproduced the character of the paper in a smaller space, using similar design elements – typography and rules – and turning them into 'thumbnails'.

The team used this common design language across a whole range of navigation models, adding to it or reducing it dependin on how much space was afforded. The models were broken dow into about four different directions; at one end a list-based method, and at the other grid-based.

The team spent a long time seeing how far down they could reduce the graphic design of the thumbnails while still maintaining *The Guardian*'s style and giving a sense of hierarch These exercises allowed them to see how long a scroll or how many pages they would need to use to reproduce the content.

The key to a lot of what the team were looking to do was presented when they discovered that they could accommodate the newspaper comfortably within a small number of screens. Of the range of navigation models they looked at, the treatment illustrated above (left) seemed very promising; a more graphica menu list on the left-hand side that opened on tap (or drag) and folding back to a 'spine' when closed, therefore allowing the rest of the screen to display article content or section fronts. The other area that looked most convincing was the one illustrated above (right). This felt like the app was trying to take on too many of the conventions of the newspaper, and was getting a little too close to the 'PDF draggers' that they were trying to avoid. However, it was popular because it removed that extra pane of navigation and focused squarely on content. Any list approach always felt a little too complex, and made the experience more akin to a chore, ticking off the stories as you went. The team were always keen to have the interface dissolve, to put the content directly under the fingertips, rather than having a separate navigation and content mode.

Match-fixing in 'fake international' friendly turns up heat on Fifa

Football

Hernández helps United forget their troubles

Football

De3 20/24p lorem ipsum dolor sit amet lorem ipsum dolor

De3 34/38p lorem ipsum dolor sit amet

De3 20/24p lorem ipsum dolor sit amet lorem ipsum dolor

De2 27/31p lorem ipsum dolor sit amet

De2 34/38p lorem ipsum dolor sit amet

De2 56/60p lorem ipsum dolor

Grid

'he designers had been experimenting with five- or six-column grids from the start, although they had been using them in the background much of the time. Mark Porter's suggestion was to bring the grid to the front and exploit it as a concept, with the size of the squares corresponding to the size of the story. The team reduced the styling of the graphic blocks further, removing rules as they let the background separate the stories, minimizing the type styles and adding colour to differentiate sections.

nterface

n parallel to the look of the app, the designers were constantly working through various navigation methods. To get and share an understanding of this model, Andy Brockie and Jack Schulze from the design consultancy Berg spent some time creating animatics (simplified paper mock-ups shot using a camera and tripod and then animated together in sequence). These helped them quickly get a sense of how a reader could navigate the app and were also useful to pass over to the development team.

Although the iPad offers a whole range of touch gestures – drag, swipe, double-tap, two-finger interaction, and in addition the option of limiting these to a particular part of the screen (some apps reveal their navigation if you double-tap only in the top area of the screen) – the designers aimed to make the app work with the most basic of these: single-tap and swipe. They wanted any navigation options to be simple enough that making them

Top left: Sketch showing how the exposed grid would work on the tablet.

Top right: A more detailed version of the grid, showing how it could be divided up in order of importance and showing relative point sizes. A minimum range of typeface styles that suited the headlines were then defined and slowly built out as the app developed. It is the first time the extensive range of fonts has been used to such effect in any of *The Guardian*'s digital products.

Above: Low-tech mock-up using card templates to show how titles may be revealed.

The mechanics of the app are based upon layers. One layer is made up of the section fronts, so a user can swipe through thes to quickly gain an overview of the news. This is the area that is the most innovative, where most of the design work went, and that differentiates this app from others. It is the layer that most reveals the hierarchy of content and allows for a degree of

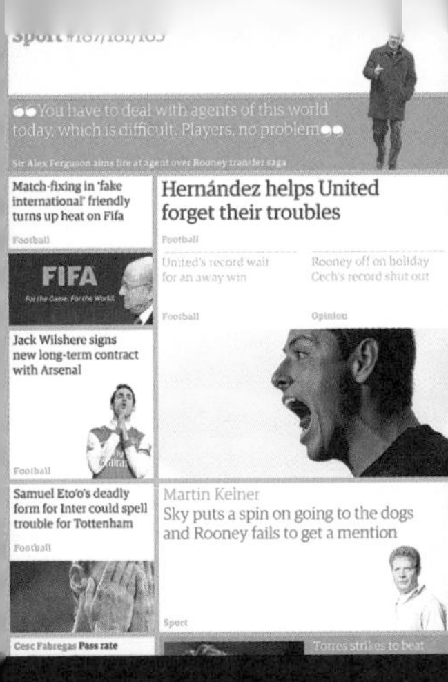

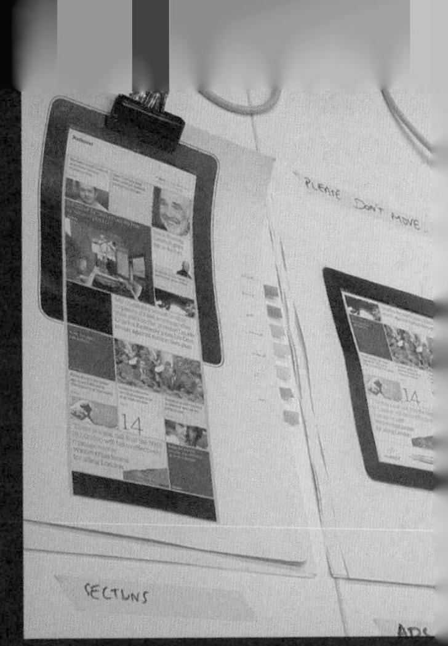

The articles deliberately draw up from the bottom of the screen and over the top of the section fronts. Once in this level, a user can choose to navigate article to article, section through section. The tab at the top allows the core navigation on the right of the app to remain available, but can also be used to indicate the section the user is in. The team spent a long time creating templates that allowed them to reflect the range of articles: large features have large pictures; comment articles make more of the typography, while regular columns are illustrated with byline pictures or other graphic devices.

Other benefits of a digital device were utilized on articles, but were deliberately limited to those features that would see the most use. Related articles are linked together (the print version would refer to page numbers, while in the app there is just a direct link), so that people can read all around the subject. Links are provided to updates on the newspaper's website in cases where the story has moved on, and to videos when they add something to the story. As the articles are delivered as HTML, the team has the benefit of sharing and copying, along with all the styling attributes offered.

Outcome

In the future the designers aim to add more interactive elements and galleries, but each time these will be very straightforward and appropriate; they resist adding bells and whistles just for the sake of it.

Andy believes that his team created something that is a new proposition, something that is different from other digital offerings. The way it is produced and built, with a small dedicated team producing a daily iPad edition, means that it can adapt to the news each day, just like a newspaper.

Top left: Mock-up of the sports section using the grid, typefaces and imagery.

Top right: Work in development pinned up on the wall to evaluate variations of the design and get input from those involved in its inception.

Right: Andy Brockie believes he helped to create something different to other digital offerings. 'It works in either orientation and nothing is sacrificed. Instead of it being based on lists, breaking news, and the fastest updates it's instead designed to be a more reflective, discoverable experience. This gives it the potential

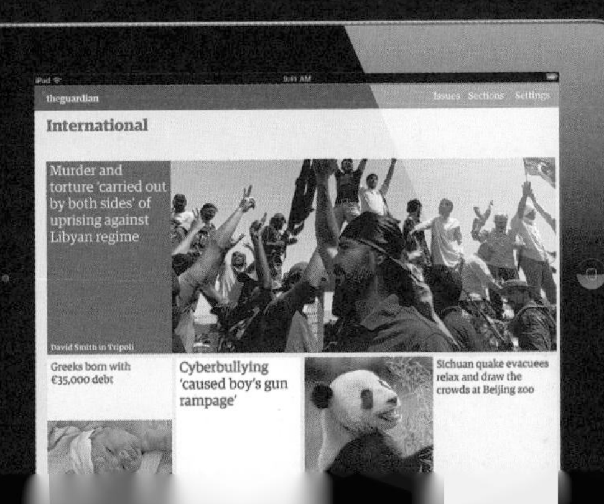

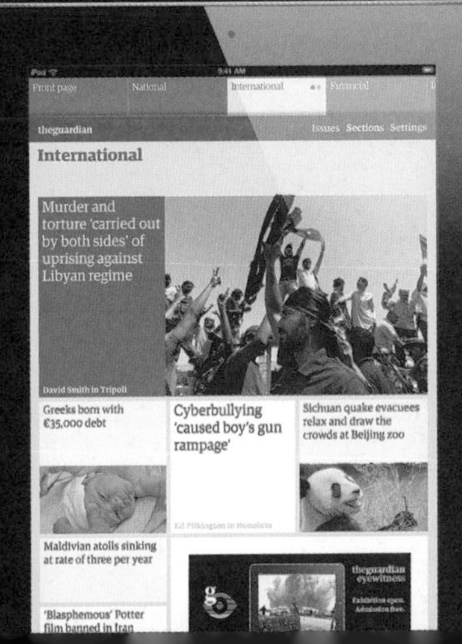

drone

① ② ③ ④ ⑤ ⑥ ⑦ ⑧ ⑨ ⑩ ⑪ ⑫ ⑬ ⑭ ⑮ ⑯

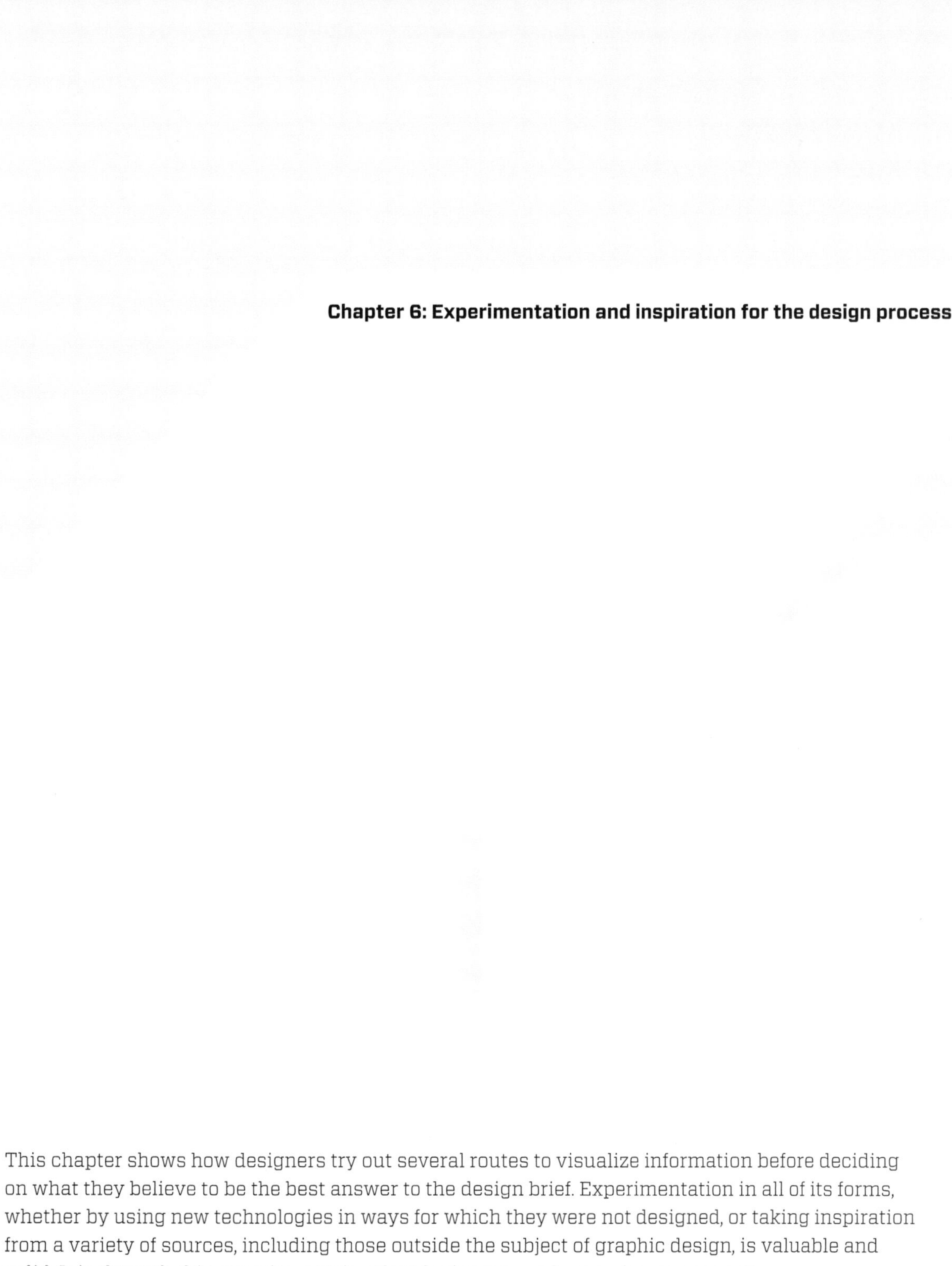

Chapter 6: Experimentation and inspiration for the design process

This chapter shows how designers try out several routes to visualize information before deciding on what they believe to be the best answer to the design brief. Experimentation in all of its forms, whether by using new technologies in ways for which they were not designed, or taking inspiration from a variety of sources, including those outside the subject of graphic design, is valuable and valid. It is through this experimentation that designers produce unforeseen results.

Why is experimentation and inspiration important?

What is the point of experimentation within the design process? Experimentation sits at the heart of the creative process. As designers we look for new ways of doing, making and ultimately communicating information and ideas. The desire to experiment is fuelled by curiosity: we look, we see, we respond to the world around us; our situations and circumstance, our likes and dislikes, our interests and experiences all shape and influence our work.

When we are experimenting we are asking questions and seeking answers. We can't expect to instinctively 'know' the best way to resolve a problem, so we ask questions of the brief and we explore and experiment to find the most appropriate answers. This is an essential part of the design process; it can lead to exciting and unexpected solutions, taking the designer into new territories that challenge the established or expected methods of communication. It can lead to new ways of doing and thinking, and new and exciting design directions and opportunities to engage and communicate with an audience.

The willingness to explore and experiment also helps you establish and define your own style and beliefs, and to find out who you are as a designer. The work we admire from our peers captures something unique. It has personality, individuality and it goes beyond the norm; it pushes or challenges the established boundaries and presents something new and unexpected.

As individuals, our experiences, opinions, inspirations and influences are all different. These will (and should) shape our approach to the way we design. Where we live or grew up, the political, social and economic climate, our beliefs and opinions, the music we like, the artists or architects we admire are all sources of inspiration and should be embraced when we are engaged in the creative process.

Student project by Sophie Garwell: D&AD/Diesel competition entry, 2011

This project was created in response to a Designers & Art Directors' (D&AD) competition brief set by the well-known brand Diesel to illustrate two songs by an artist chosen by the student. The idea was to explore new and imaginative ways in which design and illustration could be integrated into the music experience. Sophie selected two tracks she loved, 'Festival' by Sigur Rós and 'Animal Arithmetic' by Jonsi. Her response to the brief was to create an experimental illustrative book for each track that attempts to visually describe and communicate the music. The differing formats of the books reflect the structure of each track; the compositions of the visuals attempt to capture the mood, volume, rhythm and pace of each piece. They explore the possibility of the visual representation of music. As a starting point, Sophie mapped out the pitch and volume of the songs, paying particular attention to the instrumental layers. She used this as the basis to create an appropriate visual palette, experimenting with different colours, textures, materials and surfaces to use within the piece. She comments, 'The first half [of the song] is very slow and subtle, so I took soft textures to mirror the map of movements I had made. The second is much more beat-orientated with layering of instruments.'

The final pieces reflect the points of difference within the music and between each track. A single page represents 30 seconds of music in visual form; when 'read' at this pace while listening to the music it creates a multi-sensory experience for the audience.

This illustrative interpretation of musical data is the result of extensive experimentation and exploration around two pieces of music that Sophie found particularly inspirational.

'Of course design is about problem-solving, but I cannot resist adding something personal as well.'

Wim Crouwel (b. 1928), graphic designer

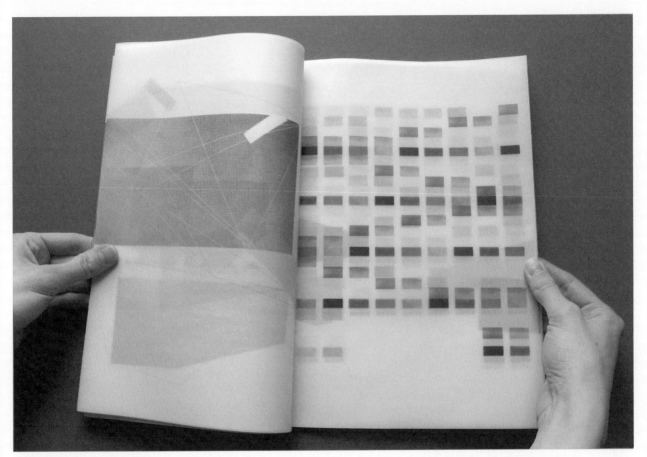

Previous page, above and right: Sophie Garwell's response to a D&AD/Diesel competition brief: 'The books are a visual description of the music of Sigur Rós and its emotive dynamics. The songs are built up with many layers of instruments, pitch and tempo, creating a unique atmosphere, which I translated into a visual format. The books follow the path of the music from start to finish in an attempt to be a visual accompaniment to such rich musical qualities.'

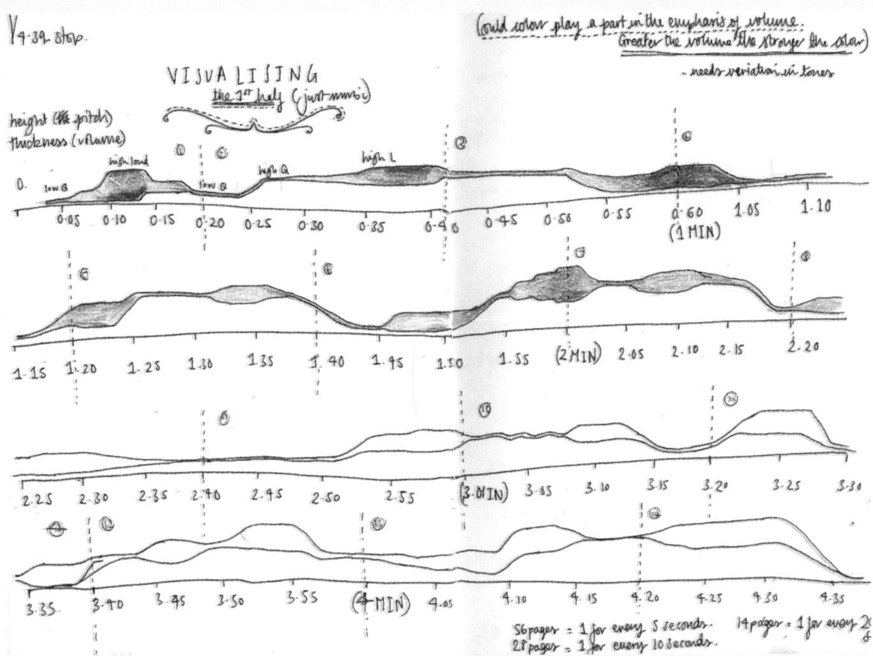

Lateral thinking

Psychologist Edward de Bono conceived the term 'lateral thinking' in 1967. In simple terms it involves thinking beyond the obvious solution, sometimes termed 'thinking outside the box'. He summarizes the approach as, 'you cannot dig a hole in a different place by digging the same hole deeper'. By this he means that changing direction cannot be achieved by putting more effort into one approach. Lateral thinking means not just accepting the pieces of a puzzle you have been given but seeking to change them. It is a technique used to shake people out of their complacency to produce something unique instead of coming up with predictable solutions.

Lateral thinking is important in information design as there is a perception that dealing with large amounts of data is relatively boring. If not presented correctly, information becomes just numbers and words with little meaning. The ability to visualize this raw data and place it into a visual form that demonstrates relationships or differences can change the audience's understanding of the subject.

Lateral thinking can be used through the process of visual exploration. In this phase designers experiment with different media, materials and ways of presenting the raw information. During this process, creatives move beyond initial concepts and explore avenues outside of the obvious choices. This can result in more innovative solutions to the problem. By sketching and prototyping, the designer can investigate various methods to present the message, using diagrams, grids, typography and imagery. This allows the information designer to compare methods in order to select the most appropriate technique.

It is during this phase that many designers 'play' with the visualization. Play means different things to different people, but psychologist Bruno Bettelheim defined it as 'freedom from all but personally imposed rules (which can be changed at will) by freewheeling fantasy involvement and by the absence of any goals outside the activity itself' ('The Importance of Play', *Atlantic Monthly*, March 1987, p. 37). Playing can result in happy accidents and keep the approach fresh and vibrant. It can involve playing with images by making collages or montages or using unfamiliar tools and design techniques.

Student project by Stephen Woowat: Urban First Aid, 2004

An example of lateral thinking is the Urban First Aid project by British graphic designer Stephen Woowat, produced when he was a student. The brief was to communicate information about roads in the city. Stephen used lateral thinking to liken the transport infrastructure of a city to that of a human circulatory system. The ring road has become the main arteries in the heart of the system. Using this simple metaphor, the reader understands the importance of roads in the city as they provide links to the outside world, bringing in valuable commodities such as food, as well as exporting waste products. If this system gets clogged, the circulation of goods slows down and causes major problems.

The visual solution is presented in the form of an installation, which uses the floor plan to show the road structure. On top of this, Stephen has used the vernacular of medical graphic design to diagnose key areas of congestion and prescribe solutions such as a bypass or rail networks to alleviate the problems. The idea that any potential problems could be diagnosed and dealt with equates town planners to doctors, as they can both alleviate problems and repair them through intervention or surgery. This way of presenting the information helps the viewer to remember the message: it is a clever idea, presented not just as facts and figures, that engages the audience.

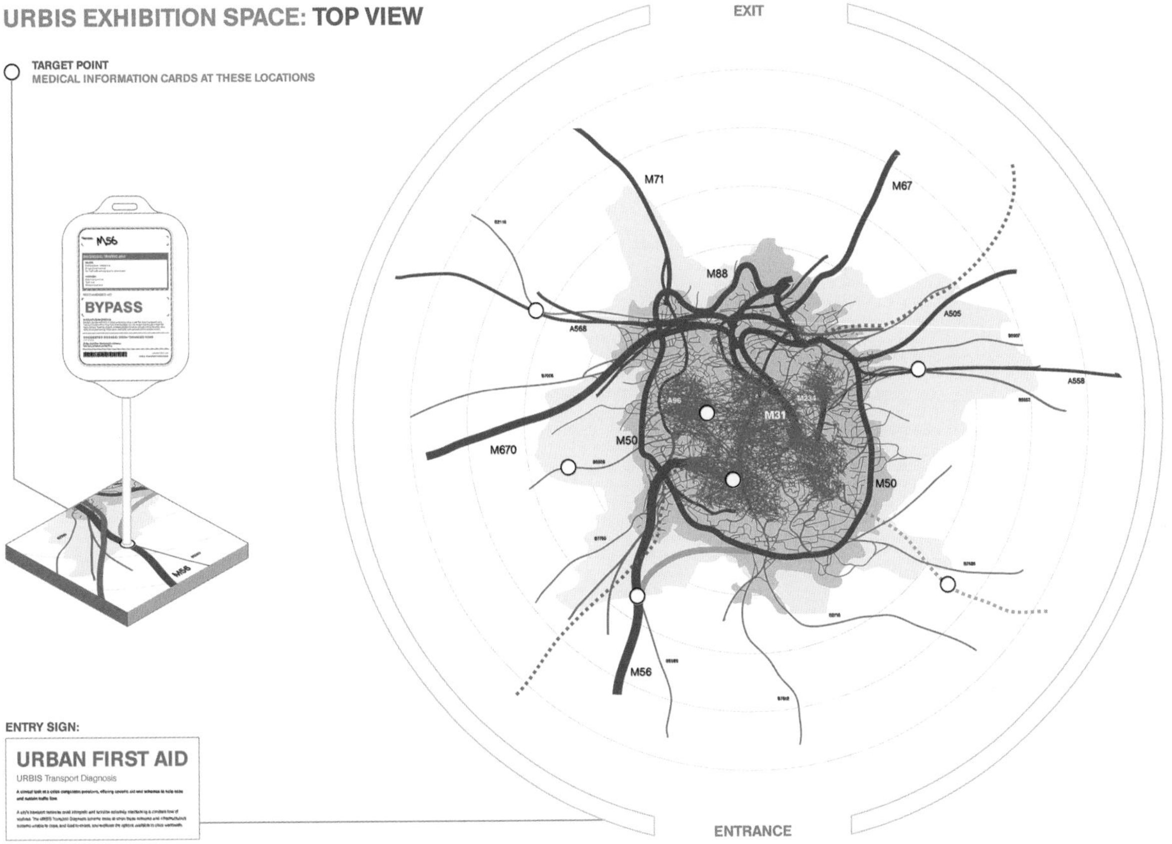

URBIS EXHIBITION SPACE: TOP VIEW

TARGET POINT
MEDICAL INFORMATION CARDS AT THESE LOCATIONS

EXIT

M71
M67
M88
A568
A505
A558
M31
M50
M670
M50
M56

ENTRANCE

ENTRY SIGN:

URBAN FIRST AID
URBIS Transport Diagnosis

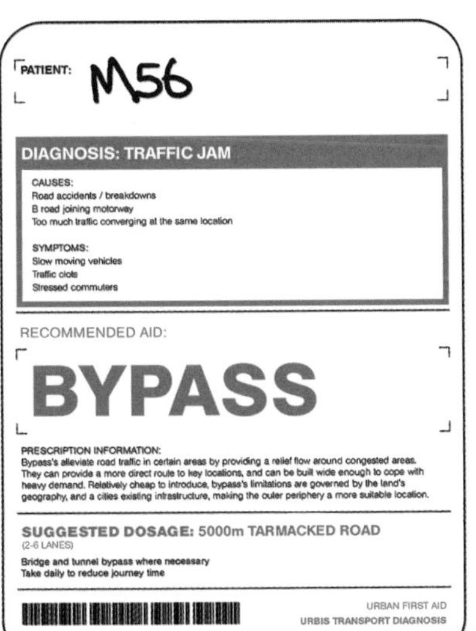

PATIENT: M56

DIAGNOSIS: TRAFFIC JAM

CAUSES:
Road accidents / breakdowns
B road joining motorway
Too much traffic converging at the same location

SYMPTOMS:
Slow moving vehicles
Traffic clots
Stressed commuters

RECOMMENDED AID:

BYPASS

PRESCRIPTION INFORMATION:
Bypass's alleviate road traffic in certain areas by providing a relief flow around congested areas. They can provide a more direct route to key locations, and can be built wide enough to cope with heavy demand. Relatively cheap to introduce, bypass's limitations are governed by the land's geography, and a cities existing infrastructure, making the outer periphery a more suitable location.

SUGGESTED DOSAGE: 5000m TARMACKED ROAD
(2-6 LANES)
Bridge and tunnel bypass where necessary
Take daily to reduce journey time

URBAN FIRST AID
URBIS TRANSPORT DIAGNOSIS

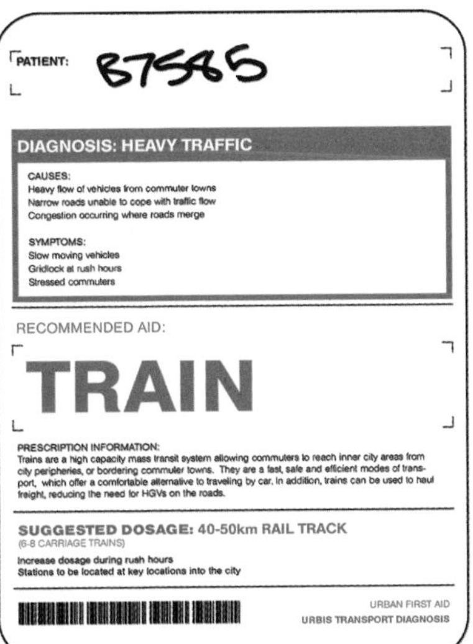

PATIENT: B7585

DIAGNOSIS: HEAVY TRAFFIC

CAUSES:
Heavy flow of vehicles from commuter towns
Narrow roads unable to cope with traffic flow
Congestion occurring where roads merge

SYMPTOMS:
Slow moving vehicles
Gridlock at rush hours
Stressed commuters

RECOMMENDED AID:

TRAIN

PRESCRIPTION INFORMATION:
Trains are a high capacity mass transit system allowing commuters to reach inner city areas from city peripheries, or bordering commuter towns. They are a fast, safe and efficient modes of transport, which offer a comfortable alternative to traveling by car. In addition, trains can be used to haul freight, reducing the need for HGVs on the roads.

SUGGESTED DOSAGE: 40-50km RAIL TRACK
(6-8 CARRIAGE TRAINS)
Increase dosage during rush hours
Stations to be located at key locations into the city

URBAN FIRST AID
URBIS TRANSPORT DIAGNOSIS

Stephen Woowat's Urban First Aid project, 2004, which uses lateral thinking to liken the ring road around a city to that of the circulatory system of a human heart.

Inspiration for design

Designers are inspired by a multitude of things: it could be an environment they have experienced, such as the city they live in or their travels abroad; it may be a building, a piece of architecture, an artist and their work or their philosophy and beliefs, a particular cultural movement, a belief or ideology, a piece of music, poetry or the written word. It may be old signage, tickets collected from around the world, or sweet wrappers. In short, inspiration can be found everywhere!

We absorb our surroundings both subconsciously and consciously. As designers we should be looking, recording, collecting, drawing and photographing the things that surround us. The things that capture our interest may become the inspirations that drive and inform our work. Evidence of this can be found throughout design history and in the work of many of the designers featured in earlier chapters.

When first studying Fine Arts at the Academie Minerva in Groningen, the Netherlands, legendary graphic designer Wim Crouwel said he was more inspired by the building (the first modernist building in Holland) than by the work that went on within it. Crouwel is known for the 'architectural' use of space in his design work, and there is no doubt that this early inspiration shaped his subsequent work. In the late 1950s he read the book *Grid Systems in Graphic Design* by Josef Müller-Brockmann (see Chapter 3), and this too inspired his use of the grid in his posters. These are just two examples of the many influences on his work. Müller-Brockmann also looked beyond his own field for inspiration:

'What pleases me is that I have always sought what is better, that I have still remained self-critical, and that I am still interested in things outside my own field. My library is the expression of my curiosity. I would advise young people to look at everything they encounter in a critical light and try to find a better solution.'

Josef Müller-Brockmann, in an interview with Yvonne Schwemer-Scheddin, © *Eye* magazine, 2001

US designer David Carson, who is best known for his influential magazine designs, is also clear on the potential sources of inspiration:

'My environment always influences me. I'm always taking photos and I believe the things I see and experience influence my work. ... I think it is really important that designers put themselves into the work. No one else has your background, upbringing, life experiences, and if you can put a bit of that into your work, two things will happen; you'll enjoy the work more and you'll do your best work.'

David Carson, *Layers* magazine, 2007

The world that surrounds a designer can shape his or her ideas. The agency Idiom in Bangalore looked to Otl Aicher's 1972 Munich Olympics pictograms (see p. 41) and to Sanjhi, a form of Indian folk art, when they were commissioned to design the pictograms for the 2010 Commonwealth Games in Delhi. The shape of the logo for the 2016 Olympic Games in Rio, created by design studio Tátil, was inspired by the Brazilian environment; it is based on the famous Rio landmark of Sugarloaf Mountain.

Look around you, think, respond, and be curious. Being open to the influences and inspirations that surround you is essential to creating work that has a sense of personality and individuality; something that can make the work distinct and unique.

To give you some examples of how this awareness can inspire and drive the direction and content of projects, we show the work of William Cottam and Holly Langford, two recent graphic design graduates from Nottingham Trent University. These illustrate how a personal interest in or response to an issue can provide the basis for interesting and compelling visual communications.

Revealed:
CCTV Locations

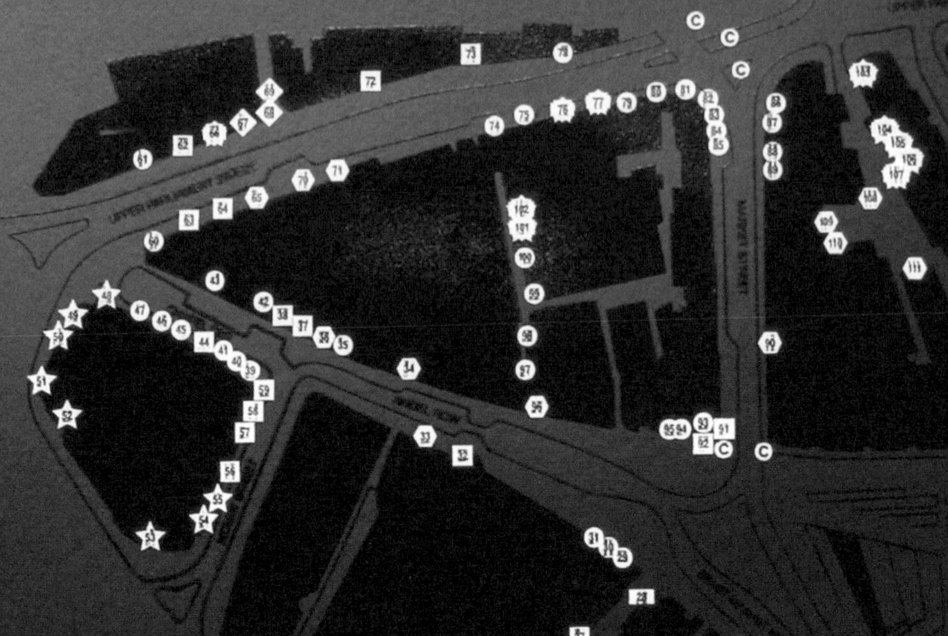

This map depicts the locations of the majority of CCTV cameras within a 200 meter radius of Nottingham's Old Market Square, whilst it also identifies whether they belong to private businesses or Nottingham City Council.

In total, of the CCTV cameras found, 149 belonged to private businesses and 16 to Nottingham City Council which works out to be approximately 14 CCTV cameras per street. This means that whilst we are in the city centre, its possible to walk past up to 50 cameras, unaware that we are being watched. This is without even considering the CCTV installed within premises which would at the very least, quadruple this figure.

The amount of CCTV that surrounds us cannot be ignored. How much longer can we live in a society where we are under constant surveillance? The UK is already the most watched nation with an estimated 4.5 million CCTV cameras and alarmingly this number is increasing. Lets put a stop to CCTV expansion and reveal the truth.

Bars/ Clubs/ Pubs	●	Casinos	◆
Restaurants	■	Banks	▬
Shops	⬢	Other	⬟
Hotels	★	Council	Ⓒ

Bars/ Clubs/ Pubs

5. The Approach
6. The Approach
7. The Approach
8. Walkabout
9. Walkabout
10. Walkabout
18. Up and Down Under
19. Bar Schnapps
20. Cookie Club
21. Bla Bla Bar
22. Bla Bla Bar
23. Weatherspoon Free House
24. Weatherspoon Free House
30. The Bell Inn
31. The Bell Inn
35. The Dragon
39. The Fat Cat Bar
40. The Fat Cat Bar
41. The Fat Cat Bar
42. Bar Bistro and Restaurant
43. Bar Bistro and Restaurant
45. Bar Tonic
46. Bar Tonic
47. Bar Tonic
74. Foxy's
75. Foxy's
78. The Stage
79. Flares
81. Flares
82. Reflex
83. Reflex
84. Reflex
85. Reflex
86. Shameless
87. Shameless
88. Bar Circle
89. Bar Circle
93. Yates
94. Yates
95. Yates
97. Cucamaras
98. Cucamaras
99. Plan B
112. Gatecrasher
113. Gatecrasher
127. Coach and Horses
128. Coach and Horses
135. The Bank
136. The Bank
137. The Bank
139. The Joseph Else
140. The Joseph Else

Restaurants

12. Citi Restaurant Buffet
13. Chutney
32. McDonalds
37. Umami Curry House
38. Umami Curry House
44. Ask
56. China China
57. China China
58. Las Iguanas
59. Las Iguanas
60. Las Iguanas
61. Big Wok
62. Big Wok
64. Kismet Kebabs
72. May Sum
73. May Sum
91. Subway
92. Subway
115. Vienna Bar and Grill
116. Vienna Bar and Grill
117. Vienna Bar and Grill
118. Vienna Bar and Grill
119. Vienna Bar and Grill
120. Zizi
121. Zizi
122. Antalya Takeaway
129. Subway
134. Pizza Hut

Shops

1. Cruise
2. Bag and Leat
3. Specsaver
4. HMV
11. Rohan Haird
33. Alpha Graph
34. Tescos
36. Sky News
65. Kaya Food C
96. Boots
108. Debenhams
109. Debenhams
110. Debenhams

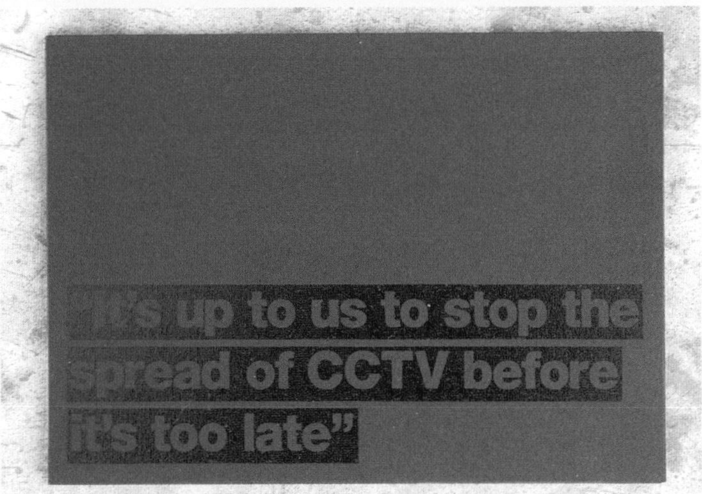

Student project by William Cottam: Revealed, 2010

While walking around the city centre of Nottingham, William began to notice the number of CCTV cameras located in a very small area. On further investigation he discovered there were very few locations where one was not being watched within this area, yet people seemed unconcerned – or maybe they were just unaware. Many people assume that the reason for the cameras is to reduce crime; however, evidence indicates that CCTV is not effective in reducing or solving crime.

So who is watching us and why? Shouldn't modern citizens feel trusted to go about their daily lives in a law-abiding manner? Isn't camera surveillance just another form of spying and an infringement and erosion of our civil liberties?

William decided he should use his skills as a graphic designer to initiate a response to this issue and create a campaign to stop the expansion of CCTV. He experimented and explored the best way to communicate this information. After trying and testing several routes it was clear that using a well-known area within the city as the basis for his campaign would offer the most effective and compelling content as well as providing a meaningful context for the final communications. Many people would have walked, shopped or sat waiting to catch a bus without realizing that their every move was being watched.

A poster mapping the location of CCTV cameras within the area was created; the visual language of existing warning posters was utilized and new versions produced carrying an alternative warning message to the public. Finally, a set of 'opinionated postcards' were made to reinforce the message of the campaign.

William experimented in his design process to find an appropriate and balanced visual language and tone to communicate with. Measuring the right tone and selecting the most effective formats to carry a message or information is a vital part of the overall design process. In many instances this can only be established through active experimentation with materials, media and formats, and testing how these different approaches communicate with the desired audience.

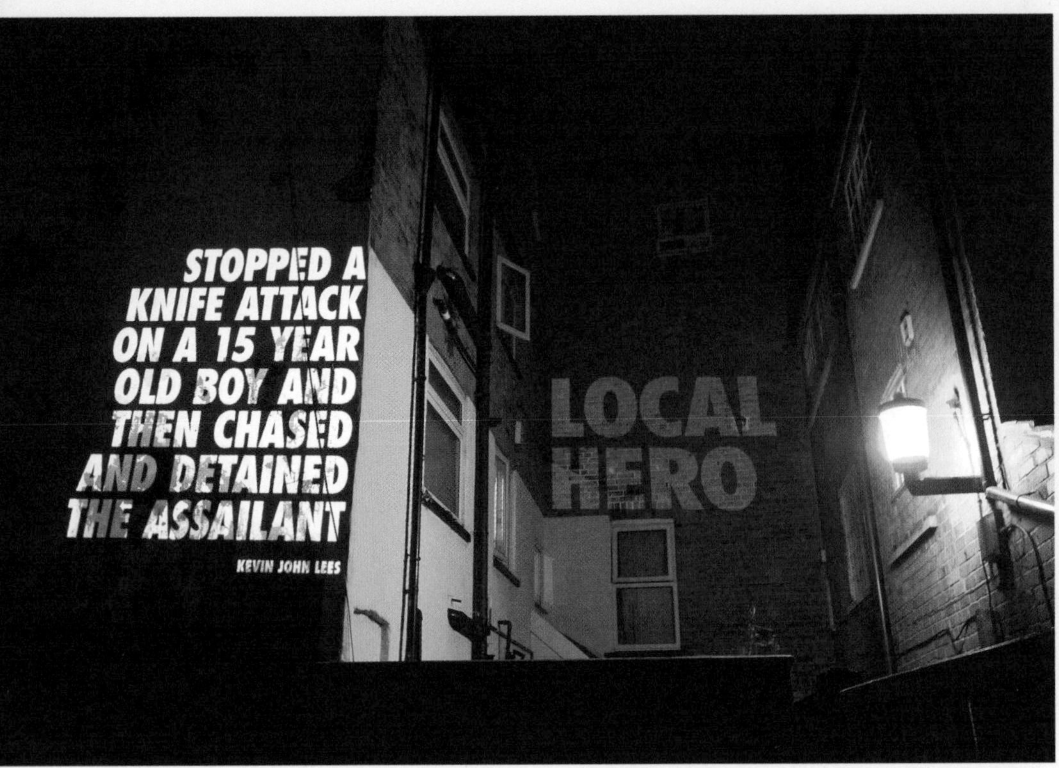

Student project by Holly Langford: Local Heroes, 2010

This project was a campaign created in an attempt to bring together urban communities in the East Midlands, to raise awareness within the community of individuals who have acted in challenging situations rather than turning a blind eye. Its ambition was to tackle the attitude of 'someone else will help'. The campaign set out to communicate directly with the audience in their environment. The sites selected were in urban areas where the street lighting was poor. Holly had discovered through her research and exploration the effectiveness of good lighting as a tool to deter crime. As a result the project developed two purposes: 'To take the message to the street and create an impact, I projected stories of local heroes' great achievements into the areas where they live. This idea was based on the fact that street lighting is more effective than CCTV at fighting crime. So by projecting the stories they are inspiring hope and are also protecting the area.'

Holly created the Local Heroes brand with the hope that it would inspire people, improve the sense of community spirit, ownership and strength. The brar would extend across other platforms as it progresse using both direct mail and an interactive interface t engage people. The direct mail would be an annual publication that would celebrate 'Heroes' and their stories, bringing the local heroes to the attention of a national audience. The proposed website and app would offer people the opportunity to post their stor The interface is live and charts each story's location and details on a national map. As time passes, the online community grows and the map fills with locators that can be clicked to gain access to the stc it is a 'good news' site, an online beacon bringing positivity and hope.

This project was the result of a great deal of research, experimentation and development in Holly's final year. She tried out numerous ideas before settling on this approach. Holly went out into the local community with projectors and set up the environmental graphics to see if the idea of using light as part of the message delivery would work. She tested out her ideas and analyzed and adapted the outcomes according to her findings. Her use of media is driven by experimentation; she uses established channels to communicate where appropriate but also exploits the potential of new media alongside this to ensure effective delivery of the message.

So far we have looked at student projects within these pages, but this does not mean that these are the only projects where inspiration and experimentation play a key role! The practices we begin as students will continue throughout our careers as professional designers. If we maintain the willingness to look, explore and experiment with ideas and approaches to our work we will continue to evolve, and new ideas may be found or inspired by a multitude of things.

Editing data for inspiration

Data is collected from a variety of sources. Increasingly, our experiences are documented through data that is collected on the most mundane of items, such as our mobile phones. How many calls we make, their duration, the number of text messages, even how many photographs we have taken and where, along with what music we have listened to, all go some way to recording our daily lives. The data tells stories about us. It is the job of the information designer to edit and interpret these stories visually for the audience to clearly understand. The designer filters out the unnecessary information and concentrates on finding the interesting points, so that the story is communicated succinctly without any interference.

Information designers explore and understand data through visualization. By presenting facts, figures or statistics in space rather than as numbers or text, the viewer finds it easier to understand. Humans have an innate ability to recognize patterns and relationships. When information is depicted visually, these relationships and patterns become easier to identify. The designer has the task of disassembling the data, analyzing it and then reassembling it in a simplified form. By doing this the stories buried within the data become visible through the graphic abilities the designer employs, such as navigation and abstraction. The facts and the interrelationships between them become transparent.

Creative use of data: Nicholas Felton

Nicholas Felton and his annual reports are a prime example of how showing data creatively tells stories. Felton documents personal events, such as social relationships, travel, food and emotions for each year, and presents them as a printed document.

This began in 2004, when Nicholas produced an end-of-year report called 'Best of 04'. In it he included some statistics about his year, such as how many air miles he had travelled. The following year he produced his first annual report. Within the report he detailed several categories he thought would be of interest to family and friends. These included his photographs, music he had listened to and books he had read throughout the year. By 2007 he was documenting his habits scrupulously. Online services such as Flickr and Last FM kept records of his photographic experiences and listening habits, while his computer calendar kept records of meetings and events. Along with information from free sites about weather and maps, Felton compiled a huge amount of information about his daily life. He then input the data into spreadsheets to enable comparisons and patterns to be identified within the material. Once the focal points had been identified he began the design phase. He says: 'My chief concern is that the finished graphic should be highly scannable and easily digested. For me this means the elimination of keys and fiddly lines attaching labels to items. Relationships should be as direct and unadorned as possible' (*IDN* magazine interview, 2008, vol. 15, no. 4, p. 32). In his 2010 annual report, Nicholas documented his father's life after he had passed away. It was compiled from the physical ephemera, such as calendars, slides and other artifacts, in his possession. Nicholas has since published a stunning report for 2010/2011.

2010–2011 annual report by Nicholas Felton.

In New York City

2010—2011

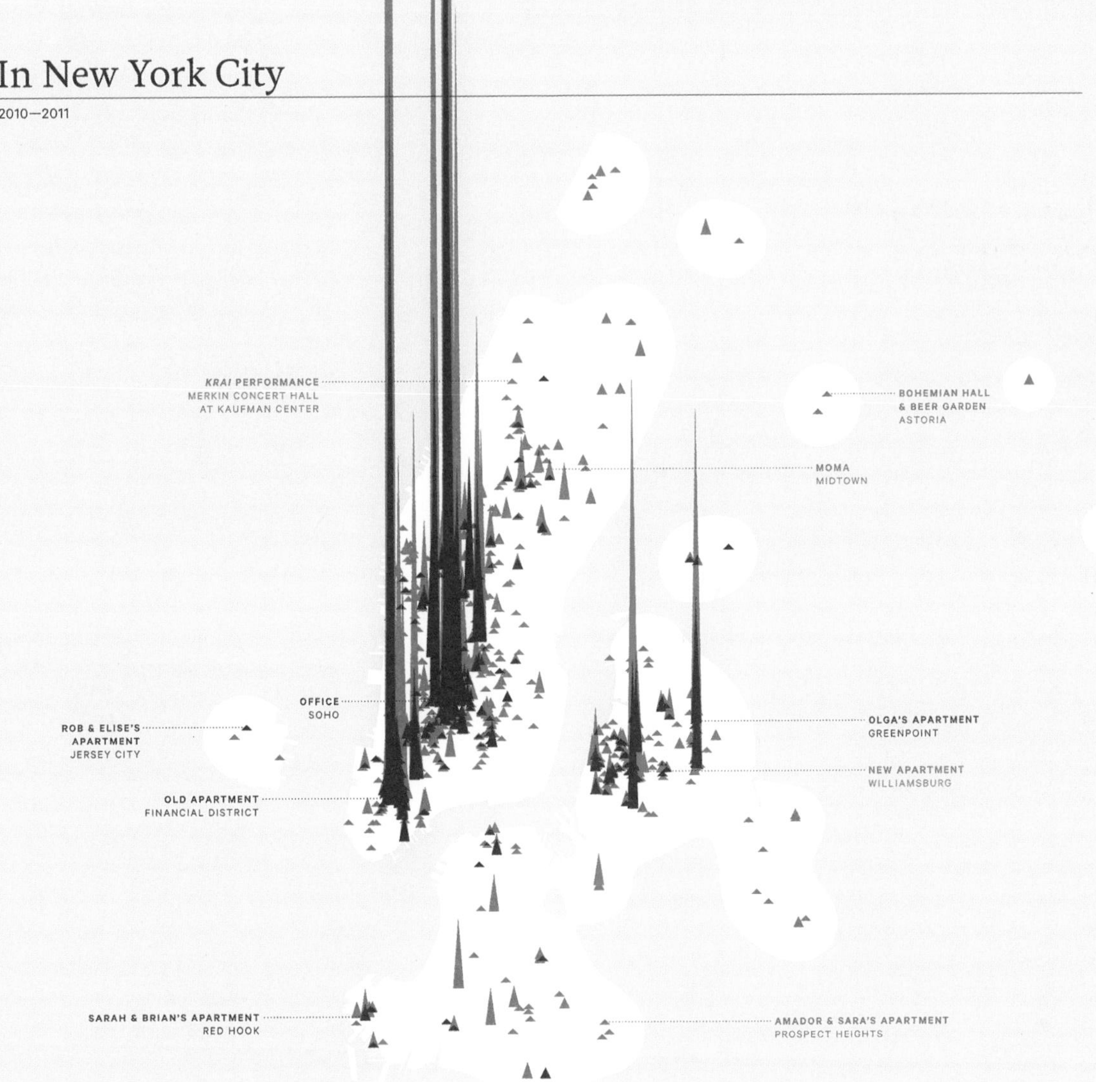

DAYS SPENT IN NEW YORK CITY

442¾

61% of each year

TIME IN NYC BOROUGHS

MANHATTAN — 377¾ DAYS

BROOKLYN — 61½ DAYS

QUEENS — 3½ DAYS

BRONX

STATEN ISLAND

NYC PLACES VISITED

648

173 restaurants, 121 shops, 55 bars, 41 outdoor places, 39 offices, 35 delis, 34 coffee shops, 22 homes, 20 venues, 16 grocery stores, 13 galleries, 11 banks, 9 museums, 8 airport terminals, 7 hotels, 7 liquor stores, 7 schools, 6 drug stores, 4 train stations, 4 open houses, 4 post offices, 3 laundromats, 3 movie theaters, 2 parks, 2 rental car locations, a dance studio, a gas station, a gym, mini-storage and work

MOST VISITED NYC SHOPS

FEDEX, SPRING STREET — 9 VISITS

J. CREW LIQUOR STORE — 8 VISITS

PETLAND DISCOUNTS — 7 VISITS

VITSOE — 7 VISITS

APPLE STORE SOHO — 6 VISITS

MOST VISITED DELI

Broadway Gourmet Food Market

584–588 Broadway — 30 visits

RATIO OF NYC SUBWAY TO TAXI TRIPS

5¾:1

1,147 subway vs. 202 taxi trips

FAVORITE NYC BEVERAGE

Filter Coffee

296 servings

TIME IN NYC SPENT IN RESTAURANTS

5%

Twenty Eleven

EVERYTHING

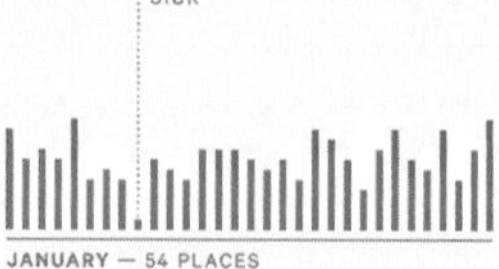

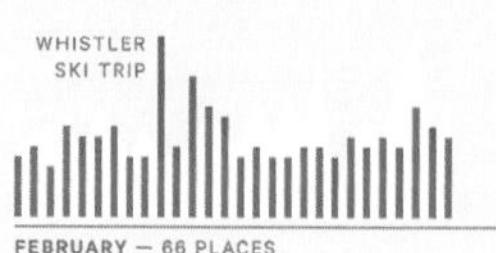

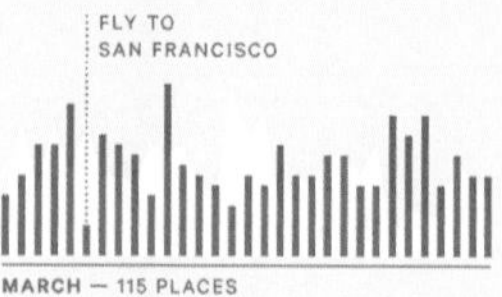

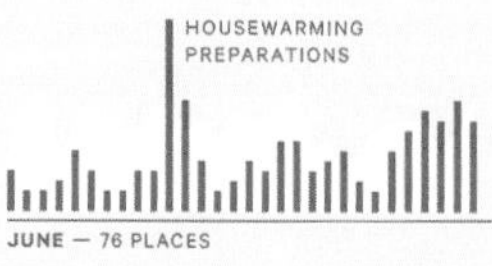

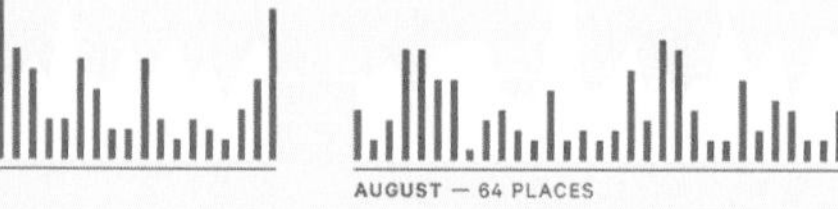

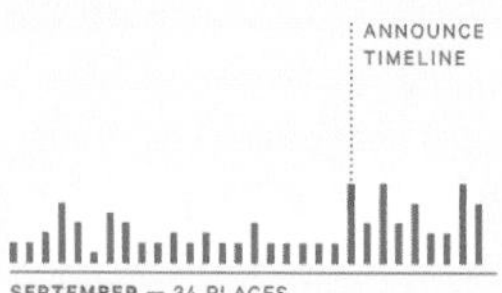

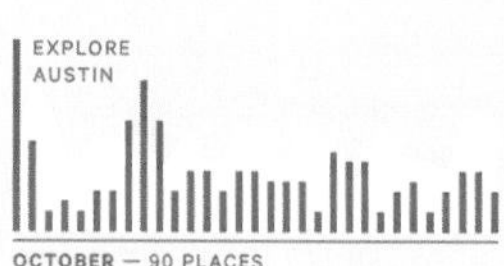

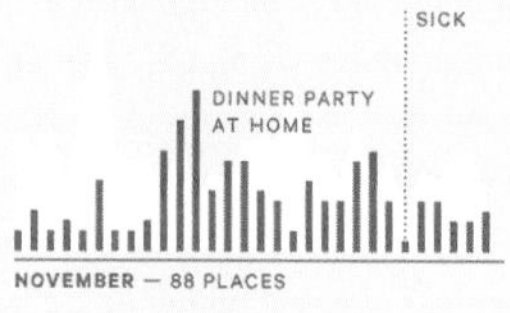

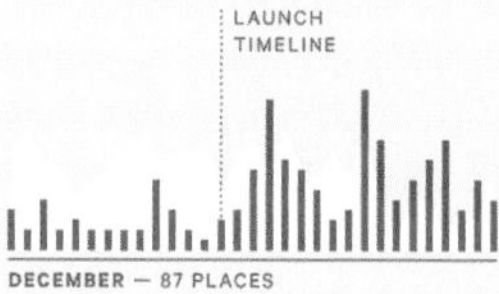

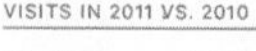

PLACES VISITED

in 63 cities, 10 states and 3 countries

MOST FREQUENTED PLACES

OFFICE — 242 VISITS

FACEBOOK 1601 — 189 VISITS

OLD APARTMENT — 138 VISITS

PALO ALTO APARTMENT — 132 VISITS

LA COLOMBE SOHO — 104 VISITS

HOURS AT WORK

2,567½

Approximately 49 hours a week

HARDEST WORKING DAY OF THE WEEK

Tuesday

505 hours worked in 2011

MILES RUN

88¾

Approximately 3 miles per run

TEETH LOST BY CAT

One

June 4, 2011 — his remaining canine

TIME WITH FRIENDS AND FAMILY

BEVERAGES RECORDED

1,916

256 different types

FAVORITE BEVERAGE

Filter Coffee

649 consumed

ALCOHOLIC BEVERAGES

806

42% of all beverages excluding water

MEDIAN BEER TIME

7:30 PM

For 521 beers

MILES WALKED

1,009

Approximately 2¾ miles a day

TIME SPENT WITH...

OLGA — 75¾ DAYS

RYAN — 70 DAYS

MATT — 19 DAYS

AMADOR — 15 DAYS

MOM — 14¾ DAYS

ROB — 7¼ DAYS

MARINA — 5¾ DAYS

SARAH — 3½ DAYS

BRIAN — 3½ DAYS

OLGA'S MOM — 3¼ DAYS

DAYS SPENT IN TRANSIT

33¼

11 days spent flying

BEST CELEBRITY ENCOUNTER

Dieter Rams

May 5, 2011 — at NYC Vitsœ Shop

MOST AVOIDABLE INJURY

Split Eyebrow

Walked into a door in Whistler Village

PRESIDENTIAL CHOCOLATES ENJOYED

One

April 26, 2011 — shared by Mark

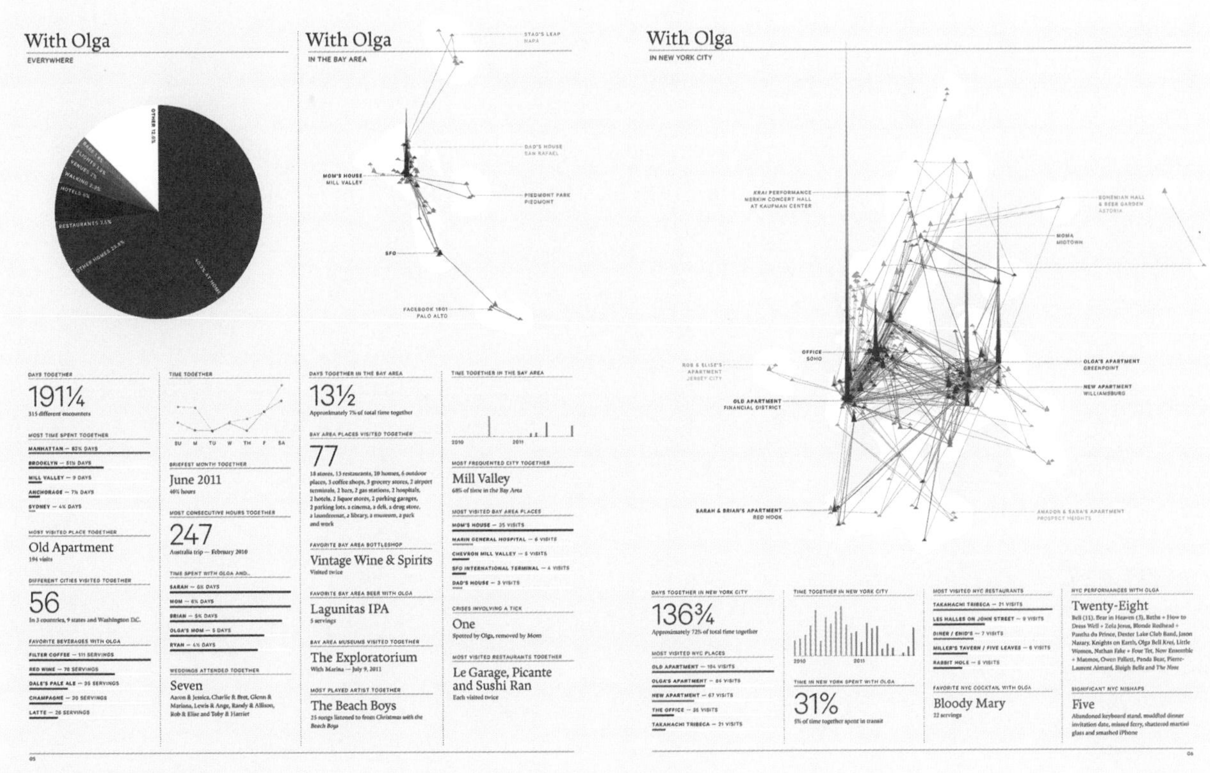

2010–2011 annual report by Nicholas Felton.

The importance of trying out ideas

Once the data has been collected and edited, the information is used to generate ideas. In this phase, the designer attempts several concepts in order to communicate the data. The designer will often explore structure, image and typography, developing grids, styles of imagery and typographic elements, which will help the clear communication of the message. The more ideas the designer generates, the greater the ability to compare their effectiveness and analyze the possibilities to ensure they are fit for purpose.

Sketching is one of the most immediate ways for a designer to explore their ideas by visually building and refining them. It is a valuable tool to rough out and develop ideas for a brief. It is simple and cheap and the process allows the designer to resolve issues quickly. Some designers keep sketchbooks to develop ideas; others work on separate sheets of paper. Whichever method is used, the premise of refining through progressive drawing remains the same.

Trying out ideas: Tanya Holbrook

Tanya Holbrook is a designer for Fallon in London. While studying for her degree in graphic design she completed a project that mapped her carbon footprint for the year 2007. This project looked at the journeys she had undertaken within that year, such as walking, driving and flying.

While developing the project, Tanya tried out several ways to interpret the data she had collected. It had to be analyzed and edited to pick out the most relevant facts and statistics in order to tell the story of her travels for the year. Certain pieces of information appeared too detailed, others not detailed enough. The comparison of local, national and international had to be made and then some way to portray the data coherently to an audience had to be found. She analyzed the mileage from her cars, looked at the travel tickets she had kept and also looked at the work of other designers.

She went through the data and edited it, looking at various stereotypical ways that most designers would use to depict it. The process of editing can be very difficult, as the designer is trying to select facts, figures or statistics that indicate relationships or facilitate some sort of comparison. Just telling someone you have travelled 20,000 miles in a year in your car doesn't mean much until you realize the national average is 8,000 miles. The data needs to be set in context to make it meaningful.

The sketchbook Tanya produced for this project is interesting because she has included her references from contemporary design along with drawings and notes on the data that helped her arrive at her final solution.

Since the project was about distance travelled and destinations, the inclusion of a map was explored to give a sense of distance and direction. Tanya experimented with how much of the map she could show without it becoming the focal point of the information. By reducing and simplifying the map, Tanya was able to suggest distances by looking at the relative positioning between destinations and their orientation to each other. She decided to use directional lines to suggest the pathways and used different thicknesses to denote frequency. All of this was arrived at through a process of trial and error in the sketchbook, constantly analyzing and evaluating the visuals to make sure they communicated the key information clearly and consistently. The final poster

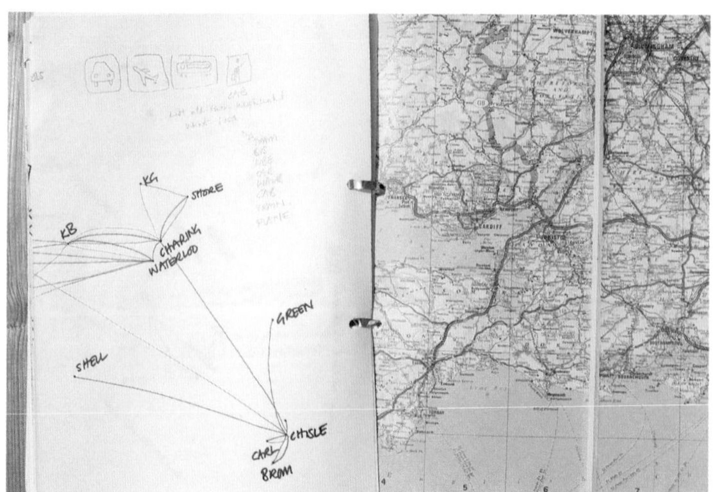

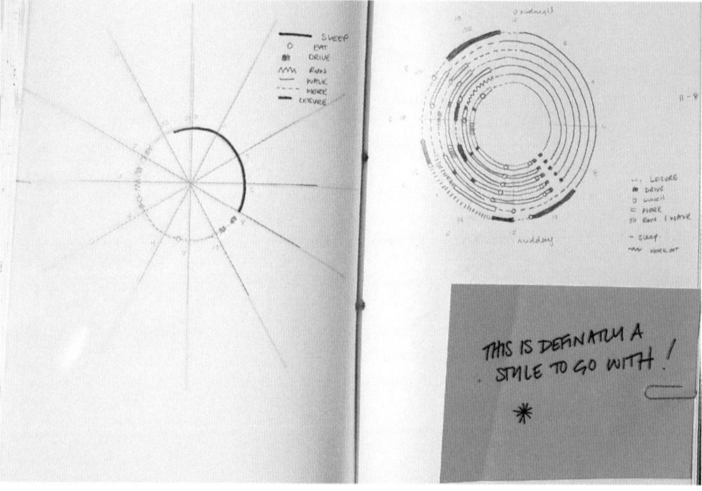

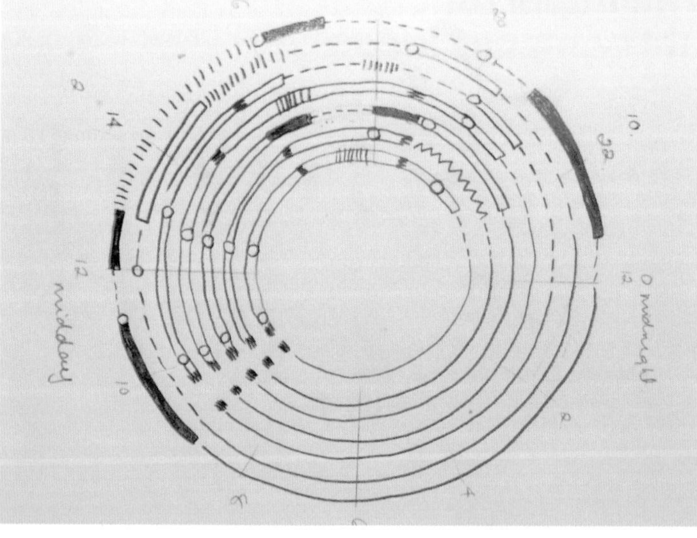

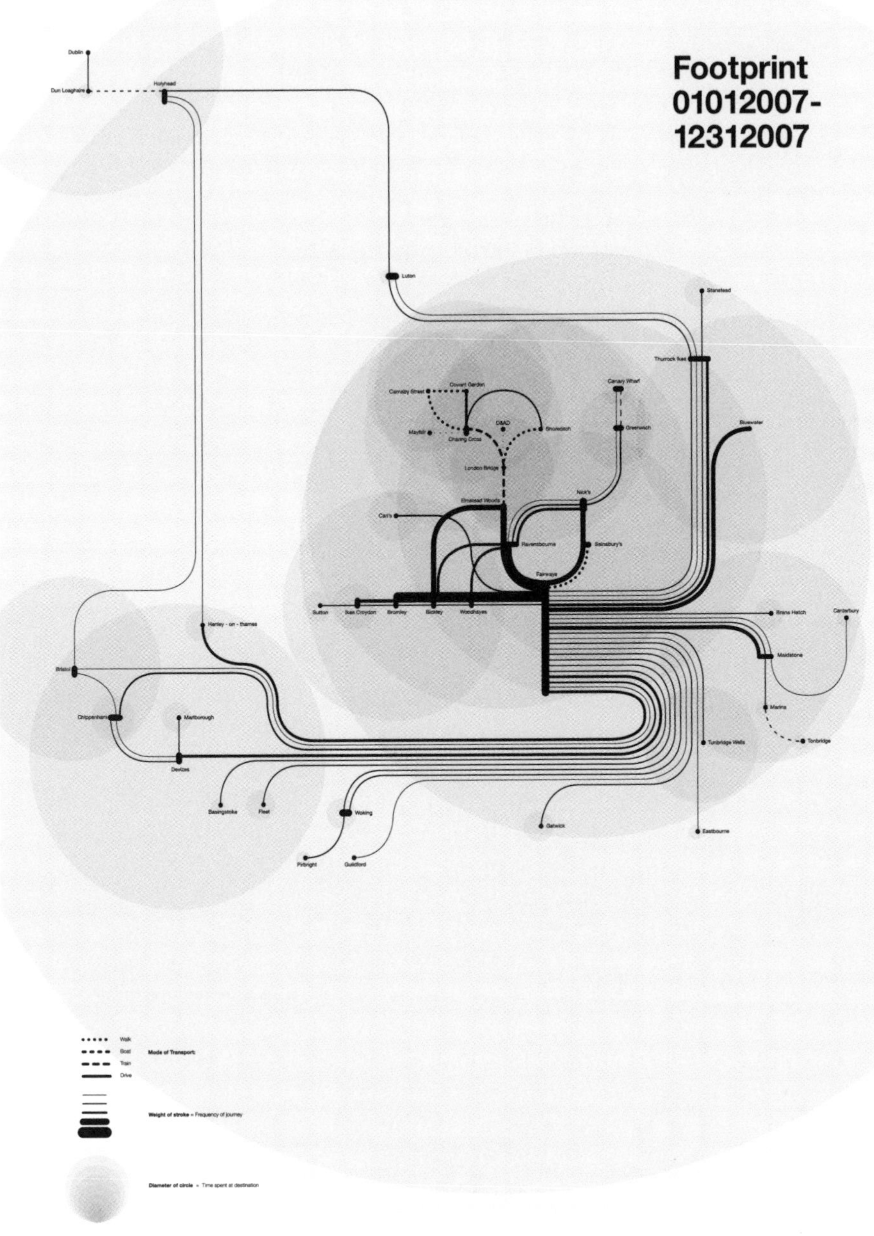

Opposite, top: In her sketchbook, alongside a map, Tanya looks at destinations and relative distances travelled locally and develops icons for mode of transport.

Opposite, centre: The development work continues by looking at radial designs to map out and categorize daily routines and the amount of time spent walking, driving, running, etc.

Opposite, bottom: Radial design exploring the time spent undertaking different activities in a day.

Left: Tanya's final design, which demonstrates the various destinations visited in a year, the mode of transport, frequency of visits and amount of time spent at each one.

is produced in black, white and shades of grey and uses minimal text. Tanya has commented that although she likes the poster aesthetically, the process of designing it was far more interesting and challenging. The project shows that there are stories hidden in seemingly mundane data. She realized that she had driven a half-mile stretch of road between her home and college an awful lot. It made her more aware of her habits and behaviour. Today, devices such as the Nike+ Sportswatch GPS are tracking, recording and presenting data. Through sensors, the watch records calories burnt, location and distance moved. As a result it can tell our stories automatically.

HINTS & TIPS

Taking inspiration from the world around you

Information design is no different from other design disciplines: it is a creative endeavour that has a rational outcome. Inspiration is key to any creative activity, but it does not come about through divine intervention. Designers naturally tend to be curious individuals; this curiosity can be beneficial as they can take inspiration from areas other than graphic design. If you keep an open mind you may find that the past and the present offer a rich source of inspiration for designs. Art, film, culture, music, architecture, sculpture, furniture and fashion all influence how we view the world. In turn, they provide us with visual shapes, forms, colours, textures, type forms and organizational structures, if you look closely enough.

Taking inspiration: News Knitter

One such project that takes inspiration from an unusual source is that of News Knitter. This piece of data visualization by Mahir M. Yavuz and Ebru Kurbak at the University of Art and Design in Linz, Austria, started as a quest for an alternative medium to envisage live data streams. They realized that text and imagery designs on clothes were quite common. They asked themselves, 'How can ephemeral information, which is generated, absorbed and evaluated by real people on a daily basis, be materialized, attached back to the physical body and enter urban daily life?'

Diagram showing the process of the News Knitter project. This details gathering the data, analyzing and generating the patterns from it, and finally sending that information to the knitting machine to produce the garments.

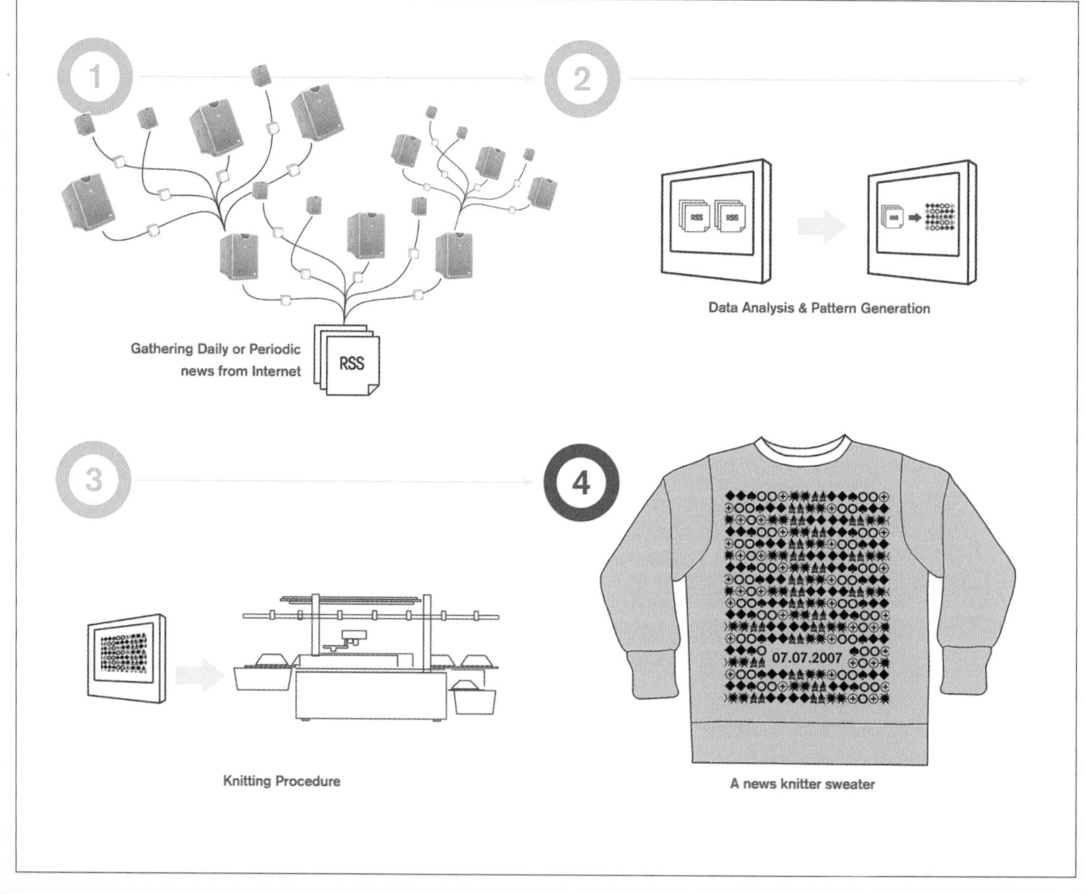

The key idea was to translate digital data into the physical world. Since all digital information is in the form of binary code consisting of just 1s and 0s, the information can be readily converted into an analogue format via a piece of software.

The project uses the form of knitted garments, in this case sweaters, as an alternate way to present and visualize large amounts of data. Through the means of knitting, digital information is visualized as a three-dimensional tactile item. Ebru and Mahir have commented, 'Knitting builds up a meaningful whole from a mass of strings, just like information networks of virtual space are made up from digital bits. Knitting is very different to printing, as it has a structural order that can be constructed and deconstructed at any time.'

Fashion is always looking at other disciplines such as architecture and pattern for inspiration. In this instance, the tables have been turned and it is the information designers finding inspiration in the pattern and make-up of the fashion item.

Top: The garments on display at Ars Electronica Festival in Linz in 2007. The exhibition consists of ten unique sweaters that are produced as sample outputs of the News Knitter project. Using online global or local Turkish news from a particular day or a time period generated the patterns of the sweaters.

Above: Garments being produced in Istanbul using Shima Seiki's computerized flat knitting machines.

The project takes live data streams of news stories around the world and translates them into a pattern to be used in the construction of the garments. The nature of the data streams means the patterns generated are all unique and unpredictable. The software Processing (see Chapter 5) takes information from live news feeds from the internet, filters them and then converts the results into different visual patterns, both graphical and typographic. Typographic patterns are composed according to their time of publication, point size of headline and popularity. Graphical patterns are generated by the popularity of the news items and particular keywords. The frequency of these keywords denotes the colour and scale of the shapes used to depict them – in this case, a plus sign or bar.

Once the patterns have been generated, a knitting machine is used to produce the final items of clothing. Each sweater is the culmination and interpretation of a specific period or day. The designers used online global news or local Turkish news to generate the patterns.

The final presentation of these garments was through an exhibition shown at the Ars Electronica Festival in Linz in 2007. Ten unique sweaters were produced as sample outputs of the News Knitter project. Following this first exhibition, News Knitter was exhibited all around the world, including at the electronic arts festivals Siggraph and Isea.

This project proves that you shouldn't be afraid to seek stimulation from unusual or unrelated sources. Although you may have to adapt or compromise your interpretation of them within the design process, the resulting solution turns out to be more engaging and unique if you look beyond the obvious places for inspiration.

Top: Sweater showing a typographic pattern, generated using the point size of the text to show a story's popularity among global news items.

Above: Sweater showing a graphical pattern, generated by the popularity of news items and particular keywords. The frequency of these keywords denotes the colour and scale of the shapes used to depict them, in this case, a plus sign or bar.

HINTS & TIPS

Some ideas on finding inspiration

Look beyond your own subject area for inspiration (architecture, art, music, philosophy, nature).

Be aware: engage with politics, culture and news.

Know your subject: designers past and present, the way they work, their attitudes, opinions and approaches.

Record your experiences: listen, photograph, collect, observe and explore.

Travel: inspiration can be found on the journey, not just at the destination (international or local); a ticket (the paper, colour or type); a conversation with a fellow passenger; the type of people you observe getting on or off the bus at different points; how and where they sit and what they do while in transit; the environments you travel through; the signs/typography you see outside the windows.

Sometimes the mundane can provide great inspiration and fascination.

Most importantly: be curious.

Some ideas on experimentation

Be open-minded and willing to explore diverse design directions. This may lead you to discover new and interesting ways to communicate, as well as shaping your own practice in unexpected ways.

Explore the potential of materials, media, formats and technologies within your design process.

Get your hands dirty; don't just talk or sketch what you might do: do it!

Don't be frightened of trying out new things; working beyond your comfort zone will ensure your practice evolves and improves.

Try out different approaches within your design process; ideas can be enhanced and communication improved by the selection of the most interesting and effective media, materials and format.

Guidelines on designing with information

KISS

Keep it Simple, Stupid (KISS). This guide is about simplifying elements and only including the essentials. This is so the audience is guided to the important data and not confused by any unnecessary information.

FOCUS

Select a particular element or elements to provide a focal point. That way it is easier for the viewer to decipher the message.

If possible, visualizations of data should:

- Have a clear purpose, such as a description, comparison or contextualization.
- Show the data and allow the audience to think about what the data means and not how it was made.
- Don't distort the information or mislead.
- Permit the viewer to uncover several layers of data from a broad overview to specific detail without confusing.
- Let the user compare different facts or statistics.
- Allow the audience to remember the data or facts clearly.
- Appreciate the user's intelligence.

Inspiration for the design process

Project: Wayfinding and signage for Great Ormond Street Hospital, London

Design: Landor Associates, London

Overview

For more than 150 years, Great Ormond Street Hospital for Children (GOSH) has been one of the world's leading children's hospitals, offering the highest levels of medical care. Over that time the hospital has grown to encompass many buildings across one central London site, all of which make it very difficult for visitors, patients and staff to find their way around. Due to a major redevelopment program that took place in 2012, GOSH felt it was the perfect opportunity to review their wayfinding and signage strategy.

GOSH approached Landor back in 2008, and a small team volunteered to work on the project. Landor's office was then located nearby, so the designers were able to get on-site quickly and often, enabling them to get a feel for the full extent of the hospital. A number of the Landor team had friends or relatives who had been patients at GOSH, so the team were able to understand the emotional needs all the more quickly.

Approach

Hospitals can be lonely, scary places, especially when you're a child. It can be hard to find your way around, and even harder to find a place to belong. The brief was to provide a theme, naming solution and guidelines for the floors and wards, to aid wayfinding. It needed to interest children of all ages, families and staff and have long-term appeal.

The hospital's philosophy, 'the child first and always', was at the heart of the strategy. There needed to be a theme that everyone could relate to, yet would be fun for children. With naming, the designers had to be creative while adhering to strict criteria – no negative cultural connotations, not too abstract, and be simple for non-English-language speakers to pronounce. The designers drew inspiration from the natural world – a theme that was already established within the hospital and one that gave the team the richness and diversity to create a captivating environment.

How's it
going dude?

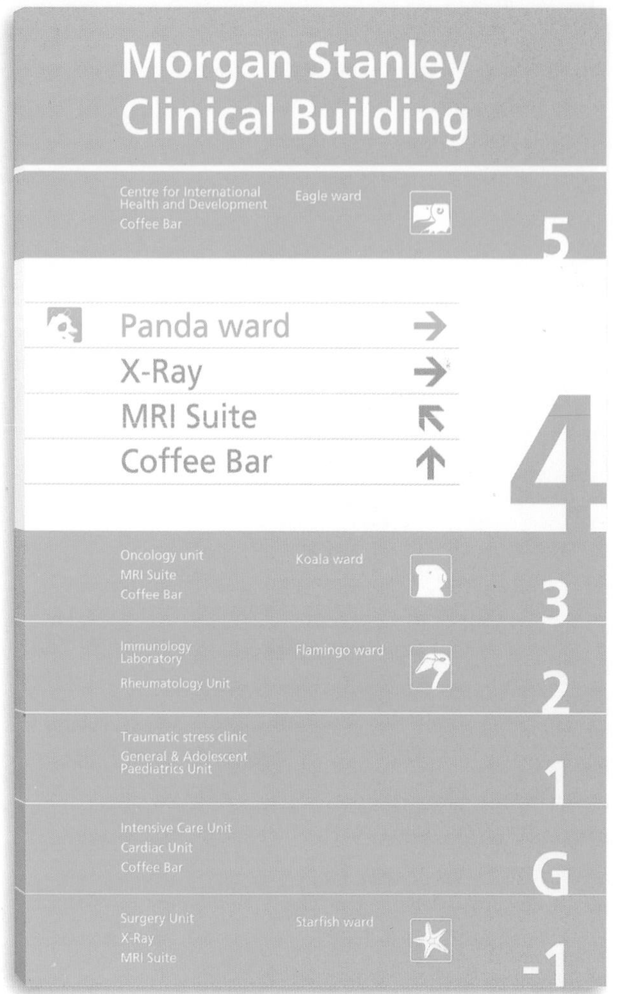

The team faced the challenge of producing a scheme that succeeded in the practical sense but that also appealed to the visitors/patients (the audience) who had to navigate the environment. The patients at GOSH range from newborn to 18 years old. Landor needed to create characters that would appeal to very young children – simple, recognizable shapes – but that also had an attitude and an aesthetic cool that would appeal to the older age group. As such, they tried to ensure that the animals had enough character to be unique to GOSH, but offered plenty of opportunity for people to project their own thoughts and stories onto them. In the end the team developed some rules of thumb: distinctive silhouettes that would work well as signage icons and also engage very young children, nothing overly abstracted to ensure recognition. They enjoyed adding small details and behaviours to the characters that would engage older children and adults.

Outcome

The new theme and wayfinding system provide clear direction in ways children understand, and animal characters appealing to all ages of the hospital's patients provide therapeutic distraction throughout the journey. Not just how to get there, but entertainment, education and a community of friends.

Landor split floors into natural habitats, from living in the oceans (lower ground floor) to living in the skies (top floor). The work has had a positive response from patients and families and the client is delighted with the new system, which will be implemented throughout the hospital as new buildings open.

Above left: Great Ormond Street wayfinding system, showing how the habitats are used on the ascending floors from oceans on the lower ground to skies on the fifth floor.

Left: Pictograms showing the various animals used for the ward names. The use of imagery means that visitors and patients can find their way easily without having to rely on text.

Opposite: The combination of traditional wayfinding system and expressive illustrative elements makes the environment pleasant as well as functional.

Frontage Building
The Morgan Stanley Clinical Building
Cardiac Wing
Variety Club Buildi
Follow me!
Toucan Ward
SCRABBLE

Project: Innovative approaches to information design research

Design: Dr Alison Barnes

Overview

Dr Alison Barnes is a practising designer and senior lecturer at the University of Western Sydney in Australia. She completed her PhD at the London College of Communication in London in 2011. Her thesis focused on the potential of interdisciplinary collaboration between graphic designers and cultural geographers, and in particular the communicative possibilities of typography and graphic design when used in relation to the understanding and representation of place.

Alison's work centres on exploring notions of everyday life and place through print-based graphic design. By everyday life, she means the kind of daily routines or things that we tend to take for granted. For her, these seemingly inconsequential events or items are fascinating. Whether it is a favourite ornament on a mantelpiece or the recycling of unwanted household goods, there is always a story waiting to be revealed. These stories, and the work that develops through them, are not driven by a commercial perspective, but by Alison's own personal interest. However, that is not to say that she would describe her work as 'self-indulgent'.

Below: The design of the grid and the setting of the typography have been developed conceptually. The grid is modular, designed in response to the notion of a collection being the sum of several parts. In places this is used in such a way to reference meaning within the text; for example, in the section of the essay that references collectors, the text is set in small blocks that begin to fill the page. At the end of the book, the text begins to break out of the grid, resembling a collection of separate, disconnected lines, to reflect the idea that on death, possessions that once held meaning more often than not simply revert to becoming inconsequential junk.

24
25
Collections
A collection is a self-contained entity within the stuff. It has clear parameters, defined not only by the individual,
but also by the elements of the collection itself. Unlike the imperceptible accumulation of stuff, collecting and collections
are purposeful acts. The Victorians were great collectors and at a time when the English were busy colonising the globe,
perhaps their collecting could be seen as a more local, personal element within this global exercise of power and control.
Collecting could still be seen as a way of obtaining a sense of control in our increasingly complex lives. We may not be
able to control the global economy, or even the local council, but our collection of wildlife ornaments or paperweights allows us
total control of this aspect of our own world.
Belk 1988:154

Please take
all photos
in Hackney
Your favourite place
Your favourite view
Something ordinary
Something unusual
Somewhere peaceful
Somewhere busy
What makes you happy?
What makes you sad or angry?
What do your dreams look like?
Take three pictures of anything you want to finish up the film.
Your Hackney
Daily Journey Log
Cream
memory n
remembrance, reminiscence
How has Your Hackney
changed?
recipe n
What don't you like
about Your Hackney?

Above: Cultural probes are designed to provide inspirational responses from participants, rather than the kind of information one would get from a traditional survey or questionnaire. Here, the pack includes a disposable camera, questions on postcards, a journey log, a recipe sheet and a memory sheet. However, the pack can be designed in relation to each project, so the contents can vary. The fact that the tasks are often quite creative, or more interesting than simply answering questions on a sheet of A4 paper, engages the participants in the research and makes the researchers seem less remote. The packs are not designed to be sent out in great numbers; this type of research is not about statistics and averages, but about more personal insights that can trigger an interesting idea for the development of the design work.

Approach

One of Alison's key motivations is to explore the potential within graphic design to communicate information or stories in ways that engage the reader in an interactive space of exploration. She is also keen to develop a broader idea of what the design process encompasses, and specifically the research aspect of that process. As a student, one is encouraged to research the brief, especially at the start of a project. However, often that goes no further than using methods such as searching the internet or library for information about the subject matter, the target audience or other examples of design work that relate to the aesthetics or style of product or artifact needing to be designed. While Alison does use secondary methods like these, she also likes to 'get out there', to site herself within the research, which enables her to develop a different perspective. By walking, photographing, taking notes, or just talking to people she builds up a range of different types of information, which she then uses to develop content for the work. These types of methods are often used in other subject areas and could be broadly defined as ethnographic. As a graphic designer, she finds crossing borders into other academic territories, like cultural geography for example, particularly interesting. She likes to take on new ideas and research methods from outside of design and interpret them from her position as a graphic designer. In a sense, she becomes something of a bricoleur, someone who constructs their approach using a range of diverse research methods specifically chosen to respond to the particular situation that is of interest

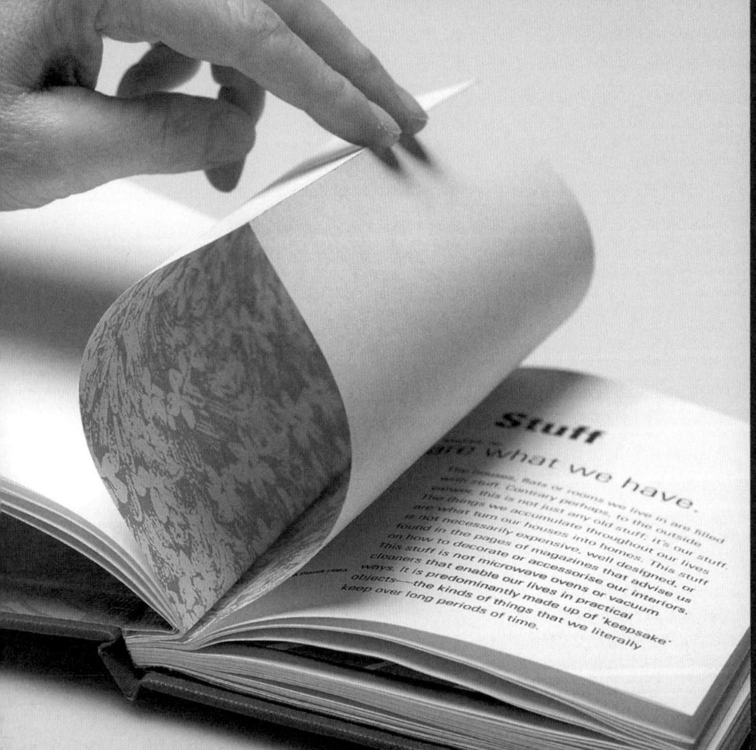

Above: *Stuff* also includes envelopes that contain ephemeral artifacts that the reader can handle; for example, old photographs, stamps, cigarette cards and handwritten cards and letters. Handling these objects creates a pause within the process of exploration of the book and enables the reader to reflect not only on these objects, but also on similar objects that may relate to their own possessions and memories.

Left: A book is essentially a collection of bound pages, and with limited-edition work it is easy to explore the potential of non-traditional materials. For example, *Stuff* includes perfumed drawer liners as pages, which bring a multi-sensory dimension to the reader's experience, and glassine paper to protect the full-bleed photographs. These pages reference the type of materials one might find in an older relative's house, which could be used when storing precious possessions in drawers or compiling a traditional family photograph album.

Much information design these days seems to be
lefined by the use of coloured graphic elements drawn n Adobe Illustrator that represent facts and nformation (often numerical), presented in large poster format. Alison finds this kind of work beautiful, out also finds herself regularly unable to sustain any nterest beyond the immediate aesthetic impact it offers. In her work, she likes to engage with elements ncluding language, typography, paper stock, folding and format to produce graphic design that attempts to go beyond this type of skeletal landscape of statistics. She likes to interpret and design with information in a way that offers the reader a more 'open' experience. Rather than 'close down' the information and suggest here is one correct reading, she prefers to edit and lesign with it in a way that enables the reader to become a more active participant in the process of engaging with the information. Sometimes this could be by using materials that engender a multi-sensory experience, with smell and touch used alongside vision. It could be through the execution of the ypography that is set within the pages so it offers nultiple reading paths through columns that run both vertically and horizontally. Within the design of books, t could perhaps be through format, by drawing the reader in to find information hidden within French olds, gatefolds or books within books. It could even be hrough the inclusion of hidden ephemeral artifacts within the piece that the reader can then find and handle. All of these types of interaction help place the reader within the story, to induce the use of a fuller range of senses that offer a more 'experiential journey', one where they not only reflect on the information, mages and stories contained within the set text, but also on how similar experiences or information mpacts on, or is present in, their own lives.

Outcome

For Alison, information and inspiration can be found everywhere, even in the seemingly most insignificant places. The challenge is to work with the methods and processes of graphic design in such a way as to nake the everyday as fascinating for the reader as t is for her; to reposition the ultra-ordinary as the extra-ordinary. That is the power of information design.

This chair makes me think of falling in love with London.
SG, 2000

Interaction can be created through the use of interesting formats and binding. Here the pages are French folded, which creates a hidden pocket in each page. These have been used to position captions that relate to the photographs on the outside of some of the pages. The photographs are seemingly ordinary as far as the reader is concerned, but for the owner they are deeply meaningful possessions that contain important memories. The reader, therefore, has to literally search beneath the surface of the image to reveal the meaning that each item holds.

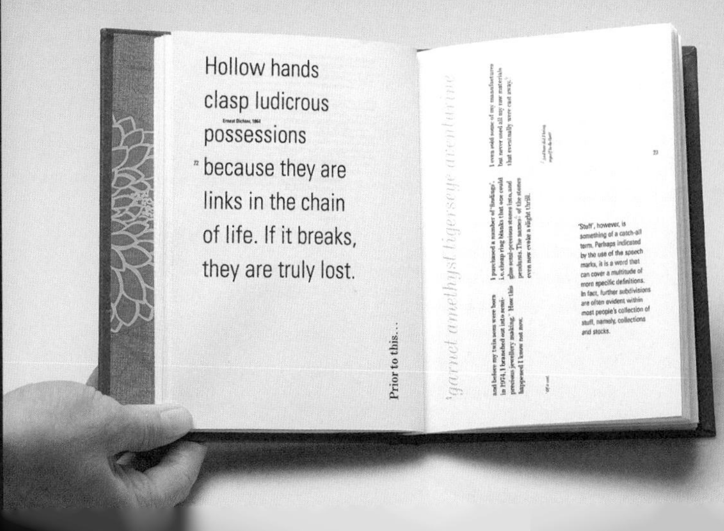

Hollow hands clasp ludicrous possessions because they are links in the chain of life. If it breaks, they are truly lost.
Prior to this...

EVERYONE EVER IN THE
3200 BCE TO
during the recorded history of humankind — 669.39 MILLION
THE LUXURY OF PROTEST
1996_Ethnic Conflict in Nagaland
1996_Naxalite–Maoist Insurgency
1996_Nepal Civil War
Civil War in Chad
2003_Islamic Insurgency in Saudi Arabia
2004_Haitian Rebellion
2007_Ingushetia Civil War
2008_Invasion of Anjouan

Chapter 7: Information design in practice: print, interactive and environmental

In this chapter, we focus on how the final outcomes were achieved on a diverse range of projects. These have been selected to represent three areas: print, interactive and environmental design. We explore the problem-solving routes the designers have taken on each project. The case studies discuss what challenges have been faced and, in some instances, what the restrictions or opportunities may have been when designing for one of these specific modes of delivery.

Design outcomes

In this chapter, we seek to highlight and identify the different considerations that have to be taken into account when designing information for a particular medium. The creators of each project featured offer insights into their approach and what their intentions and ambitions were when working on these specific briefs. We ask what inspires them and what influences their initial ideas and subsequent design directions, and ultimately how they realized these in the final outcome.

We hope you agree that the diversity of the work featured in this chapter is testament to the possibilities and the breadth of outcomes achievable within these three distinct fields of information design.

Routes for print-based information design

Information design in print takes many forms. It is often considered to be mainly charts and diagrams in books, but, as we have established in earlier chapters, a page in a newspaper is a form of information design just as a printed sign in the city centre is. We are surrounded by pieces of information every day in the form of printed matter: the books we read; the printed bus timetable at the bus stop, and even the nutritional information on the chocolate bar we eat.

When we talk about print, though, we are not just talking about ink on paper. The very fabric of print can be used to explore and explain a concept. The medium can be part of the message communicated. Printed matter uses ink on a substrate or stock to generate the image or design. However, there are other ways of generating a design on a surface. This could be offset lithography, screen-printed, etched, laser- or die-cut, embossed or debossed. The stock itself can be opaque, semi-translucent or completely transparent.

Over the following pages we have showcased some examples of innovative print design. These discuss how to structure information and also how to use the medium itself as a way of enhancing and communicating a message.

Previous page: Everyone Ever in the World, poster designed by The Luxury of Protest (see pp. 170–73).

Opposite: Printed clothing label with washing instructions.

30°
MACHINE WASH COLD 30°
DO NOT BLEACH
WARM IRON
DO NOT DRY CLEAN

Print-based information design

Project: *Culture and Climate Change: Recordings*, book produced for The Open University, UK, 2011

Design: Hyperkit, London

Hyperkit are a London-based design studio founded in 2001 by Kate Sclater and Tim Balaam. They describe their work as 'good-natured, useful design, often bringing together a love of material, process and functionality'. Hyperkit produce work across a variety of platforms including print, digital, exhibition and interiors. Here we feature a printed editorial outcome.

Overview

Culture and Climate Change: Recordings is a book produced for The Open University, the largest distance learning university in the UK. Kate Sclater describes the project: 'The subject of this book is cultural responses to climate change. The challenge of the brief was to create a publication that, whilst being made up solely of text, was visually engaging. It had to be clearly laid out and easy to read, but with a personality that reflected the nature of the content.'

The book contains a mix of essays, transcripts and information, with no images, only text. The largest section of the book features transcripts of four discussions that took place between artists, academics, producers and journalists. Each discussion includes mention of various exhibitions, performances and publications, most of which needed expanding upon through the use of fairly lengthy footnotes. The editors were keen to give the footnotes a presence alongside the main text, not simply list them at the back of the volume.

Approach

Hyperkit took on board these intentions. Their response was to create structure within the pages through the use of a grid, typefaces and limited colour; these 'tools' combined to create an effective hierarchy. Different typefaces were selected and applied to distinguish content type; this helps the reader navigate the information effectively, but also provides visual interest and personality to the overall piece.

To communicate the fact that the book is intended to be a practical resource, the designers decided to use a soft cover reminiscent of a textbook, with a cloth spine to add interest. They also listed the names of all the contributors on the cover.

Kate explains, 'Using a palette restricted to two colours, we employed various techniques to navigate the publication and to differentiate between these types of content. There are changes in type size, grid and colour, of both the text and the page background. We also employed three different typefaces – a serif face, a sans serif face and a typewriter-style face – each of which acts as a visual device in communicating the different types of content. In order to allow for the extensive footnotes, two of the columns in the three-column grid are used for the transcript, while the third is used for the notes. The notes appear in the highlight colour and employ the typewriter-style typeface, giving a hint to their purpose. Within the main text, the word or phrase relevant to the note is highlighted in blue and this, along with the proximity of the note, eliminates the need for numbering, thereby reducing visual clutter.'

At the start, a series of essays use the full width of the page and appear in the serif typeface Galaxie Copernicus. The middle section, the transcripts, uses the sans-serif face Aperçu. The back section of the book, which includes a timeline and other resources, uses a tinted background and makes use of the typewriter-style face Elementa. New sections are denoted by a page of fully bled colour.

Outcome

The project is a good example of a simple and elegant use of colour, typeface and grid structure to add order and hierarchy to a design. The text-only book could have appeared rather daunting and visually unappealing to read. Hyperkit have, however, produced a piece that is pleasing to the eye and easy for the audience to navigate and decode. The understanding of the content and the need for the extensive footnotes has been interpreted visually to strong effect. The rationale for the proximity of positioning and colour-coding means the need for a key or numbering system is no longer necessary, making for pages that are less text-heavy and clearly show what is important.

This 112-page soft-cover book, perfect bound (a solely adhesive-based binding) and with a cloth spine, is printed in two colours throughout. The main body of the book is a series of transcripts presented in black text. These contain extended footnotes by the authors, which are presented in blue copy.

Culture and Climate Change: Recordings

Contributors

BERGIT ARENDS
MARCUS BRIGSTOCKE
ROBERT BUTLER
NIGEL CLARK
QUENTIN COOPER
SIOBHAN DAVIES
BETH DERBYSHIRE
ROGER HARRABIN
WALLACE HEIM
MIKE HULME
CHARLIE KRONICK
RUTH LITTLE
DIANA LIVERMAN
VICKY LONG
ELEANOR MARGOLIES
OLIVER MORTON
TIM SMIT
JOE SMITH
CAROLYN STEEL
RENATA TYSZCZUK

History

These four discussions address a new field: 'culture and climate change'. This is a subject that considers, among other things, the response of artists, writers, performers, musicians, broadcasters and comedians (and, through them, the audiences that they reach) to the changing climatic conditions in the world and, more significantly, to the challenges that come from the new idea that we are largely responsible for these changes. As producers of the podcast, and editors of this volume, we wanted to start by asking where this subject — culture and climate change — originated and how far back it goes. We wanted to see how much it was part of other strands of political, anti-industrial or apocalyptic thinking and whether it has taken the place of other familiar and deep-rooted anxieties about the spread of germs, for instance, or nuclear proliferation. When did the subject of culture and climate change first emerge, who first engaged with it, how has it developed, and in what ways does it differ from the kinds of subjects that are closely related to it?

The first of the discussions took place in the imposing surroundings of the Examination Schools at Oxford University in September 2010. It was the opening morning of the fifth TippingPoint conference to be held in Oxford and the audience comprised 100 or so conference participants, including artists, scientists, writers and theatre directors. On the panel were Nigel Clark, senior lecturer in human geography, Siobhan Davies, choreographer, Wallace Heim, writer and editor on environment and performance, and Diana Liverman, professor in environmental policy. The discussion was chaired by Quentin Cooper, presenter of BBC Radio 4's *Material World*.

Quentin began by explaining to the audience that these discussions aimed to establish a framework for thinking about these cultural responses, for making them more engaging and more wide-reaching. This being the first of the four discussions, he wanted to discover what has been effective so far and what hasn't, what has raised awareness and what — if anything — has changed policy, practice and behaviour.

The distinctive temporalities invoked by thinking and talking about climate change represent the sixth distinctive feature of the cultural politics of climate change. Economists and policy specialists have sought ways to give future generations a voice in the present, albeit through very attenuated or clumsy proxies such as 'discount rates' and 'policy targets'. Past generations can also be heard: from our prehistoric ancestors, who coped with earlier changes in climate with doggedness and imagination, to the more recent ancestors who bequeathed inventions and discoveries that have changed both climate and our understanding of it, such as steam engines or techniques for retrieving and interpreting ice cores. Although contemporary human interests are more audible than those of the past, this expanded ethical, political and cultural community is increasingly present in our thoughts and actions. As Mike Hulme says in the discussion which is recorded here, the future 'is a place that we all live in, in our imaginations'.

Mike Hulme goes on to point out that climate change is 'both political and cultural' (page 76). It is the meeting points between these spheres which we have sought to explore in the four discussions documented in this publication. The six features I have outlined here — global pervasiveness, uncertainty, interdependency, the reverberations of history, interdisciplinarity and temporality — are shaping a new cultural politics which is, like climate itself, in a permanent state of change.

On constructing for the unforeseen
Renata Tyszczuk

When confronted by global environmental change, humanity has tended to try to forestall the predicted events — to stop the future happening. We tend to speak as if the solid certainties of our civilisation are under threat — a way of thinking that produces little more than anxiety. An alternative response might be to think in terms of 'improvisation': discussions around climate change might then serve as a context for exploring potential future worlds, opening up more promising possibilities for living on a fragile — for humans — and dynamic earth.

Our situation is precarious; several decades of earth systems science confirm that we live on an unpredictable planet. As Nigel Clark reminds us, the earth is astonishingly good at unleashing primordial forces of destruction and pulling the ground from under our feet (Clark, 2010). In the 'History' conversation documented in this book, he suggests that if we look back in time, we see evidence of our ancestors' resourceful responses to abrupt changes in climate and other natural disasters. Human existence on the planet has always been provisional; instability is in the nature of our existence.

Many of the systems and categories we assume to be fixed — whether economic, social, ecological or political — are actually 'conditions' or 'constructions', which are changeable. In recent years, the concepts of progress, modernity, the quest for certainty and the supposedly unshakeable foundations of knowledge have been questioned by philosophers such as Stephen Toulmin, who describes 'the scaffolding of modernity'

artist' label in a different way, in that theatre already has an anatomy or taxonomy. It's got a lot of different genres and any playwright writing a play that touches on climate change will either be writing a comedy or a tragedy or a farce... and that affects the way they write the play and the meaning of what they're writing. Part of *The Contingency Plan* by Steve Waters (2009) is set in Westminster and Whitehall. At one point a drink is spilt over the Cabinet Minister's trousers and he has to take his trousers off and hang them on the radiator to dry. Well, now we're drawing on the Whitehall farce, the Brian Rix farce, of people walking around in their underpants. So the form of the play is also a part of the meaning of the play.

Does anything that is labelled as climate change art automatically lose some of its power because it will turn off those who are not interested in the subject?

Charlie I think it loses its power by becoming polemic. It can be great polemic but it loses its power to speak to a broader audience because it will categorise and polarise the response. It doesn't matter who labels it — it will still have the same effect. It has a divisive effect not just on the viewer but also on the makers. I've met artists who are profoundly moved by the impacts of climate change and are very, very worried about the implications, not just for their own family but for society at large, but the last thing they want is to be described as a climate change artist. They feel quite strongly that it undermines the integrity and authenticity of their own work. It's the composite societal impact that interests me: what brings the work into that wider conversation, to the wider political reaction you have as a viewer, as a voter, as a citizen, as a consumer.

Just as there will be scientists who choose to step beyond science and towards activism because they see climate change as a clear and present danger and want to alert people around the world, there may be artists who choose to go beyond being an artist and step towards activism. Do they risk the negative categorisation Charlie has just described?

Beth This issue is emotional, and it's human. You may as an artist or a scientist have a particular discipline, but this is something that affects us all and it's emotional because it questions our future.

Robert Climate and discussion about climate will percolate all through different artists' lives and the way they think. It's impossible not to think about it. So it will surface in many different ways, in very different genres. You don't want people to go and see a work of art and think because it's about climate or climate change it's part of a small group of works. You want to think that it's more like the impact of Darwin in the nineteenth century: it impacts right across the range.

Bergit If we take apart this idea of 'climate change art', it's looking at systems, because climate change is understanding systems; it's looking at our relationship to nature, and our observation of nature; it's looking at the impact of climate change, what caused it in the first place, at energy use and how we can address that. It's all of these. It's a term that needs so much unpacking that it's not very helpful to call something 'climate change art', because you want to look at all these different aspects. We can trace our cultural evolution, and look at our place in nature for a start. Where do we think we are within the natural environment? We

Contributors
Resources
Timeline

Resources

Selected organisations

Selected reading

Selected viewing

Print-based information design

Project: Everyone Ever in the World, poster, 2010

Design: Peter Crnokrak of The Luxury of Protest, London

As this book demonstrates, there are many ways to communicate information to an audience, and print is just one of them. The possibilities offered within the printed medium can be investigated and experimented with; they can become key to the effectiveness and success of the overall communication of an idea or concept.

Peter Crnokrak is the Canadian designer and artist behind The Luxury of Protest, an experimental design platform founded in 2009. Originally a research scientist in the field of quantitative genetics, Crnokrak designs highly complex data visualizations. In his piece Everyone Ever in the World, Crnokrak takes a complex piece of data and explores the possibilities of print, format and composition. He utilizes a variety of materials, techniques and print finishes that relate to the content he is communicating within the piece. Nothing is purely decorative, everything is considered, evaluated and reasoned. The use of paper, spot varnish, die- and laser-cutting are an intrinsic part of the overall communication; they all carry meaning and help convey the information within the piece to the audience.

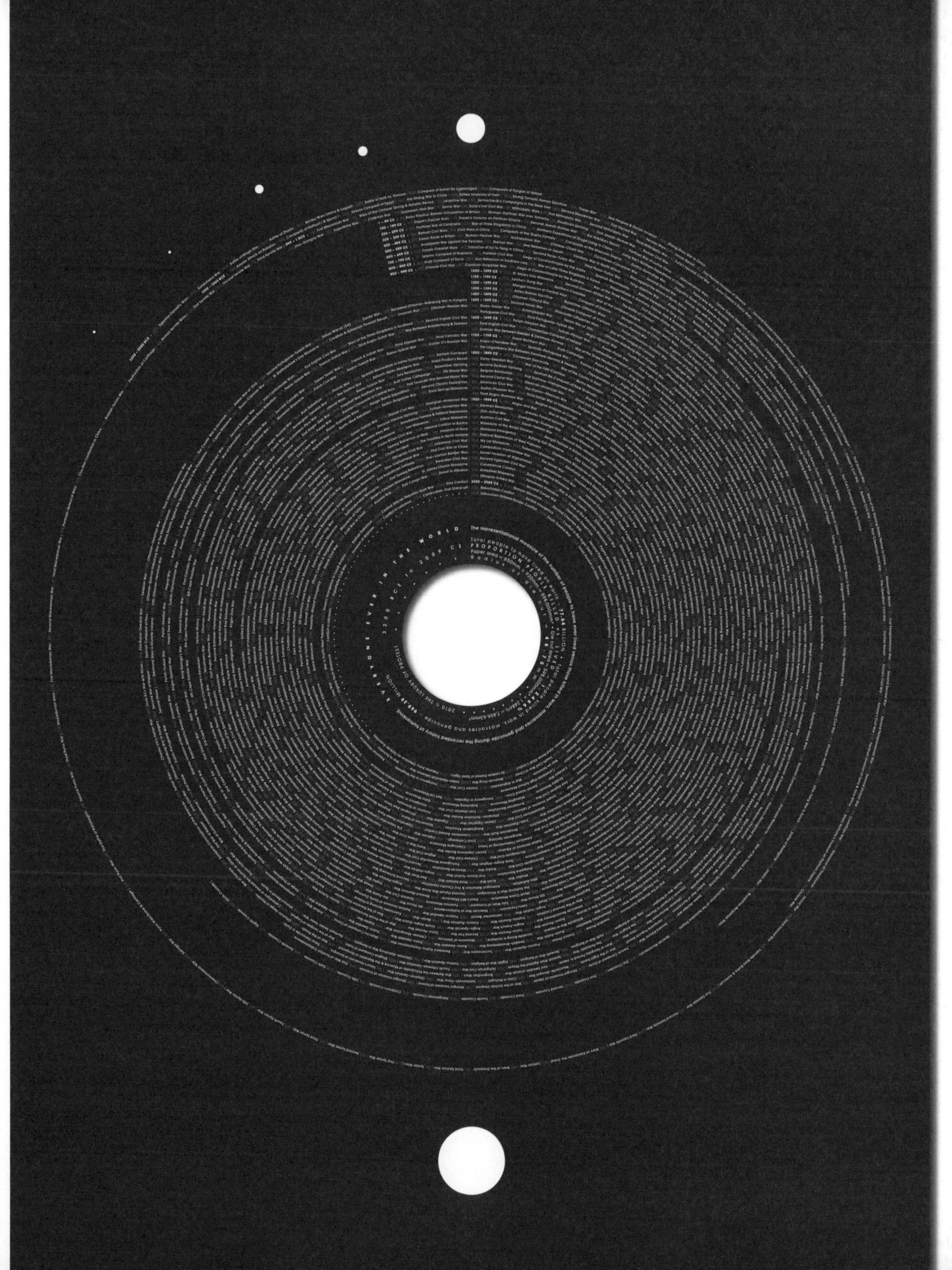

Overview

Peter has commented that his intention is to communicate to a broad spectrum of people engaged in political issues on a global scale. Everyone Ever in the World was a self-generated project to visually represent the number of people to have ever lived versus those killed in wars, massacres and genocides during the recorded history of humankind. The format is a type-based poster that represents the concepts of life and death. The poster is printed with semi-transparent ink with circles cut directly out of the material.

Peter has a very logical rationale for the poster and represents factual evidence through graphic representations. The user has to decode the poster in order to understand the statistics portrayed. It is a complex piece of data visualization that has been designed to be viewed in person, as a poster, rather than online. This summary below helps to explain what the data represents:

- Total paper area = 650 x 920mm (represents the 77.6 billion people to have ever lived).
- Die-cut circle (the centre white circle) represents the 969 million people who have died in wars, massacres and genocides.
- Area of the die-cut circle = 969 million/77.6 billion = 1.25% of the paper area (650mm x 920mm x 0.0125). All this information is shown on the poster.
- The text lists all recorded conflicts – it is a list, but grouped by millennia – allowing for a visual representation of counts. Lines stop as the earlier millennia have fewer recorded conflicts.

The text emanating from the centre lists wars from 3200 BCE to 2009 CE. The sequence of dots to the top left of the graph shows the dramatic increase in the number of conflicts over the past five millennia (left to right: from 3200 BCE to 2009 CE), one dot for each millennia, with the most recent 1,000 years being the most violent. The large dot below the graph represents the 1,000 years to come: a predicted startling increase in the frequency of human conflict.

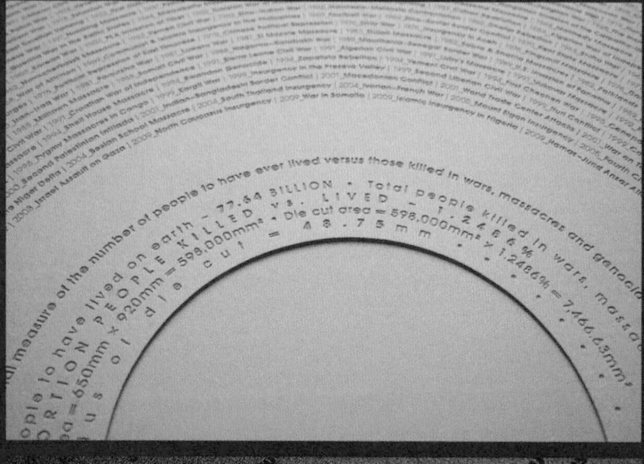

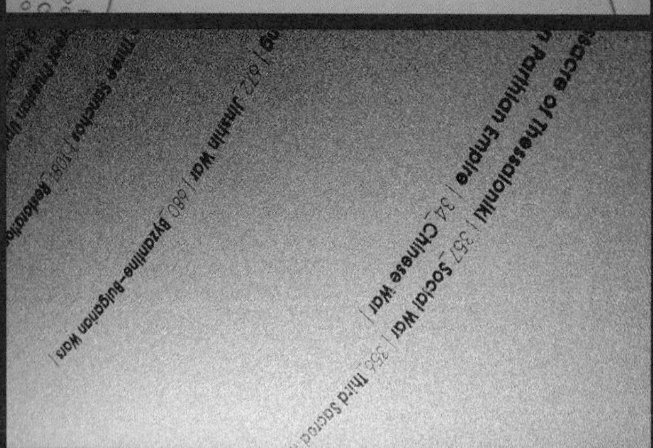

Approach

Everyone Ever in the World is as much about the content of the data presented as it is an exercise in the use of unique materials and print processes to express a concept. An early incarnation of the piece used a list arrangement for the text, where the conflicts had virtually no relation to the die-cut form. Crnokrak revisited this and has since produced three editions of the project, each using different materials and printing techniques. These show the concept of life contrasted with death in a manner that brings meaning and understanding to the data.

The first edition incorporated the basic elements that were necessary to convey the concept – the physical poster material represented the total number of people born and the die-cut circle the total number of people killed. The spiral arrangement of text was primarily a graphic tool to tie in the list of conflicts with the sum total of people killed in those conflicts, as represented by the die-cut centre.

Printing the text in clear gloss ink was a device to allow for the text to disappear when the poster is viewed head-on, but be readable at an angle. This is an important concession to the massive list of text that, if printed in standard white ink, would visually obscure the form relationship between total poster area versus die-cut area – the single most important data relationship represented in the piece.

As a contrast to the heaviness of the first 'black' edition (which in itself has a direct symbolic relationship to the void of death), the second edition, printed on frosted semi-clear plastic, takes on a ghost-like transparency to express the same concept, but using diametrically opposite language. The fundamental relationship of poster area to die-cut area remains, but the lightness of the milk-white ink on semi-clear plastic conveys the fleeting nature of existence and the symbolism of loss – that life disappears as easily as it is created.

Outcome

Everyone Ever in the World won an award in the 2010 International Science and Engineering Visualization Challenge, won a premier award from the International Society of Typographic Designers, and was published in the prestigious journal *Science*.

Crnokrak printed a special edition of the poster to commemorate winning the award. The entire poster is laser-engraved and laser-cut in heavy cotton paper. Laser engraving produces a distinctive burn pattern with subtle smoke-like wisps that are particularly pronounced on white paper. The designer chose this process as it perfectly conveys the notion of loss, destruction and death. The graphic simplicity of the poster imparts a sombre and respectful tone to such a weighty subject matter.

Opposite, top: An early version of the poster presents the copy as a list rather than a series of lines radiating out from the centre.

Opposite, centre: Detail of the laser-engraved edition of Everyone Ever in the World.

Opposite, bottom: Detail of the printed edition of Everyone Ever in the World.

Right: Everyone Ever in the World, second edition, printed on frosted semi-clear plastic.

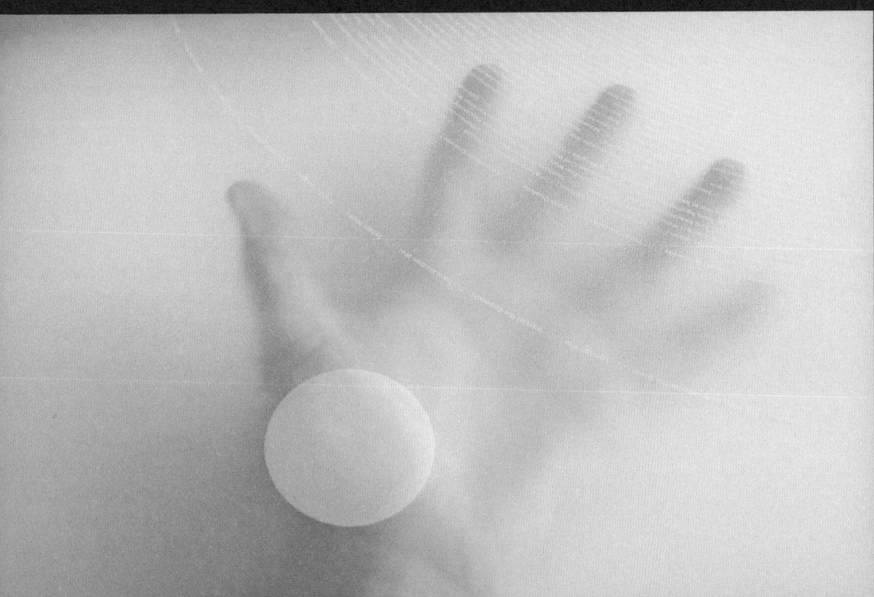

Routes for interactive information design

By definition, interactive design requires the user to interact with the information presented. By making choices the user is in control of the experience and not just a passive receiver. The user is allowed to browse the material at their leisure in the order they choose and not follow set routes.

The world we inhabit has become increasingly reliant on technology, and as a result we have developed more familiarity with the design of interfaces. For example, we are now accustomed to navigating information on a website in an order or sequence to break down experiences into meaningful steps to input or receive data. It is important to note that interactive information design is not just about computer technology, however. Many perceive it as screen-based design including design for mobile phone apps or websites. Although these are included in interactive design, we must remember that any kind of interaction, even something as simple as moving, folding or revealing, can be classified as interactive design, including items such as pop-up books.

The element of choice is very important, as it allows the user to have a personalized experience. Many of us learn by doing, not by watching or listening. The experience of interacting means the user will learn and retain the information in a memorable way.

The case study featured overleaf (pp. 176–77) shows how information can be presented in an engaging way without being too complicated. UK-based Studio Tonne designed a web interface for users to select, play and download music.

Interactive design is at the heart of the Science Museum's 'Who Am I?' gallery. It consists of a series of interactive exhibits created by UK agency AllofUs, Graphic Thought Facility and Casson Mann. The exhibition explores genetics, sociology and anthropology. It consists of an interconnected installation in three parts, inviting visitors of all ages to discover what makes each of them unique. A reactive wall entices visitors inside, where the gallery's 'molecule' graphic identity responds to each visitor's movement, creating a live representation of their silhouette. Once inside there are two large multiplayer interactive tabletops. These allow 16 people to enter a series of inquisitive challenges that delve into the strange mystery of why we are who we are. Finally there is an 8-metre-wide backdrop, on which visitor data and input is aggregated and visualized as dynamic, playful projections, vividly bringing to life the topics, ideas and responses being generated in the gallery, as each individual steers the exhibition's course. This exhibition demonstrates the scope of interactive design and its ability to use fun to engage an otherwise passive viewer. In this way information learned will almost certainly be remembered.

Interactive information design

Project: Interactive website for Dan Rose Music, 2008

Design: Paul Farrington of Studio Tonne, Brighton, UK

Paul Farrington, founder of Studio Tonne, based in Brighton, UK, is well known for his playful and eclectic body of interactive design work. The project presented here is an interactive website for Dan Rose Music. Dan is a music consultant for the television and film industry.

Overview

In his briefing to Paul, Dan had recognized that radio and television are no longer the only channels for introducing new music to fans. Social networking and online file-sharing sites have had a huge influence on music sharing and as a tool for marketing and distribution. Dan asked Paul to design a web-based application for clients to connect to a music library via the internet. Usability was a key factor for the site: he wanted a simple interface that didn't require a lot of thought to use.

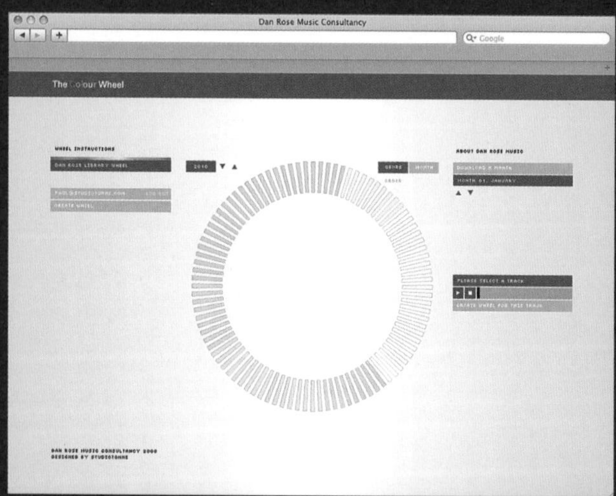

Colour wheel designed for the Dan Rose Music website by Paul Farrington of Studio Tonne.

Approach

Dan wanted a 'sampler' idea whereby clients could listen to examples of the music without compromising the integrity and copyright of the artist. Instead of listing tracks by artist or genre, Dan wanted the audience to experience the music without any preconceived notions. Dan felt that if you categorize by genre such as drum and bass or rock, it gives people an idea of a sound even before they hear the music.

Paul had an interest in the condition synaesthesia, which he discussed with Dan. This is a neurological condition where the stimulation of one sense can lead to involuntary stimulation of another sense. Phrases such as 'loud shirt', 'bitter wind' or 'prickly laugh' are examples of metaphors influenced by synaesthetic experiences where the senses can become mixed up and amplified. Paul was particularly interested in sound and colour synaesthesia. As the title suggests, people with this condition have a unique relationship between sight and sound. The condition has been described as 'something like fireworks'. A voice, piece of music, or even ambient environmental sounds such as dogs barking can trigger colour and firework shapes that arise, move around, and then fade when the sound ends. Synaesthetes comment that sound often changes the perceived hue, brightness and directional movement of a colour. Most say that loud tones are brighter than soft tones, and that lower tones are darker than higher tones.

Paul proposed a solution using synaesthesia and also the book *Reinventing the Wheel* by Jessica Helfand as inspiration. The solution involved using a colour wheel to organize the music. The samples would be categorized and arranged via colour. This would allow the user to navigate the music via mood suggested by the colour choice, thereby eliminating any preconceived notions of artist or genre. Paul said, 'I have used wheels or circles a lot in my work; for me they are perfect when you have a load of content that you want to put into a small confined space. The client wanted a site that was compact and wasn't a scrolling site.'

Paul commented, 'The wheel came out of the idea of how the client would actually use the site, as I find a lot of clients don't use sites when you build them, so I thought, "how can we make Dan use the site to add new music on a regular basis?"'

Below: Early design based on pipes rather than a wheel.

Right: The presentation of the track information in development.

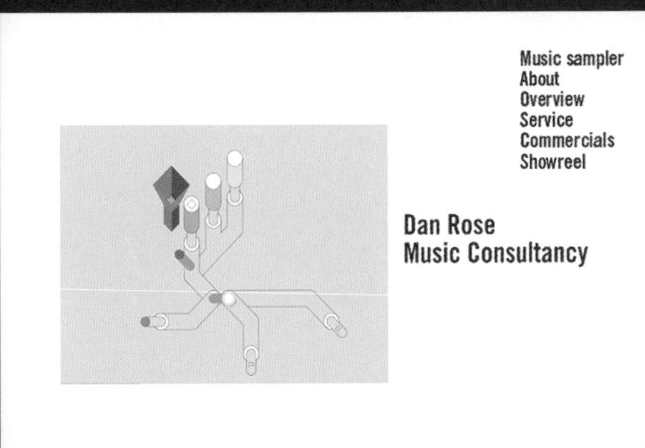

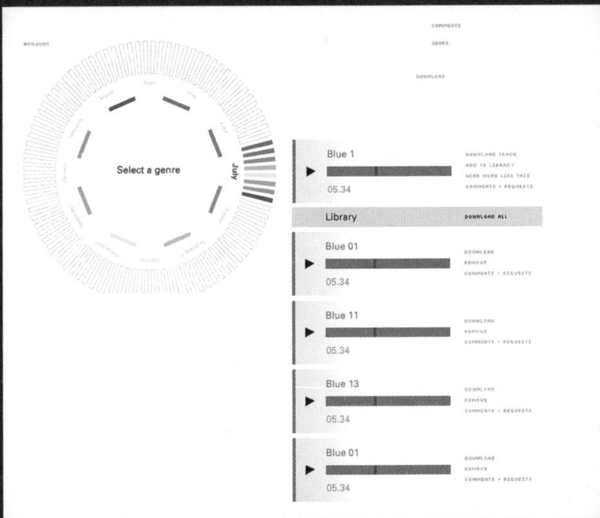

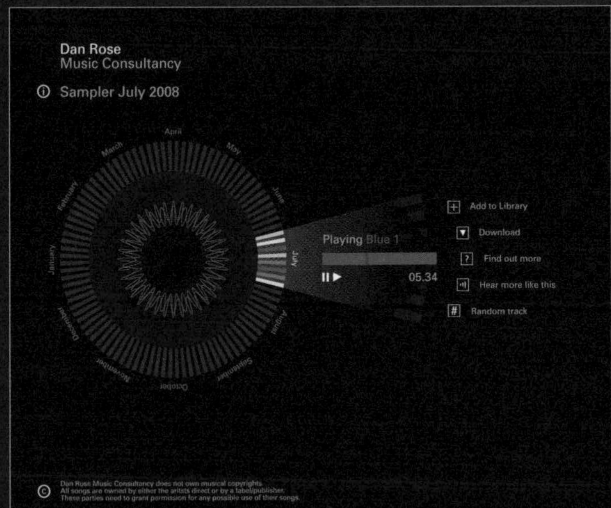

Above: Early version of the wheel and interface showing a radial grid structure and simple media player timeline with play and pause buttons.

Below: Early versions of the wheel.

As a result of this, the next system proposed was on what sort of schedule new music would be added to the wheel. Should it simply be a case of when it was new or had just been discovered? Paul felt that this would get lost, so he suggested using a monthly calendar system whereby new music would be added at the beginning of each month and clients would be informed.

There are two ways in which you can interact with the colour wheel:

1) Simply download the tracks to your desktop every time there is a monthly update.

2) As a personalized online music library using the functions currently available and only downloading when wanted.

Paul consulted with Dan and together they selected eight colours, each based loosely around a genre of music. They then arranged the music via colour according to their personal interpretation of it, such as orange for up-tempo, etc. Most of the arrangement was intuitive. They devised a colour system by selecting hues that looked good on screen and had enough contrast from each other for them to be easily recognizable.

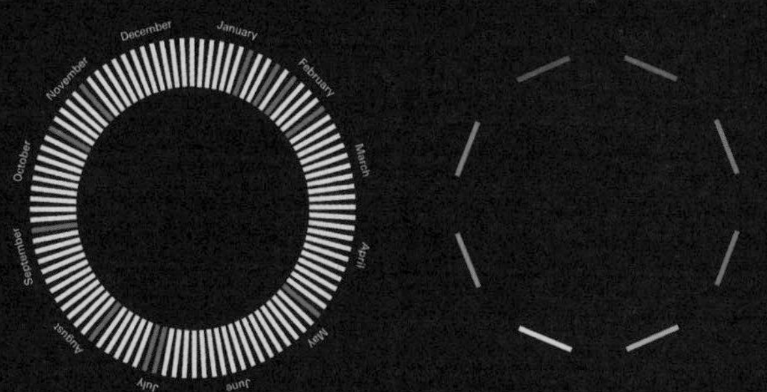

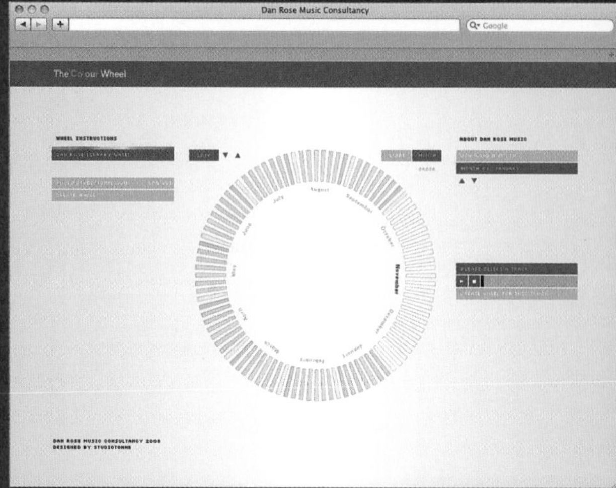

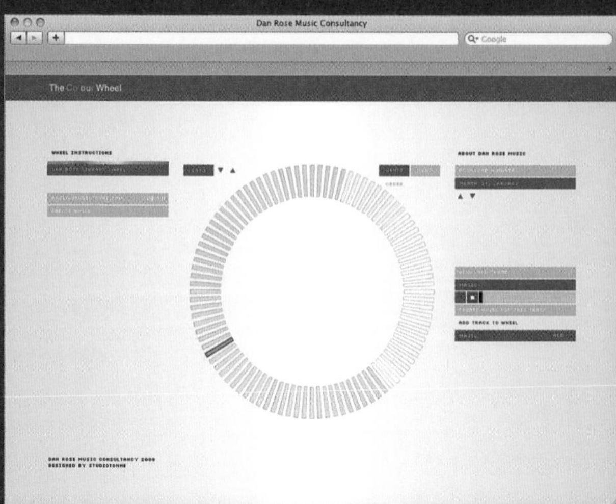

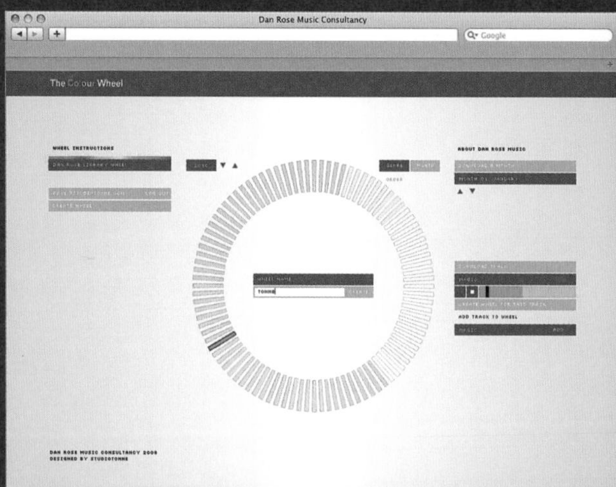

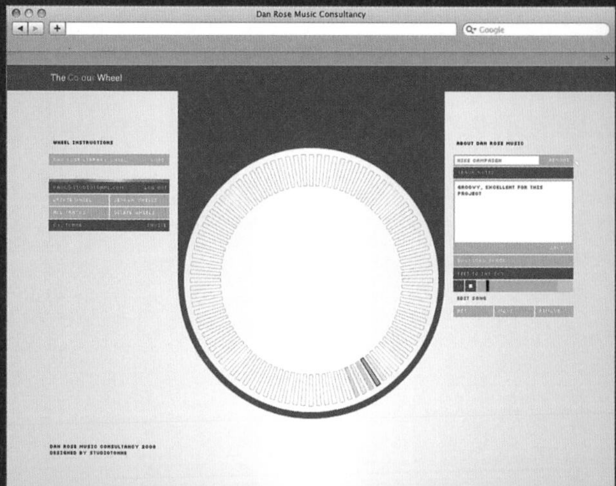

Top: When logged in the user can view the tracks either by month (**left**) or by genre (**right**) with the click of a button.

Above left: The user is presented with their own colour wheel on logging into the website.

Above right and opposite: The process of setting up your own music wheel on the site. The black carrier shaper makes it clear that you are in the website's personal area.

When you first enter the site, you are presented with a wheel of music chosen by Dan Rose. The user can listen to the samples and then build their own wheels based on their preferences. Paul played with the navigation of the site looking at the placement of the information and the various functions that needed to be included, such as the ability to download tracks to the desktop. The site went through several versions before the final one was settled upon, but the basic premise of the wheel remained the same. The user wouldn't see the tracks arranged alphabetically or via name, but through colour association. The tracks were grouped via month for the general interface and then in a circular 'holder' for the personal wheels where the user was selecting and saving tracks to listen to at a later date.

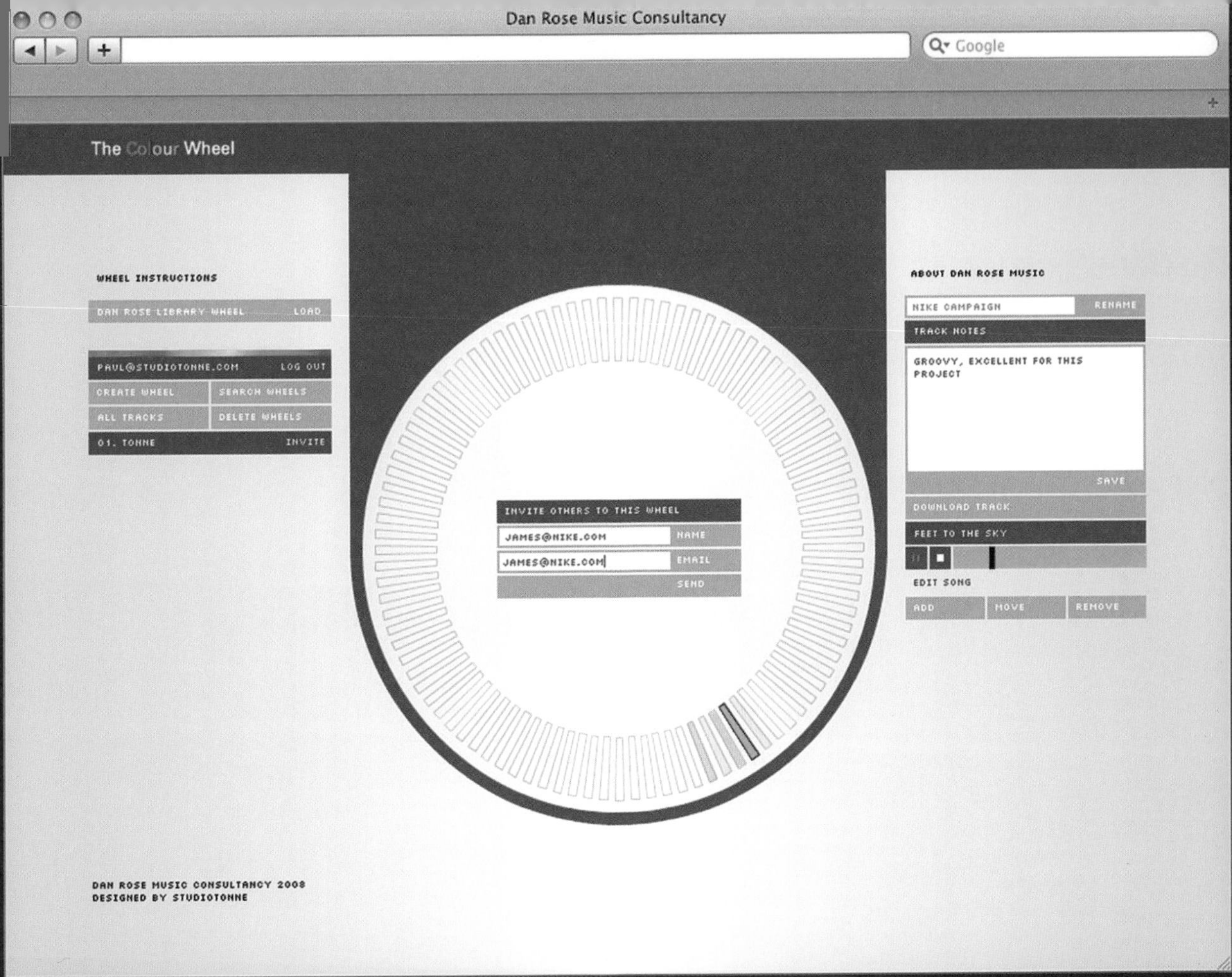

Outcome

Paul comments that they could have done lots of research into colour theory, but the budget was small and the research not needed. 'When you design a site and then program it you have to go through a process of discovery. You can't just design a site and then tell a programmer to make it. The way it worked was that we got the general idea agreed, but when we started to program it I could see areas that had been missed and new ideas could be developed. The site has a lot of depth to it and was built for clients. We programmed the site so that Dan could see who was using the site and which tracks they were adding

There is also a full analytical system that keeps track of who is listening to the different types of library music, tailored appropriately so the right kind of music is sent to the right kind of clients.

The project was developed systematically, implementing an approach across the whole application. To make sure it worked, Dan sent out the site to trusted clients and asked for their feedback, which was positive. Paul commented, 'I think what Dan enjoyed was that when he first came to me he just thought he

Routes for environmental information design

Environmental design takes many factors into account. It is essential that the design is appropriate for its function, its audience and also its location. The design must have longevity and the materials utilized need to be considered carefully. The design may need to have specialist craftspeople to construct the proposed project. The solution has to be user-friendly and durable. Distance and scale need to be taken into account. Legibility and readability can be huge factors too, along with what is achievable in the space or site. The case studies chosen demonstrate two diverse and inventive approaches to producing environmental signage and wayfinding. Adi Stern's project for Design Museum Holon and Bikeway Belém in Portugal both consider, respond to and reflect their surrounding environments within their solutions. The projects are very different in their approach: one seeks to guide and create an experience for its users with its playful use of typography and pictograms on a cycle route; the other discreetly but effectively guides them through a space. They both go beyond what we may consider a traditional or obvious approach and, one could argue, they challenge the established conventions or 'rules' of information design. We believe they demonstrate concepts and applications that have successfully understood the needs of the environment that contain them and the audience who will use them.

Environmental information design

Project: Signage and wayfinding system for Design Museum Holon, Tel Aviv, Israel, 2010

Design: Adi Stern Design, Tel Aviv, Israel

Adi Stern is principal at Adi Stern Design, based in Tel Aviv, Israel. Here, Adi explains the approach he took to tackling the complexities of designing a signage and wayfinding system for the Design Museum Holon in Tel Aviv.

Overview

The signage and wayfinding system of the Design Museum Holon challenges common approaches by using white arrows on white walls. The arrows, which are primarily discernible because of the shadow they cast, emerge from the museum walls and are transformed from two- to three-dimensional forms. The shape of the arrows echo the flow and movement of the Corten weathering steel bands that surround the museum building, creating a unity of design throughout the museum.

Adi Stern's wayfinding system at Design Museum Holon, Tel Aviv, Israel.

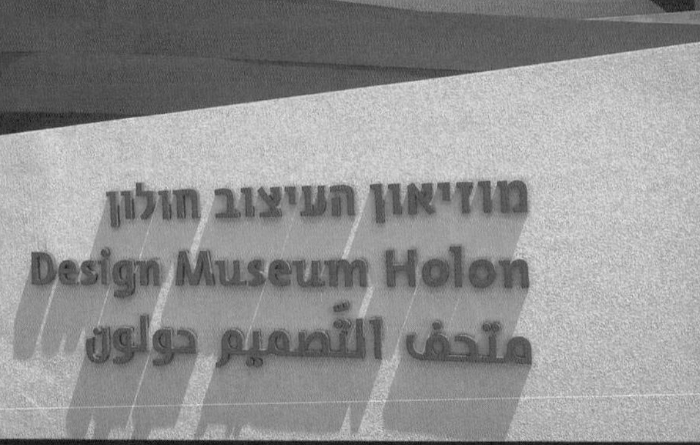

Approach

A major challenge in this project was to create a system that would be visible and easy to use, while not competing with Ron Arad's dynamic architecture. The museum building is a very expressive and intensive edifice. Its unique character and spirit was unmistakable from the very early stages of the process. Thus, it was clear to Adi that the signage and environmental graphics in and around it should be as low-key as possible. On one hand, the designers looked for a system that would harmonize with the building. On the other hand, they clearly aimed at a system that would be functional and therefore noticeable and easily understood.

Design Museum Holon's visual identity system uses the three languages prevalent in Israel: Hebrew, Arabic and English. The decision to use these three languages (which meant also using three very different scripts) is pivotal and worth mentioning. Most Israeli institutions do not apply Arabic – one of the two official languages of Israel – in their visual identity. Apart from the significant political nature of the decision to use Arabic, it created an interesting design challenge: devising a three-scripts typographic system. Moreover, it needed to be a non-hierarchical system where no language was superior to the others and all had a similar visual weight and presence. Such a system did not exist at the time and therefore it became clear that a new custom Hebrew typeface was needed.

The DMH Hebrew typeface brings the Hebrew as close as possible to the Latin font (The Mix by Lucas de Groot), but without betraying the script's authentic nature and tradition. Adi's goal was to create a Hebrew typeface that could stand on its own right; the Hebrew should not be apparent as Latin-influenced, nor the Latin to look Hebrew-influenced.

When designing the system, Adi didn't want a 'sign', a three-dimensional object, hung or stuck on the wall. He says, 'I looked for an elegant, quiet and harmonious solution that would fuse with the wall. In a sense, my approach to the design was two-dimensional. I wanted to think of the entire wall as my

אבגדהוזחטיכל
מנסעפצקרשת

format. The wall was treated as paper, as a poster or a magazine page. Above all, my wish was to create a system that would be on one hand very simple and basic while on the other hand unconventional, interesting and unique.'

To blend with the building, one thing that was crucial was to make the arrow look as if it is part of the wall. The designers needed to find a way to hide the seam between the arrow and the wall, so they used the same paint, with the same colour and texture, to make the connection as smooth as possible.

In producing the signage, several sizes of the typefaces and arrows were tested in situ with mock-ups. The difference in size between the planned arrows (based on architectural plans and simulations) and what was eventually produced was immense. By the end of the process, the final arrows were roughly double in size compared to the initial intention.

Outcome

The solution for the wayfinding system is an unusual one. The choice of the white arrows, which seem to emerge from the wall, goes against what you might expect from an interior signage scheme. Although this is a break from convention, the signage system is straightforward to use. It is quiet and does not compete with the dramatic architecture of the building itself. It is a clever, imaginative and highly original result that integrates seamlessly into the interior space. Most wayfinding is designed by its functionality, which can lead to outcomes that are visually unattractive. On the other hand, to disregard functionality can bring about systems that are impractical to use. The scheme imposed at Design Museum Holon balances aesthetics and functionality, while being sensitive to its environment. It is simple to navigate, using only a small number of decision points and sub-destinations. This eliminates the need to use too much directional information, keeping the signage clean and clear. The design communicates the bare minimum that the user needs and is used only where absolutely necessary to good effect.

The Society for Environmental Graphic Design jury remarked, 'A simple idea is what makes this graphic design so successful. The message is clear without distracting attention from the museum exhibits. The fact that the arrows peel away from the wall in a way that has not been done before allows them to become quiet sculptural pieces of art themselves.' This project resulted in Adi being given the Tokyo Type Directors Club Award for his design.

Environmental information design

Project: Bikeway Belém for Lisbon Harbour Association, Câmara Municipal de Lisboa (Lisbon City Hall), Portugal, 2009

Design: P-06 Atelier in collaboration with Global Landscape Architecture, Lisbon, Portugal

Founded in 2006 and based in Lisbon, Portugal, P-06 Atelier are an award-winning firm specializing in communication and environmental design. They collaborate with architects, urban designers, landscape designers and engineers on projects and are renowned for producing inventive and challenging solutions to projects with a bold and distinctive graphic style and approach.

We are featuring a project they designed and produced in collaboration with Global Landscape Architecture. Bikeway Belém is a fascinating piece, as it is an environmental wayfinding system that goes beyond pure functionality and attempts something more immersive. The Bikeway covers 7,326m (24,000ft) in the centre of Lisbon. It runs alongside the River Tagus, and crosses a variety of urban spaces. It directs cyclists but also provides its users with a graphic interpretation that is inspired by and responds to its environment. P-06 Atelier have created a scheme that demarks and defines a route but also offers an experience for users as they travel. It is inventive, visually and mentally stimulating, memorable and fun – a poetic narrative.

Founding partner Nuno Gusmão describes the project, its ambitions, intentions and the challenges.

Overview

The objective was to define a new urban environment, beyond the demands of a bikeway, in order to improve this area along the river. Alongside the cycle path the team also created a pedestrian lane. The defined path runs alongside a varied ensemble of already paved industrial and historic spaces. 60 per cent of the route can be completed on the existing asphalt paving, limestone, basalt or granite cobblestones; these are all black and white.

All the existing bikeways in Portugal have the lanes defined in red, but the designers realized that having the lane in black allowed the wayfinding system to be integrated within the existing site, and presented them with an enormous black canvas to work with. Luckily they managed to persuade the town hall authorities to consider this as a special case owing to its location and its historical surroundings. Since the 7-km ($4^{1}/_{2}$-mile) route links four local train stations, two river ferry terminals and five park and ride facilities, as well as several tourist monuments, it was important to add this information into the wayfinding, making it all part of this new urban system.

Opposite: Onomatopoeic intervention under the bridge.

MOSTEIROS
DOS JERONIMOS

Clockwise from top left: Stencils made of metal; Alberto Caeiro's poem about the river Tagus printed on a pier; a pictogram of a fish indicates an existing fishing spot; crossing different urban and historical points; white paint stencils.

Opposite: Signage system and graphic interventions invading doors and walls of abandoned warehouses and stores.

Approach

P-06 Atelier wanted more than just a basic wayfinding system; so the bikeway gives more than just directional and route nformation for its users. The project uses graphic nterpretations that encourage users further and further down he route. For example, under a bridge support, the designers created a typographic onomatopoeic interpretation that imitates he sounds of the bridge above. It is as if a story is being told along the path. Nuno Gusmão comments, 'The signs and signage ell us a story, take us, guide us, and seduce us along this stretch. All the customized signs, symbols and words establish boundaries, guidance and information, in order to determine movement and relations with the urban context that it crosses. Stopping and moving in this "installation" give form to the anguage/message of the total space, like in the pages of a book. Jnusual installations, like the poem of Portuguese poet Alberto Caeiro about the River Tagus, are used on a pier along the route, as is the pictogram of a fish indicating an existing fishing spot. These graphic narratives identify the different types of use that people gave to this stretch of riverside. With a clear intention of revitalizing this area, we "invaded" the doors and walls of abandoned warehouses and stores, using them as support for he wayfinding system and graphic interventions that run hrough the entire system and become part of the experience.'

Outcome

The solution developed presented a number of challenges to the designers, such as parked cars in the cycle lane, and periodic maintenance on pavements and other kinds of construction works that would mean the graphics would need replacing. The designers realized that the non-industrial types of graphics and text wouldn't survive with constant transit infractions. The success of the route would depend on how this was overcome. Over established pavements, mainly granite cobblestones, graphic 'incisions' were made in order to preserve the existing surface. These consisted of circles and polygons made of metal and filled with asphalt, onto which different pictograms are drawn. The existing maintenance hole covers are also filled with asphalt, making an ever-lasting system of signs. All the stencils used were made in metal, to allow for quick repair and maintenance, undertaken by Lisbon City Hall.

The team commented that, 'In terms of functionality, it was very rewarding for us to hear and read all the comments. They all emphasize the playful and meaningful side of the content we pu within the system; these engage the audience and encourage them to experience this "new" urban area.'

The final outcome is an interesting take on a traditional navigation structure for cyclists. The treatment of the route using these bold and experimental graphics gives personality to

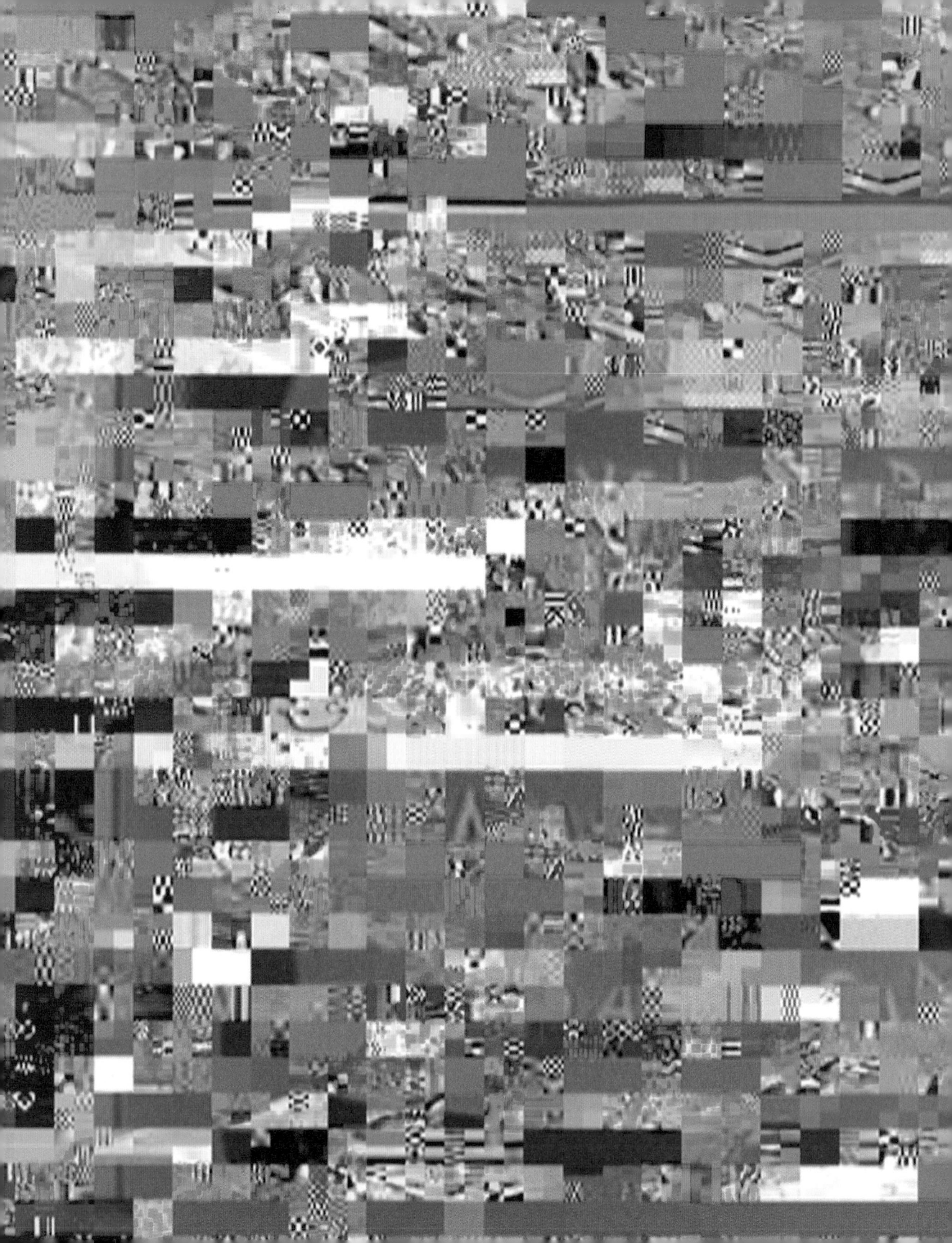

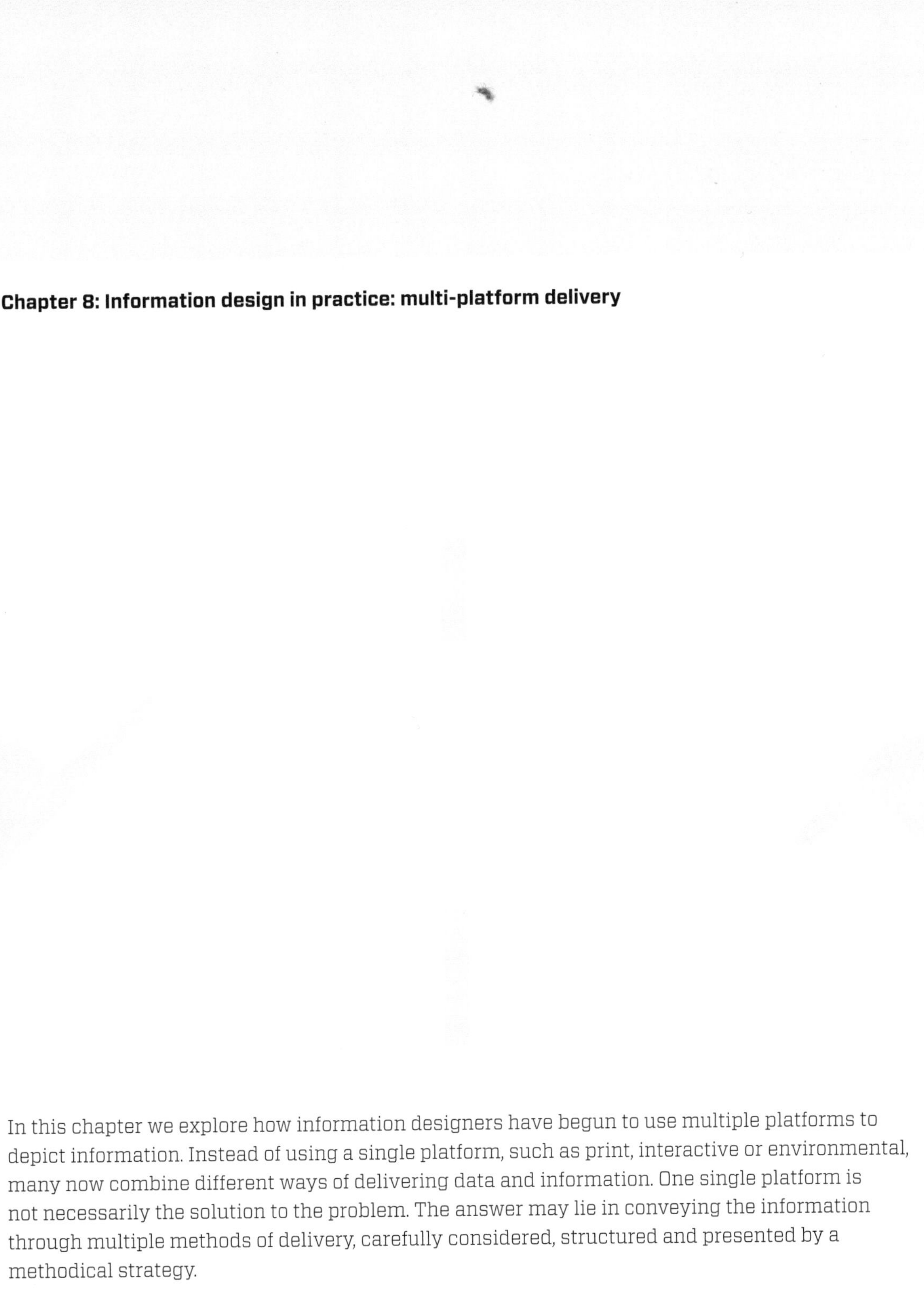

Chapter 8: Information design in practice: multi-platform delivery

In this chapter we explore how information designers have begun to use multiple platforms to depict information. Instead of using a single platform, such as print, interactive or environmental, many now combine different ways of delivering data and information. One single platform is not necessarily the solution to the problem. The answer may lie in conveying the information through multiple methods of delivery, carefully considered, structured and presented by a methodical strategy.

Using multiple platforms

The examples we have selected use more than one way to deliver a message or data. They combine and overlap platforms to ensure that the user has what they need to decode and understand the message in an appropriate form. The projects are based on solid research and understanding of the user's needs. One is a small-scale exhibition (mediaarchitecture.de's ImpulsBauhaus exhibition in Weimar, Germany); the other a large-scale wayfinding project (Two Twelve Design's proposal for the I Walk New York wayfinding system). Through these case studies we aim to demonstrate the diversity of information design and the fact that one message sometimes has to be shown in several forms depending on the user and where it is viewed.

Previous page: Digital television noise.

Interactive exhibition design

Project: ImpulsBauhaus, Bauhaus University, Weimar, Germany, 2009

Design: mediaarchitecture.de, Germany

Jens Weber and Andreas Wolter founded mediaarchitecture.de in Weimar, Germany, in 2006. They have been described as 'operating at the intersection of art, design and technology'. The award-winning partnership works mainly on commercial projects, but also ventures into art and design research.

Overall concept image for the exhibition.

The project showcased here is the ImpulsBauhaus display at the Bauhaus University in Weimar. It conveys information in the form of a physical installation. The exhibition is dedicated to the examination of the social networks of the Bauhaus movement and its global influence. It combines static and kinetic information presented within a dedicated space. The exhibition was designed to mark the 90th anniversary of the establishment of the Bauhaus School and its principles.

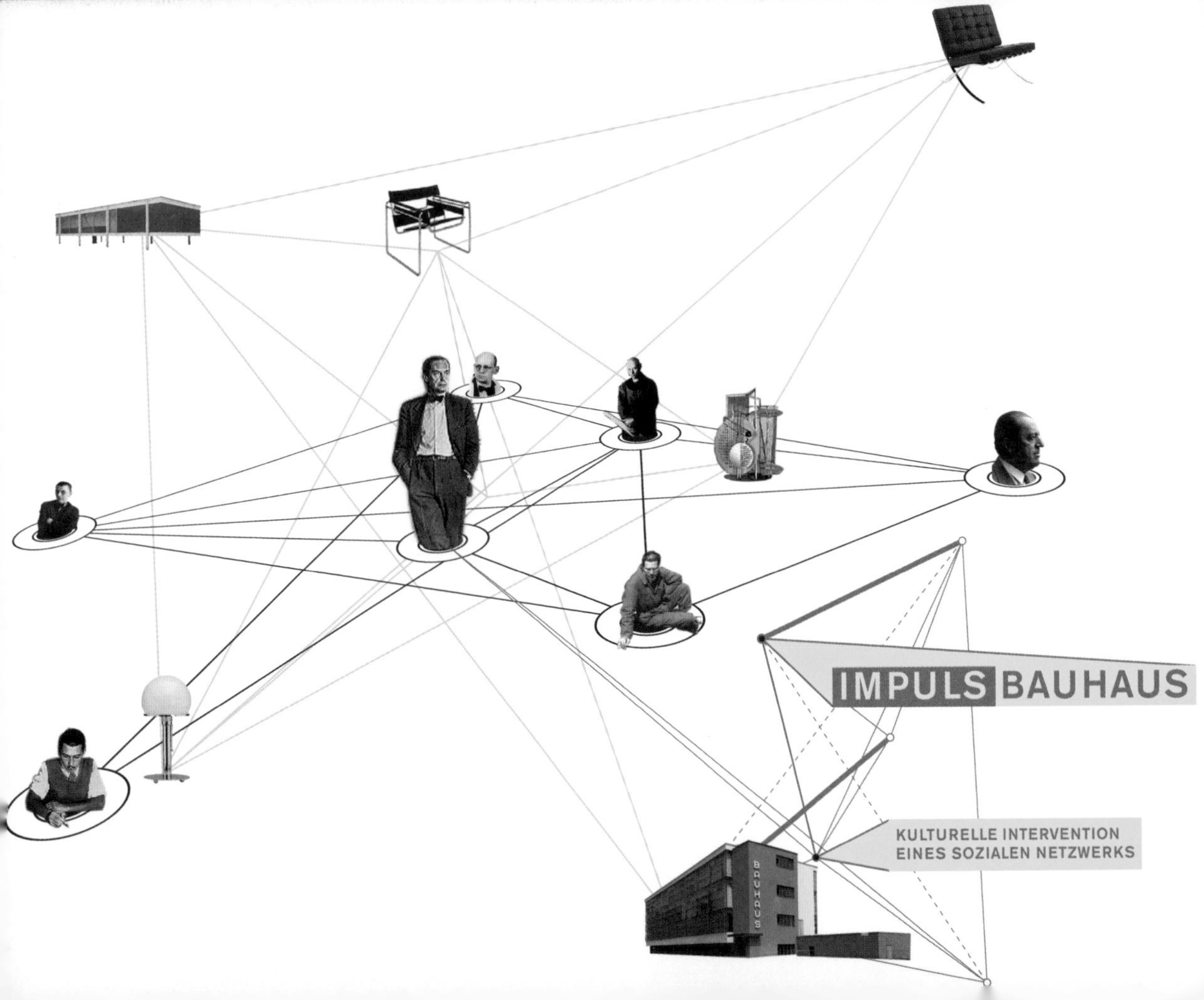

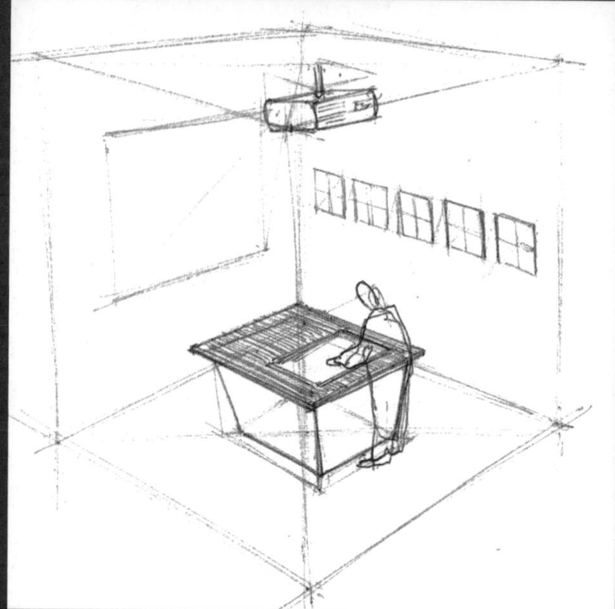

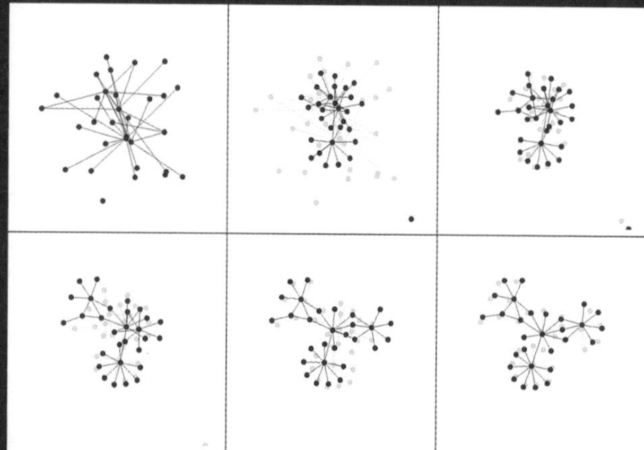

Left, above: Concept sketch showing the original idea of how the exhibition would occupy the white cube structure.

Left, centre: This image sequence shows how the arrangement of networks was created with a self-developed algorithm based on a simulation of physical forces, in which all nodes repel.

Left, below: Map showing the migration of various members of the Bauhaus to their final destinations.

The Bauhaus School was founded in 1919 by German architect Walter Gropius (1883–1969). Around 1,300 students and their instructors belonged to the State Bauhaus in Weimar, Dessau and Berlin between 1919 and 1933. Their ideas were among the most influential in the fields of architecture and design of the 20th century and spread swiftly throughout the world. After the Bauhaus was permanently shut down in 1933, many of its followers were forced into exile. The Bauhaus ideas, however, survived in countries beyond Germany and Europe.

Overview

The proposition of the exhibition was to communicate this content in an innovative and engaging way. Both new and traditional media were used for their potential to convey complex information in an exhibition context. The result was presented within an illuminated 4 x 4m (13ft) cube in the grounds of the university. The aim was for the user to be able to plot the social history, influences and links of the Bauhaus network.

Approach

Jens and Andreas took a quote from Ben Fry as a starting point for the project: 'All data problems begin with a question. The answer to the question is a kind of narrative, a piece that describes a clear answer to the question without extraneous details' (*Computational Information Design*, 2004). Jens and Andreas had to think carefully about how to manage, analyze and visualize large amounts of information by digital means. It became clear that the social network of the Bauhaus movement could only be understood in single manageable sections. An interactive exhibit would give visitors the opportunity to break down and view the network based on their individual interests.

In order for this to be achieved, the designers had to gather all the data they could about the Bauhaus members. Dr Folke Dietzsch provided some of this information in his PhD thesis *The Students of the Bauhaus* (1991), which contained extensive data about the students. The ability to present the Bauhaus social network and their different geographical locations at specific times was a challenge. It became necessary to develop a special web-based database, which became the core of the project. This database has been updated with relevant information since 2008. It includes information about all the representatives of the Bauhaus, such as where they were born, where they lived and any significant events they experienced. Interpersonal relationships have also been stored and categorized, such as working relationships and close friendships. It was important to build a flexible and extensive data structure that could be expanded over time. The database is fed by a web application; this in turn generates information for the printed matter and the exhibition.

The acquisition of this data allowed the designers to show insights into this social network and present them graphically. Analyzing the data gave rise to complex visuals so that users could be presented with information as a dynamic network and not in a static form. This needed a graphical interface that could distinguish between individual members of the Bauhaus and depict the relationships among them.

The concept for the exhibition interior was broken down into three parts: the chronological archive, the interpersonal archives, and the network archive, including the interactive table.

The chronological archive on the left of the cube presents biographies of 60 selected representatives of the Bauhaus in a grid of 20 wide by 3 high. This is a summary of the lives of these members. The text is presented as bar graphs that represent the length of certain portions of their lives. As a result it is possible for the viewer to gain a quick overview and compare these different individuals. The tables were produced as transparencies to guarantee high contrast and sharpness, so that even the smallest fonts could be displayed accurately.

On the opposite side wall to the chronological archive is an evaluation of the data that was gathered from the Bauhaus research platform. It shows the static representations of the interpersonal links between the Bauhaus representatives. These are broken down into eight types. The circle diagrams show relationships of 130 individuals and are categorized as: spouses, relatives, close friends, acquaintances, opponents, teacher/student, business partners and employers/employees. The second diagram contrasts Walter Gropius's links with those of the students. The third shows geographical locations plotted from birth to death. The final diagram, or socio-gram, shows the frequency of relationships/links of the key 60 members and plots them in terms of importance. The most sociable members are in the centre and the less social on the periphery.

Infographic showing the interpersonal relationships of the Bauhaus members.

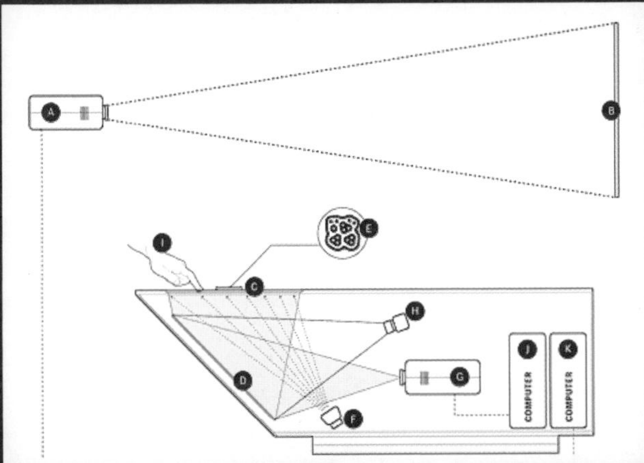

The illustration above demonstrates the workings of the interactive table. It is comprised of two components: the table and a projection screen. One section of the tabletop (C) is comprised of a matte projection surface, on which an image is projected. The objects on the interactive tabletop (C) are imprinted with fiducial markers, which the computer can recognize as individual elements. They are visible through the projection surface from beneath and are illuminated by infrared lamps (F). The camera (H) captures the reflected image of the underside of the projection surface (C) from the mirror (D). An infrared filter blocks out the light of the projector, allowing only the infrared light from the lamps (F) to pass through. The camera not only captures the image of the markers, but also fingertips as they come in contact with the interactive tabletop. Because of the matte surface, the fingertip is visible as a sharply defined point of light only when it is right above the surface. The computer (J) processes the data from the camera and creates an animated version of the tabletop for the beamer (G). It then sends the current status of the table to the computer (K), which controls the second beamer (A), which projects the second image of the map onto the projection screen (B).

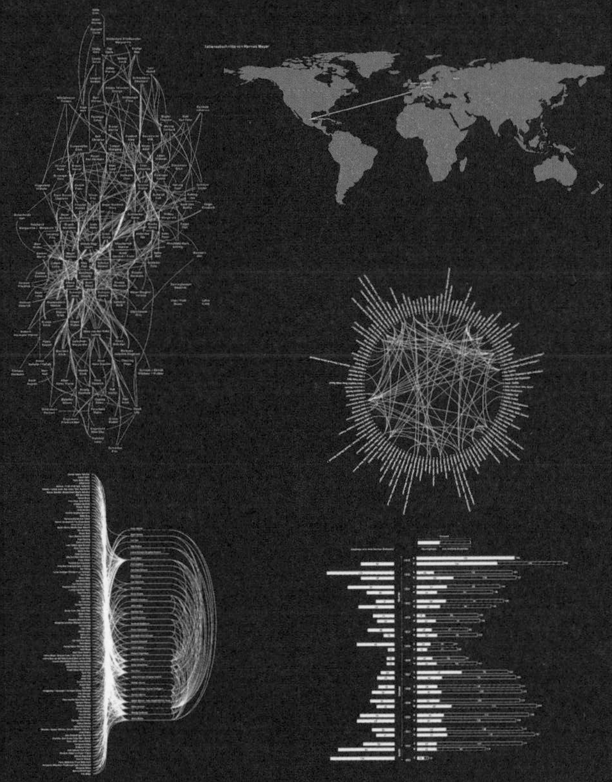

The main part of the exhibition was the interactive network archive. This was a digital interactive tabletop, where visitors could combine the two outer parts with additional information to examine biographical information and personal relationships of particular individuals, such as Walter Gropius and the artist Paul Klee. Here visitors can explore the social network of selected characters. The table reacts to the placement and movement of objects. Located at the edges of the table are ten 'tokens' with pictures of the Bauhaus protagonists printed on them. Each of these tokens represents a personality. Placing tokens onto the table creates links. This simple and direct interactive visualization has become a big attraction for visitors. The Bauhaus tokens are physical objects that act as a user element and also as part of the virtual image on the projection screen, mixing the two realities. The interactive exhibits allow the user to become immersed in the network of the Bauhaus movement. The information presented changes depending on which tokens are placed on the table.

The Bauhaus tokens serve as an input medium, but it is also possible to call up more detailed information by touching the surface of the table. When you press the yellow points in the lower section, detailed information is displayed on the wall and on the table, which users can scroll by touching. The interaction on the tabletop also calls up information projected on the wall in the form of geographical data on the token selected. One medium reacts to changes in the other, so choices on the table are visualized on the wall. As the visitor selects the Bauhaus members they create unique interactive information visualizations.

The tabletop unit was designed as an advanced graphical interface. The unit works by a camera taking an infrared image of the tabletop, which is then analyzed by a computer. It is specially designed to recognize fiducial markers on the bottom of the tokens and process multi-touch events. (A fiducial marker is an object used in the field of view of an imaging system, which

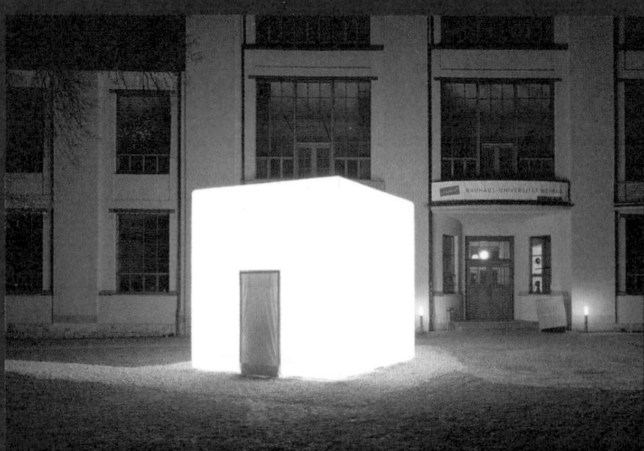
The finished white cube.

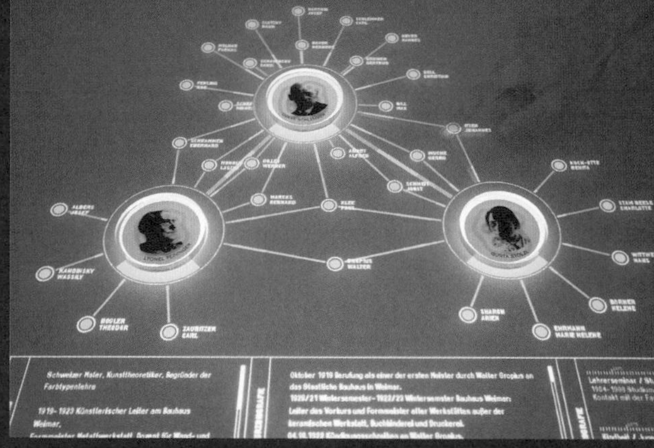
Detail of the touch table.

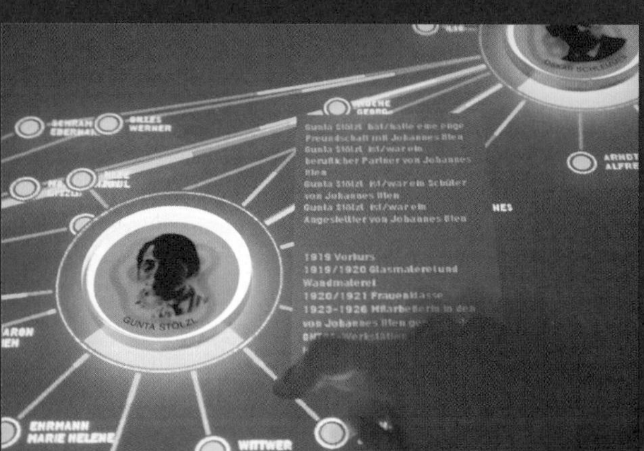

Close-up of the touch-table marker.

The exhibition in use.

The finished exhibition space.

appears in the image produced for use as a point of reference or a measure.) The system recognizes actions such as finger movements, rotating markers and other changes. It sends these interactions to the processing module, which interprets them. It recognizes when a new marker has been placed on the table and generates acoustic and visual feedback via the projector and loudspeaker. Every marker has a distinctive ID and can be assigned to each person. The software requests relevant information from the database on the research platform about each marker.

Outcome

The success of the exhibition lies in its combination of simple ways of presenting complicated data sets. The ability to isolate individual chunks of information means that the user can decode and interpret the material quickly and in a meaningful manner. Traditional means of visualization – the chronological archive and the interpersonal archive – are combined in the digital arena with the interactive network archive to form an absorbing experience. The technology is used as a way for the viewer to filter and analyze the data. It rationalizes the information and presents it as simple visual diagrams that react in real time to input from the user/viewer.

Environmental and interactive wayfinding

Project: I Walk New York, plan for pedestrian wayfinding in New York City, 2011

Design: Two Twelve, New York, USA

It may seem strange to feature a proposal rather than a finalized, fully implemented piece of information design, but we felt that this offered a fantastic opportunity to gain insight into the process of researching, analyzing and creating a strategy for the implementation of a wayfinding system delivered across a variety of platforms.

Overview

In 2011, Manhattan's Two Twelve produced a report that 'articulates the need for a unified NYC pedestrian wayfinding system'. They had been commissioned by the New York City Department of Transportation to explore the potential of a wayfinding system that covers the five boroughs of New York. Two Twelve partnered with Tim Fendley of London-based agency Applied. Both agencies are recognized as world leaders in wayfinding planning and design, Fendley being the creative force behind the highly acclaimed pedestrian wayfinding system 'Legible London'.

Approach

In order to understand the challenges involved in creating a successful wayfinding system, it is essential to have a clear understanding of the problems that currently exist for pedestrians in NYC. Gathering primary research facilitates this understanding. Current wayfinding and pedestrian behaviour was studied and analyzed. Beresford Research worked with Two Twelve to gather this information, and the findings were then used to inform the strategy of the final proposal.

So what were the issues that faced the users navigating NYC? 31 per cent of trips in New York are made on foot, and although the grid system of the city may appear to be relatively straightforward to navigate, it presents a range of problems for the pedestrian. When streets are named and numbered sequentially it is easy to navigate; however, the reality of NYC is that it contains numerous grids that merge, collide and separate. A grid system can also result in a cityscape that is indistinct, creating a challenge for the pedestrian who commonly seeks distinct landmarks to aid orientation and navigation. In the four-way intersections created by a grid system, every pathway may appear similar, leading to confusion and disorientation.

Interchanges in NYC.

500 surveys were conducted by Beresford and offered valuable insights into the pedestrian experience:

- 33% of locals didn't know which way north was.
- 24% of visitors did not know how to get to their next destination.
- 13% of locals were not familiar with the area they were surveyed in.
- 27% of visitors couldn't name the borough they were in.
- 27% of visitors and 9% of New Yorkers admitting to being lost in the previous week!

Existing wayfinding material was found to be inconsistent, as content on signs and the scale, placement and overall designs of signs varied in each neighbourhood. Digital and printed material suffered the same problem. There was also no consistent overall visual identity or 'brand' in place.

Understanding how people understand NYC

With a clear view of the problems, how do you proceed in creating meaningful solutions? The designers comment: 'In order to provide people with the right information in the right place and form, we need to assess how they create an understanding about a place for themselves.' This is crucial to the creation, construction and implementation of a wayfinding scheme: 'This understanding can guide how a city is described in a wayfinding system, for example which features are highlighted, which routes are emphasized, and which wayfinding keys are used.'

So how do residents, commuters and visitors understand New York City? They have 'pockets of knowledge' limited to places they are familiar with or need to go to. A clear picture of the city as a whole may not exist; the proximity of areas to each other and the distances between them may not be known. Research shows that we learn about places in stages: first points; then the routes between those points, then how those points and routes connect so we understand an area. We build our understanding of a place piece by piece; wayfinding works to support a partial picture in becoming a complete one.

Below: Graphic of the brain's learning process, points/routes/areas.

Bottom: Perceptions of NYC using this method.

Different users = different needs

Another key aspect of the strategy for this project was an understanding of the different needs of the range of users. The system must work for New Yorkers, commuters and the 49 million visitors to the city every year.

Often users combined the wayfinding tools they used according to their different needs. Different types of journey require different knowledge; a journey may be planned before it is travelled, but prompts may still be required while that journey is being undertaken. How do you inform, reassure and support the pedestrian at all the necessary stages of the journey? What are the scenarios that different users face? Understanding the experiences and requirements of these different groups informs the construction of layers of information within the wayfinding system and the tools selected to deliver it.

Two Twelve identified the different stages of a journey and describe what is required to support effective navigation as follows:

- Planning. These are the tools that allow people to plan a trip. They provide options regarding various travel modes. They are accessed via printed or digital media.
- Moving. These are the tools that allow people to make decisions along the way. They provide orientation, direction and identification information and are located at key landmarks, focal points, decision points and areas of rest.

THE BRAIN'S LEARNING PROCESS

We learn places through a series of stages, firstly learning points, secondly routes and finally the whole area. We need a system that helps to build this knowledge quickly and surely. The brain is like a muscle; the more we exercise certain parts of it, the more developed they become. The hippocampus is the area of the brain associated with mental mapping.

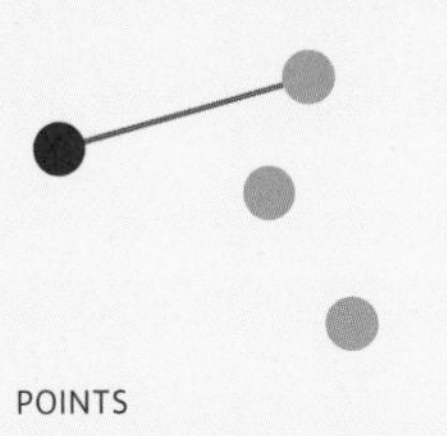

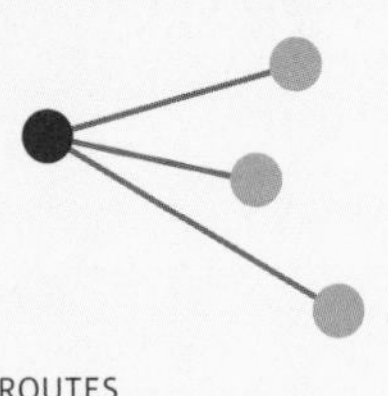

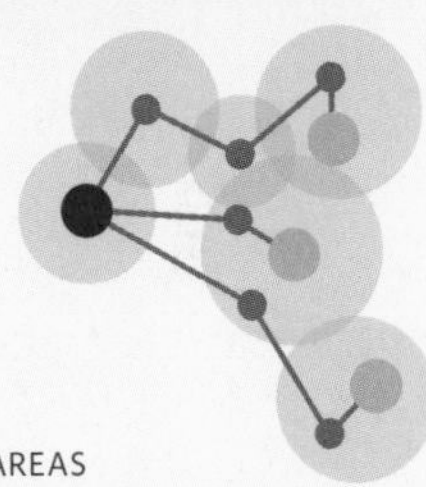

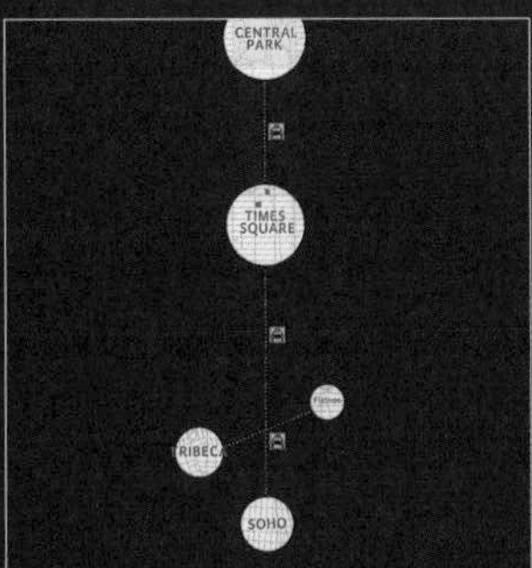

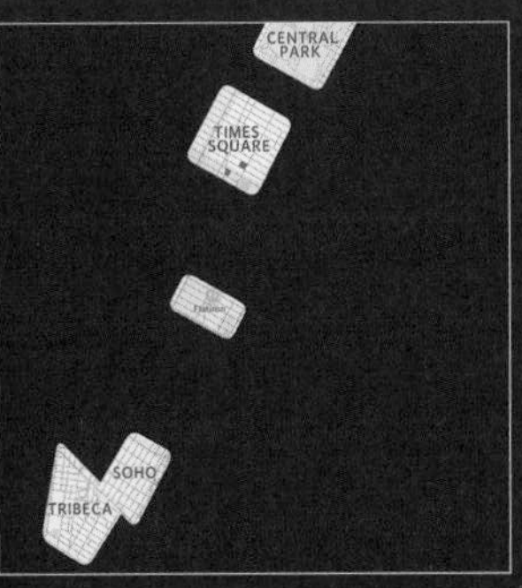

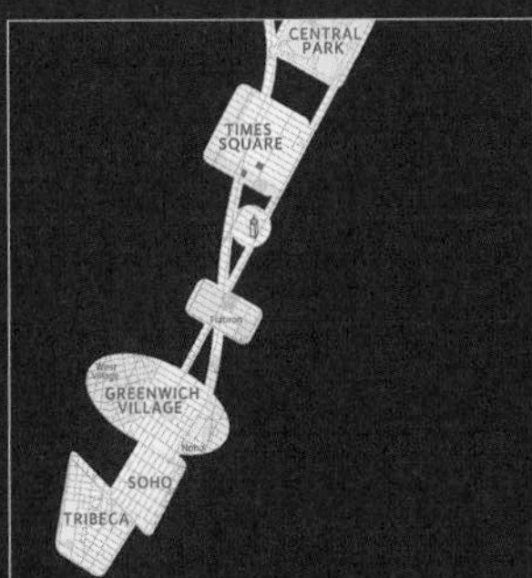

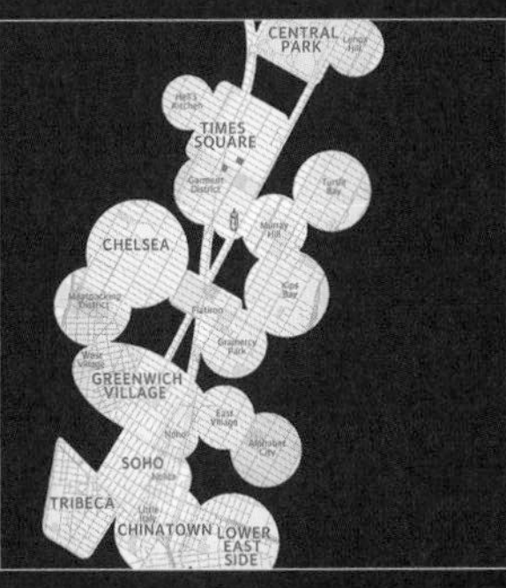

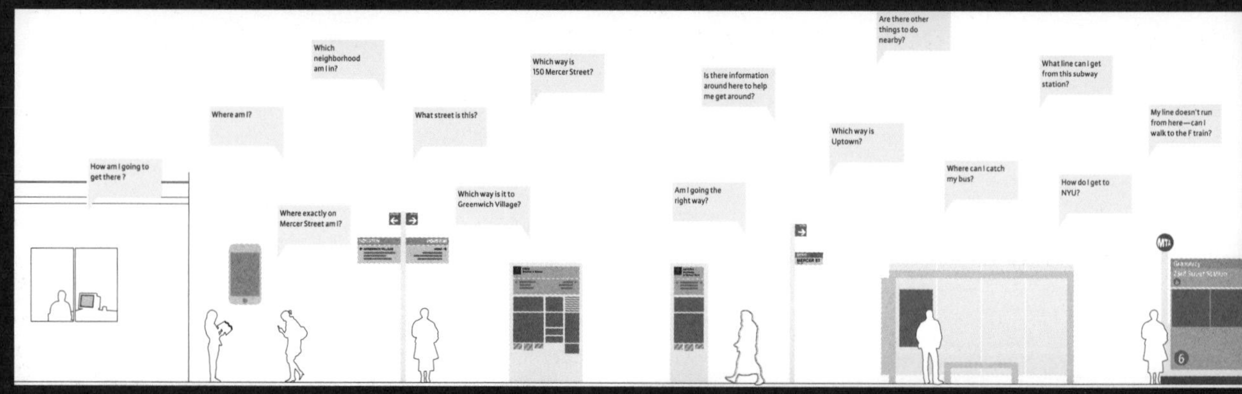

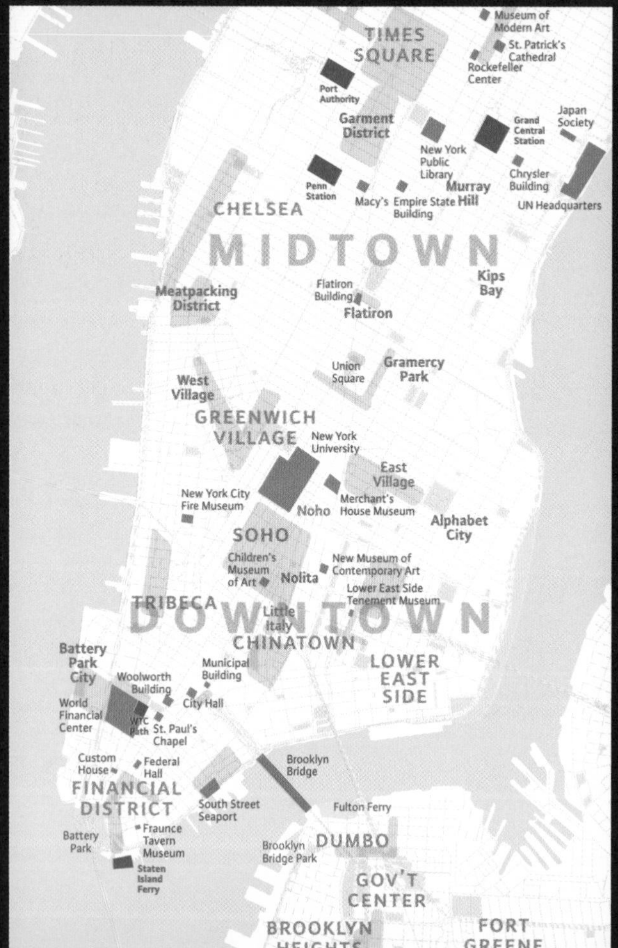

- Changing. These are the tools that allow people to make decisions about their journey when changing from one mode to another. These tools are necessary at interchanges such as subway stations and bus stops.

Different places = different needs
Once the boroughs of NYC had been assessed, it was clear they would require different implementation strategies. For example, in downtown Brooklyn business and residential areas are in clusters; in between these clusters is less developed so there is less need for pedestrian wayfinding. In contrast, Manhattan is densely populated, so this continuous pedestrian zone needs a comprehensive wayfinding system to support its users. A clear understanding of all areas must be attained in order to be implemented effectively.

The system proposed
The case for the implementation of a new wayfinding system put forward by Two Twelve is compelling. With the problems identified, the agency was able to build the foundations for a system with these ideas and guiding principles at the core:

- A branded wayfinding system: In order to be memorable and engaging, the pedestrian wayfinding system should be easily recognizable. It should be named and a symbol should be created for it.
- The street signage system: The physical manifestation of the programme is a family of on-street signage that directs and informs people on their journeys.

Top: Graphic of building a wayfinding system.

Above: Graphic map of what people are looking for in NYC.

Opposite, top left: I Walk New York symbol.

Opposite, centre: Orientation/directional wall site map.

Opposite, bottom left: Neighbourhood compass.

Opposite, right: One-directional pedestrian sign.

I NY

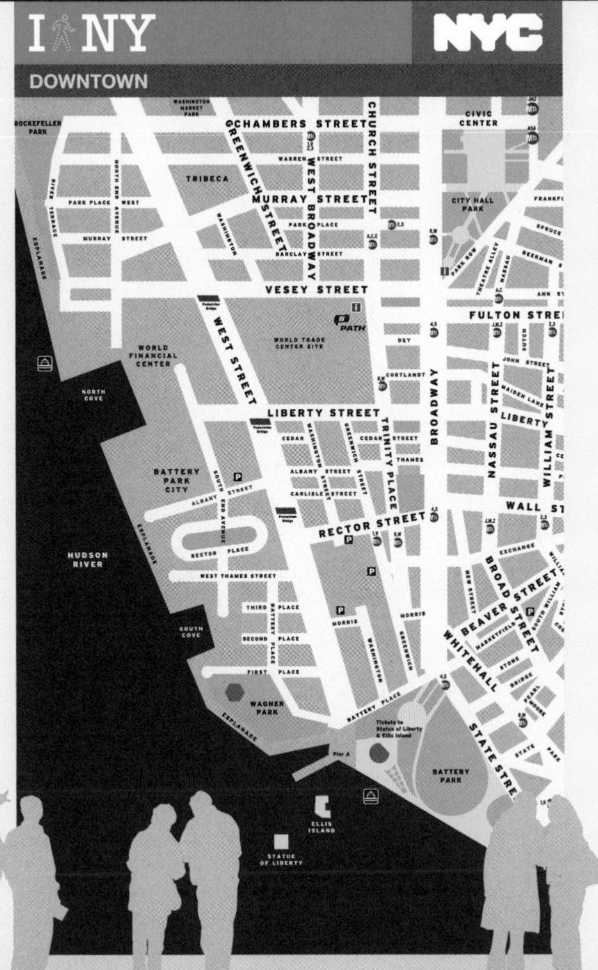

Broadway

↑ N

↑ 5 MIN
Union Square

↑ 10 MIN
Gramercy
Flatiron Building

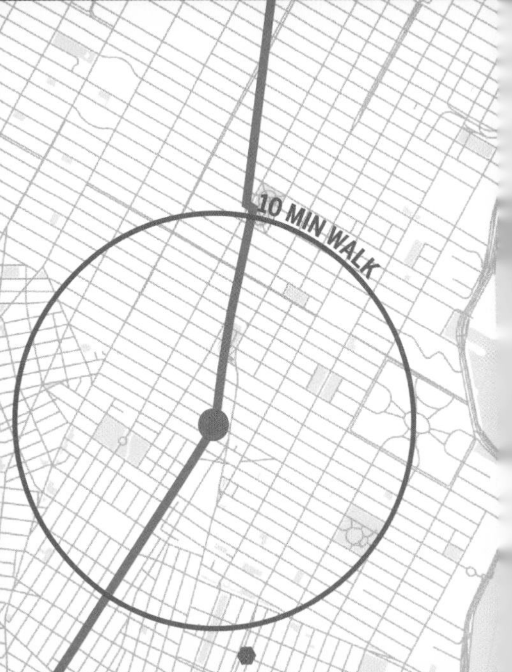

NYC

Right: Transit integration, street-level subway information.

Below: Street sign augmented with pedestrian, directional and neighbourhood information.

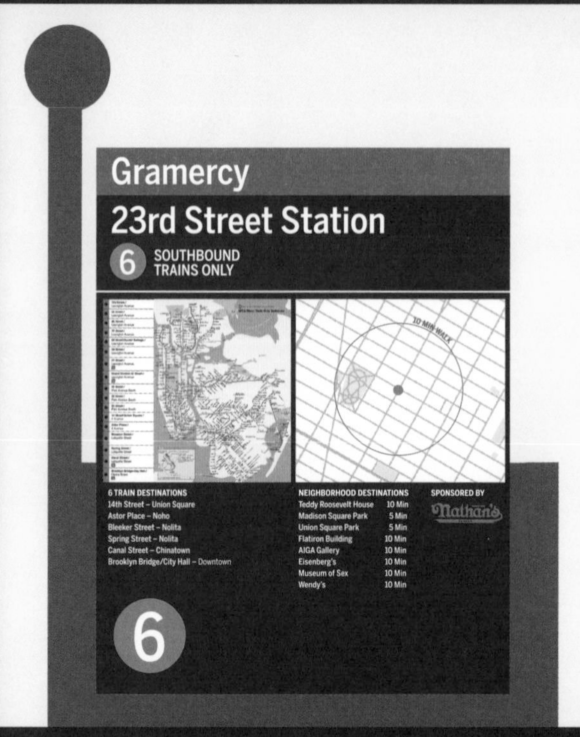

- Personal tools: The system should embrace the emergence of handheld devices and give New York a sophisticated set of digital tools to support navigation.
- Integration with public transportation: The wayfinding system elements are designed to intersect with the public transportation information infrastructure.
- Keys to the city: There is a set of simple navigation rules and insider clues that will help people understand New York City.
- The living map: A rich geographical information system (GIS) mapping database will contain the details of the city's geography and wayfinding information. This is a robust content-management tool to be used for the pedestrian wayfinding system and other related information publishers. It will also include design standards.

Guiding principles

A set of principles provides the framework for the system and helps to guide the design of its components and their functions.

- A unified language of wayfinding: The content communicated by the I Walk New York wayfinding elements should be consistent so that people have a predictable, seamless and comprehensible experience of the city.
- Wayfinding data organized: The system should be built on a foundation of information that is stored and distributed digitally. Individual agencies and neighbourhoods will update information in the same centralized database, and will use the same graphic standards in creating maps.
- Wayfinding is more than signs: The system will include a cohesive family of wayfinding elements including fixed signage, publications and digital tools.
- Information when and where you need it: The system must be user-centred so as to provide wayfinding information at key points along the way. Information should be available both while planning a trip and while conducting it.
- Better awareness of the city's riches: A broad family of elements provides visitors and residents alike the confidence to wander and explore.
- City-wide standards, allowing for local identity: The elements of the system must convey a single image of a unified city program, yet have the flexibility to respond to varying conditions throughout the city.

The first big idea put forward was the creation of a brand. A strong brand identity across all applications would bring the family of wayfinding elements together. It would identify the official city scheme and help to build recognition and confidence in the system. At the helm should be, 'A symbol that can build trust in the system, and should be instantly recognizable, iconic and memorable.' With so many elements proposed and necessary in the NYC system it was essential to have an over-arching brand to unify them.

The overall framework for 'I Walk New York' includes a comprehensive range of elements. The elements 'build on the existing city infrastructure and integrate with known recognizable information architecture'. Each element is described and has a function attached. The Brand 'I Walk New York' would have a typographic style attached to it, a typeface or faces designated for specific purposes, a colour scheme and a library of graphic elements to assist in the creation of a strong and cohesive visual identity. This would be carried across all final communication platforms.

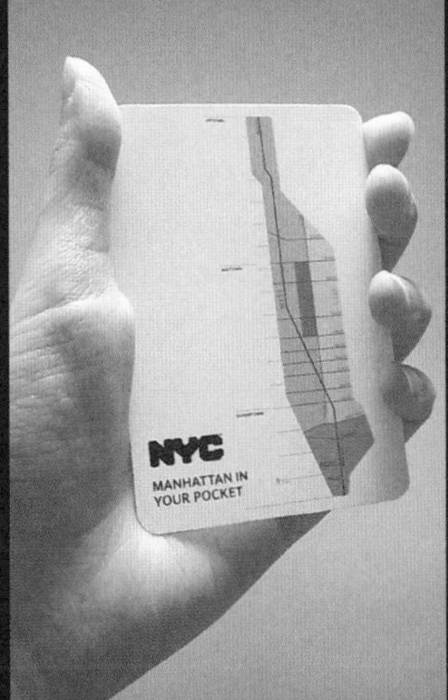

Above: Urban landscape, scaffolding.

Far left: Digital handheld application.

Left: Outreach keys to the city, 'Pocket card'.

The information architecture has to be considered carefully, as content will differ across the elements of the scheme, depending on the function identified for the specific element (a directional street sign requires a different amount of content to a wall-size map, or a handheld GPS, website or smartphone app). As with all information design, there needs to be a clear hierarchy established in line with the function of the element.

The strategy also moved the system beyond the streets of NYC; airports and train and bus stations are described as 'key points of entry' to the city and 'present an opportunity to inform the visitor about New York's offerings prior to, or at the start of

In addition to environmental wayfinding, a proposal for outreach material is presented by the agency; 'keys to the city' includes a 'Manhattan in your pocket' card and a selection of 'insider tips' to help decode the city. These are applied to a range of widely used products such as coffee cups and tickets. Printed and digital maps would be available on handheld devices and on vehicular GPS navigation systems.

Outcome

This case study demonstrates the complexity of developing a comprehensive, cohesive wayfinding system for a large city. With an understanding of the user's behaviour and analysis of the challenges NYC presents, it is possible to create a strategy for the implementation of a system that utilizes a large variety of platforms to deliver effective information to residents, commuters and visitors to the city.

Conclusion

We live in a world that is full of information. We receive this through an ever-increasing variety of media including newspapers, magazines, books, television and radio programmes, telephones, the worldwide web, the postal service and numerous other types of both solicited and unsolicited publicity, PR and marketing devices. So, how do we make sense of it all? How are we able to interpret, prioritize and digest the bits that are important? How do we recognize what is important against all the rest?

Hopefully from reading this book you have been able to see that the role of the information designer is diverse, in that there are many ways to convey data to a specific audience. There are, however, certain guiding principles that all information design conforms to. The understanding, editing and organizing of information is key to the transmission in a clear and unambiguous manner. In order to do this, the information designer uses particular tools at their disposal. These are the fundamentals of any design work: hierarchy, structure, legibility and navigation. With these guidelines, the interpretation and communication of information becomes simple to decode. When used effectively, it brings clarity and comprehension to the minds of the reader/viewer. This also brings into focus another important consideration, that of the user. The designer should produce solutions that satisfy the needs and demands of the user, not those of the designer. This requires a clear definition and understanding of the audience, so that the piece is fit for purpose.

Information designers do not just produce graphics that are pleasing to the eye; they have to ensure that the piece functions first and foremost. Aesthetics are part of it, but it is the communication of the data that is paramount.

Currently within graphic design, and to some extent information design, there is a convergence of technology and a proliferation of multiple platforms. Messages are no longer delivered through just one medium. The web, smartphones, GPS tracking and environments, along with print solutions, may have to be considered when communicating with an audience.

A good information designer will analyze the information and then propose the most logical and appropriate way or ways in which to present it. This can be quite comprehensive, as we have seen with the I Walk New York case study (see pp. 196–201), or quite simple, in the case of a book.

There are some issues you should consider when producing a comprehensive piece of information design. This is not a definitive list, but here are ten guidelines that may help.

Ten things to consider

1) Be systematic in your thinking.

2) Be as well informed as you can about the subject you are working in.

3) Be familiar with the technical requirements of the visual media you are working with.

4) Be familiar with human communication capabilities so that users can perceive and understand the information using appropriate senses.

5) Be able to consider the possible benefits of the communicated information to the users.

6) Be knowledgeable about the creation of pictures and text, static and animated, for the presentation of the information and how they can be balanced to achieve optimal effects.

7) Be able to design information in an interesting and attractive way to grab attention but still be appropriate to the required message.

8) Be able to communicate effectively in both your mother tongue and English.

9) Be able to co-operate with specialists to evaluate and improve the design of messages with regard to the different cultural sensitivities of the user.

10) Behave in a responsible manner with regard to the needs of the target users and society as a whole.

With these principles in mind, it is possible to produce beautiful and functional design that can help the audience to understand information in all its assorted forms.

Glossary

Animatic
A simplified mock-up of a piece of animation or motion design. Its purpose is to give a better idea of how the scene will look and feel with motion and timing. Often it can be a series of still images edited together and displayed in a sequence with a soundtrack or rough dialogue added. This is to test that the sound and images are working together effectively.

Bauhaus
A famous art school in Germany from 1919 to 1933. It combined fine arts and crafts and was notable for its unique approach to design, using the guiding principle that 'form follows function'. It had a profound influence on art, architecture, graphic design, industrial design and typography.

Branding
The devising of a name, symbol, or feature that identifies one company or seller's goods or services from those of its competitors.

Cartography
The study and practice of making maps.

Composition
The placement or arrangement of visual elements in a piece of design or work of art. The term composition means 'putting together', and can apply to any work of art, from music to writing to photography, that is arranged or put together using conscious thought. In graphic design composition can often refer to page layout.

Cuneiform
An ancient phonographic writing system in which sounds and syllables are represented by images.

Data
Defined as individual facts, statistics or items of information. In visual terms data is collected information that can be measured, quantified and portrayed using graphs, charts or images.

Die cut
A manufacturing process whereby a custom shape is cut into a piece of paper or card using a specially made metal 'die'.

D&AD (Designers and Art Directors)
A UK design organization, which exists to inform, educate and inspire those who work in and around the creative industries.

Egyptian font
Most often called a slab serif, Egyptian fonts have heavy serifs and were used for decorative purposes and headlines because the heavy serifs proved to be less legible at small point sizes.

Ethnography
A field of design research aimed at exploring qualitative cultural experiences. This often takes the form of a field study, from which knowledge about the target group is gained. It is a way in which designers can establish the user experience and be able to design with specific needs in mind.

Flickr
A popular photo-sharing website, which allows its members to upload their own photos into specific albums that can then be labelled, organized and tagged.

French fold
A piece of paper that is only printed on one side, then folded in half and bound at the open edge, leaving the crease on the outer edge of the page. Sheets folded this way can be glued together or stitched.

Gatefold
This is where both the left and right pages are cut longer and folded on the outer edge to meet in the middle of the document. The resulting flap means that the designer can reveal information by unfolding the pages.

Graphical User Interface (GUI)
A type of user interface that allows people to interact with electronic devices using images rather than text commands.

GPS (Global Positioning System)
A navigation system that uses satellites in the Earth's orbit to provide the user with their precise location on a map.

Grid
A two-dimensional structure made up of a series of intersecting vertical and horizontal axes used to structure content. The grid is similar to that of scaffolding when constructing a building in that it serves as a framework on which a designer can organize text and images in a way the viewer finds easy to decode.

Hierarchy
The arrangement or organization of items (objects, names, values, categories, etc.) in which the items are represented as being 'above', 'below' or 'at the same level' as one another. In graphic design we apply this to typography and graphic elements, which the viewer is required to see in a particular order or sequence.

Histogram
A graphical representation, similar in structure to a bar chart. It condenses a data series into a visual that can by easily understood by taking many data points and grouping them into logical ranges.

HTML (Hypertext Mark-up Language)
The main computer language for creating web pages on the internet and other information that can be displayed via any web browser.

Hyperlink
An element in an electronic document which links to another place in the same document or to an entirely different document. It is usually a piece of text that the user clicks to link to another web page.

Icon
An image that conveys its meaning through its pictorial resemblance to a physical object (also referred to as a **pictogram** or **pictograph**).

Ideogram
A graphic symbol that represents an idea or concept.

Infographic
A representation of information in a graphic format designed to make the data easily understandable at a glance. Infographics are used to communicate a message quickly, to simplify the presentation of large amounts of data, to see data patterns and relationships, and to monitor changes in variables over time.

ISOTYPE (International System of Typographic Picture Education)
A method of showing social, technological, biological and historical connections in pictorial form, initiated by Otto Neurath.

Lasercut
An aperture cut into paper or card using a laser cutter. The cutter uses a focused beam of light to melt or burn through a target material. Laser cutters are computer-controlled to maintain precision.

Last.fm
A music website, founded in 2002, which builds a detailed profile of each user's musical taste by recording details of the tracks the user listens to when logged into the site.

Legibility
The degree to which glyphs (individual characters) in text are understandable or recognizable based on appearance.

Modernism
In the arts, Modernism is used to describe a radical break with the past and the search for new forms of expression. It was inspired by industrialization and is often characterized by its simplicity and functionality, with a distinct lack of decoration for its own sake.

Persona
In marketing a persona represents a group of customers on which a company can focus its efforts. By understanding a customer's character, a company can predict and design for specific habits.

Pictogram/pictograph
See **icon**.

Prototype
An original, full-scale, and usually working model of a new product or an updated version of an existing product.

Readability
This refers to how easy it is to read and understand large passages of text. It can often be confused with **legibility**, which refers to the recognition of individual characters, not whole words or paragraphs.

Rebus
A device that uses pictures to represent words or parts of words.

RSS Reader (Rich Site Summary)
A browser add-on program, sometimes called a feed reader. It is designed to gather and display news feeds from specific sites. The reader reduces the time and effort needed to check for updates manually.

Sandblasting
The act of propelling abrasive material under high pressure against a specific surface to either roughen or smooth it, or to remove surface contamination.

Semiotics
The study of signs and symbols.

Signage
The collective term for signs used to display information, such as giving directions or advertising.

Smartphone
A mobile or cell phone that includes features such as a portable media player, camera, web browser and GPS.

Spot varnish
A clear varnish applied to a specific area of a printed piece.

Stock
Paper which is to be printed on.

Substrate
A specific surface to be printed on.

Swiss Style (also known as the International Typographic Style)
A style of graphic design developed in Switzerland in the 1950s which emphasized cleanliness and readability over decoration. Its main indicators are asymmetric layouts, use of a grid structure and sans serif typefaces such as Helvetica and Futura with flush left, ragged right text. The style is also associated with a preference for photography in place of illustrations or drawings.

Symbol
A mark that represents an idea, a process or a physical entity. Its purpose is to communicate meaning; for example, a red octagon is used on road signs to signify 'STOP'.

Tablet computer
A one-piece mobile computer usually consisting of a flat **touch screen**; sometimes called simply a 'tablet'.

Thumbnail
A term used by graphic designers and photographers for a small image representation of a larger image, usually intended to make it easier and faster to look at or manage a group of larger images.

Timeline
A sequence of related events arranged in a chronological order and displayed along a line, usually drawn left to right or top to bottom.

Touch screen
An electronic visual display that the user controls by touching the screen with one or more fingers and using gestures.

Vernacular
A term referring to the commonly spoken language or dialect of a particular people or place. Graphic examples of this include hand-drawn signs, street signs and found items from other countries and cultures that can be reinterpreted.

Visual impairment
A loss of vision to such a degree that the person will require additional support, as their visual capabilities are so significantly reduced that they cannot be corrected by conventional means, such as refractive correction or medication.

Visual identity
The visible elements of a brand, such as form, shape and colour, which summarize and communicate meaning that cannot be imparted through words alone.

Visual language
A system of communication that relies on visual elements to convey meaning.

Wayfinding
A term used to describe the way in which people orient themselves in a physical space and navigate from one place to another.

Further reading

Ambrose, Gavin and Paul Harris. *The Visual Dictionary of Typography*, AVA Publishing, 2010

Baer, Kim. *Information Design Workbook: Graphic Approaches, Solutions, and Inspiration + 30 Case Studies*, reprint edition, Rockport, 2010

Baines, Phil and Andrew Haslam. *Type & Typography*, 2nd edition, Laurence King Publishing, 2005

Clarkson, John, Roger Coleman, Ian Hosking and Sam Waller (eds). *Inclusive Design Toolkit*, Engineering Design Centre, University of Cambridge, 2007

Eskilson, Stephen J. *Graphic Design: A History*, 2nd edition, Laurence King Publishing, 2012

Ford, Rob and Julius Wiedemann (eds). *The App and Mobile Case Study Book*, Taschen, 2011

Gibson, David. *The Wayfinding Handbook: Information Design for Public Places*, Princeton Architectural Press, 2009

Hollis, Richard. *Swiss Graphic Design: The Origins and Growth of an International Style 1920–1965*, Laurence King Publishing, 2005

Inclusive Design, ISTD/RNIB, 2007

Kane, John. *A Type Primer*, 2nd edition, Laurence King Publishing, 2011

Klanten, Robert. *Data Flow: Visualising Information in Graphic Design*, Die Gestalten Verlag, 2008

Klanten, Robert. *Data Flow 2: Visualising Information in Graphic Design*, Die Gestalten Verlag, 2010

Knight, Carolyn and Jessica Glaser. *Diagrams*, RotoVision, 2009

Lima, Manuel. *Visual Complexity: Mapping Patterns of Information*, Princeton Architectural Press, 2011

Lorenc, Jan, Lee Skolnick and Craig Berger. *What is Exhibition Design?*, RotoVision, 2007

Lupton, Ellen. *Thinking with Type: A Critical Guide for Designers, Writers, Editors, and Students*, Princeton Architectural Press, 2004

Lupton, Ellen and Jennifer Cole Phillips. *Graphic Design: The New Basics*, Princeton Architectural Press, 2008

Malamed, Connie. *Visual Language for Designers*, reprint edition, Rockport, 2011

Marshall, Lindsey and Lester Meachem. *How to Use Images*, Laurence King Publishing, 2010

McCandless, David. *Information is Beautiful*, new edition, Collins, 2012

Meggs, Philip B. and Alston W. Purvis. *Meggs' History of Graphic Design*, 5th edition, John Wiley & Sons, 2011

Millman, Debbie. *The Essential Principles of Graphic Design*, RotoVision, 2008

Müller-Brockmann, Josef. *Grid Systems in Graphic Design*, 7th edition, Verlag Niggli, 2010

Neurath, Otto. *From Hieroglyphics to Isotype: A Visual Autobiography*, Hyphen Press, 2010

Noel, Hayden. *Marketing Basics: Consumer Behaviour*, AVA Publishing, 2009

Rathgeb, Markus. *Otl Aicher*, Phaidon Press, 2006

Reas, Casey and Chandler McWilliams. *Form+Code in Design, Art, and Architecture*, Princeton Architectural Press, 2010

Samara, Timothy. *Making and Breaking the Grid: A Graphic Design Layout Workshop*, Rockport, 2005

Spence, Robert. *Information Visualization: Design for Interaction*, 2nd edition, Prentice Hall, 2007

Squire, Victoria. *Getting it Right with Type: The Dos and Don'ts of Typography*, Laurence King Publishing, 2006

Swann, Cal. *Language and Typography*, John Wiley & Sons, 1991

Ten Have, Paul. *Understanding Qualitative Research and Ethnomethodology*, Sage Publications, 2004

Uebele, Andreas. *Signage Systems & Information Graphics*, Thames & Hudson, 2009

Visocky O'Grady, Jenn and Ken Visocky O'Grady. *The Information Design Handbook*, RotoVision, 2008

Wildbur, Peter and Michael Burke. *Information Graphics: Innovative Solutions in Contemporary Design*, Thames & Hudson, 1999

Yau, Nathan. *Visualize This: The FlowingData Guide to Design, Visualization, and Statistics*, John Wiley & Sons, 2011

Websites

Design associations and societies

International Design Network
www.idnworld.com

International Institute for Information Design
www.iiid.net

International Society of Typographic Designers
www.istd.org.uk

Society for Environmental Graphic Design (SEGD)
www.segd.org

Magazines

www.creativereview.co.uk

www.eyemagazine.com

Index

Acknowledgements

We would like to thank all the contributors; without them this book would not have been possible. In no particular order, they are: Peter Crnokrak at The Luxury of Protest; Paul Farrington at Studio Tonne; Emmi Salonen at Studio EMMI; Barbara Glauber at Heavy Meta; Tim Beard and Mason Wells at Bibliothèque; Ryan Pescatore Frisk and Catelijne van Middelkoop at Strange Attractors; David Gibson, Kamdyn Moore, Zoe Viklund and Emily Tam at Two Twelve; Shari Berman at Evidence Design (photographer Sean Hemmerle); Andy Brockie at The Guardian; Adi Stern; Maya Hart at Landor Associates; Kate and Grant Alexander at Studio Alexander; Dr Alison Barnes; Vince Frost at Frost Design; John McMillan at ISTD; John Batson at LCC; Kate Sclater at Hyperkit; Holger Jacobs at Mind Design; Jer Thorp at Blprnt; Aaron Koblin at Google; Ebru Kurbak and Mahir M. Yavuz; Mariana Rosa and Nuno Gusmão at P-06 Atelier; Jens Weber and Andreas Wolter at mediaarchitecture.de; Tanya Holbrook at Fallon; Nicholas Felton at Feltron; Stephen Woowat at Elmwood; Chris Elphick at 100 Shapes; Phil McNeill at Kin Design; and Holly Langford, Sophie Garwell and William Cottam.

All the contributors were generous with their time, advice and insights into their work. Students past and present at Nottingham Trent University have inspired us with their sense of enquiry and enthusiasm, which in turn has motivated us to push the boundaries of our knowledge as both lecturers and practitioners.

We would like to thank Laurence King Publishing for giving us this opportunity. I am sure at moments they regretted the decision!

Andy would like to thank Canice for all his patience and support, while being neglected! My mum, Iris, who passed away while completing the project; I will miss you. Kathryn for keeping me sane when I was being too anal, shabba! Phil Jarman and Dr Chris Brown for being so helpful in the office and all those colleagues and contacts I cajoled and badgered to contribute when they could have been doing real work. Thanks a million.

Kathryn would like to thank Martin, Noah and Darcey, my mum and uncle Boo for their support, encouragement and belief in me. Mr Ellison for giving me this opportunity and for putting up with my random thought processes, shabba. Phil and Brownie for their help and advice, and all the lovely designers out there who answered my emails and agreed to be part of this project ... and a shout-out to my careers advisor at school, who told me to be more realistic when I declared I wanted to be a designer or writer. Never say never ...

Picture credits

t = top, b = bottom, c = centre, l = left, r = right

Chapter 1
8: © The Trustees of the British Museum / 11: Pascal Goetgheluck/Science Photo Library / 12: © The Trustees of the British Museum / 13 l: Courtesy of the Semitic Museum, Harvard University (object no. SMN 4172) / 13 r: © 2012 The Metropolitan Museum of Art/Photo SCALA, Florence / 14 t, b: From William Playfair, *The Commercial and Political Atlas* (1786) / 15 t: From Otto Neurath, *From Hieroglyphics to Isotype*, p. 106, courtesy Otto & Marie Neurath Isotype Collection, University of Reading / 15 b: Arntz Archive, Gemeentemuseum, The Hague, The Netherlands; © DACS 2012 / 16 tl: © TfL from the London Transport Museum Collection / 16 tr: New York City Subway Map © MTA New York City Transit. Used with permission of the Metropolitan Transportation Authority / 16 b: Reproduced by courtesy of RATP / 17 t: PARC, a Xerox company / 17 c: © Roger Ressmeyer/CORBIS / 17 b: Used with permission from Microsoft. *An Introduction to Information Design* is an independent publication and is not affiliated with, nor has it been authorized, sponsored, or otherwise approved by Microsoft Corporation / 18: iPad is a trademark of Apple Inc. *An Introduction to Information Design* is an independent publication and has not been authorized, sponsored, or otherwise approved by Apple Inc. / 19 l: iStock / 19 tr, br: Photographs: Lisa Ferneyhough/Baines Dixon Collection / 20 t: Shutterstock / 20 b: 123RF.com / 21 l: National Eye Institute, National Institutes of Health / 21 r: IKEA / 22 t: © Guardian News & Media Ltd 2011 / 22 b: Opower Home Energy Report, courtesy Opower / 23 t: Paul Farrington/Studio Tonne / 23 b: © 2012 Virgin Media. All Rights Reserved / 24 l, r: iStock.

Chapter 2
26: Designer: David Chavez. Appearance model: Reed Prototype + Model / 30 tl: Nokia / 30 tr: Doro AB Ltd / 30 bl: Firefly Mobile / 30 br: Courtesy Red Dot. Designer: Seon-Keun Park / 31 l: © lunamarina – Fotolia.com / 31 r: Clker.com / 34, 35: © One Laptop Per Child / 38: Courtesy of the authors, except Harry Hill photograph: Rex Features / 39: Courtesy of the authors / 40 all: Design and photographs by Lance Wyman / 41: LOCOG / 42: © 1976 by ERCO GmbH / 44, 45 t: Courtesy of the authors / 45 b: © Marcal / 47: Courtesy of the authors / 48–53: Art direction/creative direction/design/editing/type design/game design/spatial design/interactive design: Strange Attractors Design: Ryan Pescatore Frisk and Catelijine van Middelkoop. Project client: Graphic Design Museum (now Museum of the Image), Breda, The Netherlands.

Chapter 3
54: Shutterstock / 56: Courtesy of the authors / 57 l, r: Collection of the Stedelijk Museum, Amsterdam, The Netherlands / 58: Courtesy of the authors / 59 tl, bl: Courtesy of the Herb Lubalin Study Center of Design and Typography, Cooper Union School of Art / 59 r all: *Zembla* magazine. Creative Director/Designer: Vince Frost. Designer: Matt Willey. Editor: Dan Crowe (59 tr: issue 1, September 2003, pages 88–89, photo: Henri Cartier-Bresson; 59 cr: issue 5, Summer 2004, pages 6–7; 59 br: issue 3, Spring 2004, pages 24–25) / 60: Bob Van Dijk © Studio Dumbar. Photography: Deen Van Meer / 61 all: Émigré Inc. (illustrations from issue 32, pages 12–13, 'In and around', are from *Ray Gun*, issues 3 and 6) / 63: Museum für Gestaltung Zürich, Poster Collection. Franz Xaver Jaggy © ZHdK/ DACS 2012 / 64–65: Phil McNeill / 67–71: Courtesy of the authors / 72–75: Emmi Salonen. Photographs: Jere Salonen.

Chapter 4
76: Shutterstock / 79: Designer: Wade Jeffree, wadejeffree.com / 80 t, b: Shutterstock / 82 l: New York City Subway Map © MTA New York City Transit. Used with permission of the Metropolitan Transportation Authority / 82 r: Designers: Eddie Jabbour & Dan Jabbour. © 2012 Kick Design, Inc. / 83 t, c: 'Lost and Found'. Wayfinding system design: BrandCulture. Creative Director: Stephen Minning. Photographers: Stephen Minning and Kris Baum. Client: World Square car park. Architects: Brookfield Multiplex / 83 b: Creative Director: Mark Porter at Mark Porter Associates. Designers: Andy Brockie and Barry Ainslie at The Guardian. Design Consultants: Berg / 84: Courtesy of the authors / 86: Designer: Paula Scher/ Pentagram. Client: Cohen Bros. Realty. Photography: James Shank / 87 t: iStock / 87 b: © Transport for London / 88, 90, 91: Courtesy of the authors / 92: Lithograph, 38½ x 38⅜ in. (97.8 x 34 cm). Gift of the designer. Acc. no.: 1580.2000. © 2012 The Museum of Modern Art, New York/Photo SCALA, Florence / 93 tl: freeprintable.com / 93 tr, bl: Design: ZMIK. Client: Sevensisters & Handmade, Basel. Location: Art|40|Basel, Schweiz. Date of realization: June 2009. Area: 120m². Photos: Eik Frenzel & ZMIK / 93 br all: Shutterstock / 94 t: Peter Grundy: Concept & diagram. Art Director: Alex Breuer, *Esquire* Magazine / 94 b: Purpose. Creative Director: Stuart Youngs. Senior Designer: Paul Felton. Senior Project Manager: Louisa Phillips. Designer: Amie Herriott / 95 t: Design Agency: NB Studio. Client: Museum of London / 96 r: Airfix is a registered trade mark of Hornby Hobbies Ltd © 2012 / 97 t: Peter Grundy: Concept & diagram. Ezri Carlebach, Lifelong Learning UK/ The Guardian Newspaper / 97 c: Toby Bradbury, mrlerone.com / 97 b: David McCandless & Stefanie Posavec, informationisbeautiful.net / 99 l: New Order 'Power, Corruption and Lies', design by Peter Saville Associates, 1983 / 99 r: © Transport for London / 100, 101: Courtesy of the authors / 102–103: Design: Barbara Glauber and Erika Nishizato, Heavy Meta / 104–105: Client: Fletcher Construction on behalf of the Victoria Park Alliance. Design Agency: Studio Alexander. Design Team: Grant Alexander, Sam Trustrum, Richard Unsworth, Ed Prinsep, Felicity Douglas. Photography: Kristian Frires and Dave Olsen.

Chapter 5
106–109: Courtesy of the faculty and students of the University of Houston Graphic Communications, School of Art and Gerald D. Hines College of Architecture / 110–111: Mind Design. Interior design by Design Research Studio / 112: John Keatley/Wired © The Condé Nast Publications Ltd. / 114–115: The Noble Union/Mobile IQ/BBC / 116–117: Chris Elphick / 118–119: Jer Thorp / 120–121: Aaron Koblin, Flight Patterns, 2005 / 123–124: Exhibition design: Evidence Design, Brooklyn, New York. Design team: Jack Pascarosa, Shari Berman, Len Soccolich, Carlos Fierro, Laura Sheedy, Ari Nakamura, Josh Whitehead, Rondi Davies. Media production consultants: Cortina Productions, McLean, Virginia. Exhibit engineering consultants: The Wheel Thing, Glendale, California. Lighting design consultants: Focus Lighting, New York / 126–127: All design for the exhibition (both 3d and 2d) by Bibliothèque. Photography: Tom Brown & Luke Hayes / 128: © Guardian News & Media Ltd 2012 / 129: Design: Cartlidge Levene. Photography: Marcus Ginns / 130–133: Creative Director: Mark Porter at Mark Porter Associates. Designers: Andy Brockie and Barry Ainslie at *The Guardian*. Design consultants: Berg.

Chapter 6
134, 137: Sophie Garwell / 139: Stephen Woowat / 142–143: William Cottam. cargocollective.com/doubleyousee / 144–145: Holly Langford / 147–149: Nicholas Felton / 151: Tanya Holbrook, designer / 152–154: Ebru Kurbak & Mahir M. Yavuz / 156–159: Landor Associates. Creative Director: Ben Marshall. Design Director: Carl Halksworth / 160–163: Alison Barnes.

Chapter 7
164: The Luxury of Protest / 167: Shutterstock / 169: *Culture and Climate Change: Recordings*. Edited by Robert Butler, Eleanor Margolies, Joe Smith and Renata Tyszczuk. Designed by Hyperkit / 170–173: The Luxury of Protest / 174–175: AllofUs/Graphic Thought Facility/Casson Mann / 176–179: Paul Farrington/Studio Tonne / 180–183: Design: Adi Stern. Hebrew typeface design: Adi Stern. Photography: Elad Sarig / 184–187: P-06 Atelier in collaboration with Global Landscape Architecture. Design Concept: Nuno Gusmão, Pedro Anjos. Designers: Giuseppe Greco, Miguel Matos. Photographer: Joao Silveira Ramos, Giuseppe Greco (P-06). Client: APL (Lisbon Seaport), EDP (Energy of Portugal), Lisbon City Hall.

Chapter 8
188: Shutterstock / 191–195: mediaarchitecture.de/Jens Weber & Andreas Wolter / 196–201: Images prepared by Two Twelve/Applied for New York City Department of Transportation.